PRESIDENTIAL VETOES: CHALLENGES AND BIBLIOGRAPHY

PRESIDENTIAL VETOES: CHALLENGES AND BIBLIOGRAPHY

G.V. LIPSON (EDITOR)

Novinka Books
New York

Senior Editors: Susan Boriotti and Donna Dennis
Coordinating Editor: Tatiana Shohov
Office Manager: Annette Hellinger
Graphics: Wanda Serrano
Editorial Production: Jennifer Vogt, Matthew Kozlowski,
Jonathan Rose and Maya Columbus
Circulation: Ave Maria Gonzalez, Vera Popovich, Luis Aviles, Melissa Diaz,
Vladimir Klestov and Jeannie Pappas
Communications and Acquisitions: Serge P. Shohov
Marketing: Cathy DeGregory

Library of Congress Cataloging-in-Publication Data
Available Upon Request

ISBN 1-59033-380-2

Nova Science Publishers, Inc.
400 Oser Ave, Suite 1600
Hauppauge, New York 11788-3619
Tele. 631-231-7269 Fax 631-231-8175
e-mail: Novascience@earthlink.net
Web Site: http://www.novapublishers.com

Printed in the United States of America

CONTENTS

PREFACE

The veto power is one of the most important aspects of checks and balances in the United States Government, as it helps the executive branch to check the legislative. A bill presented by Congress needs the signature of the President to become law, except when the Congress successfully overrides a veto with a 2/3 majority vote in both houses. This book provides important information about vetoes from the 1st session of the 2nd Congress under George Washington to the 1st session of the 105th Congress under Bill Clinton.

Congressional Overrides of Presidential Vetoes

Gary L. Galemore

Summary

The President's veto authority is among his most significant tools in legislative dealings with Congress. It is effective not only in preventing the passage of legislation undesirable to the President, but also as a threat, sometimes forcing Congress to modify legislation before it is presented to the President. Students of executive-legislative relations suggest that Congress's strength rests with passing statutes and the President's in vetoing them. Illustrative of this point is the fact that Presidents have vetoed 1,484 bills and Congress has overridden only 106 of them.

President William Clinton has vetoed 37 bills. Congress has overridden two of these vetoes, one was pocket vetoed. As a veto threat is carried out, Congress is faced with choices: letting the veto stand, the difficult task of overriding the veto, meeting the President's objections and sending a new bill forward, or resubmitting the same provisions under a new bill number.[1] In the case of vetoed appropriations bills, the result can be the closure of

---

[1] H.R. 1854 was vetoed October 3, 1995. See: Legislative Branch Appropriations Act, 1996 – Veto Message from the President of the United States (H.Doc.No. 104-122), in *Congressional Record*, daily edition, vol. 141, Oct. 6, 1995, pp. H 9741-9742. H.R. 2492, the Legislative Branch Appropriations Act, 1996, identical to H.R. 1854, passed the House October 31, passed the Senate November 2, and was signed into law on November 19 (P.L. 104-53).

federal agencies and the furlough of hundreds of thousands of federal employees, with the inevitable disruption of federal programs and services.

BACKGROUND

Historically, the veto power granted the President in the Constitution has proven to be an effective tool for the Chief Executive in his dealings with Congress. Article I, Section 7 of the Constitution provides, in effect, that a President needs the vote of only one more than one-third in either the House of Representatives or the Senate to sustain a veto. Congressional procedure and tradition, not the Constitution, have determined that a vote of two-thirds of either or both houses of Congress means a vote of two-thirds of those Members present and voting (provided there is a quorum) and not, as is the practice in some states, two-thirds of those elected.

The Constitution states that, when the President vetoes a bill, "he shall return it with his objections to the House in which is shall have originated." This type of veto is referred to as a regular or return veto. The returned veto then becomes a question of "high privilege," or, in other words, takes precedence over other pending business before Congress. Neither house, however, is under any legal, constitutional, or procedural obligation to schedule an override vote attempt, but may do so anytime during a Congress. It is not unusual for Congress to make no effort to override a President's veto if party leaders feel they do not have sufficient votes. In still other cases, vetoes have been challenged and sustained in one house, eliminating the need for a vote in the other chamber.

Although a measure may have passed originally by a large majority vote in both Houses, a two-thirds majority of those present in each chamber is required to override the President's veto. Prior to 1969, Congress overrode approximately 1 of every 18 (5.7%) regular vetoes. Since 1969, Congress has been more successful, overriding about 1 out of every 5 (18.3%) regular vetoes. See Table 1.

1. Vetoes Overridden, 1789-Present

President	Regular Veto	Override	President	Regular Veto	Override
Washington	2	–	B. Harrison	19	1
Adams	–	–	Cleveland	–	–
Jefferson	–	–	(2nd term)	42	5
Madison	5	–	McKinley	6	–
Monroe	1	–	T. Roosevelt	42	1
J.Q. Adams	–	–	Taft	30	1
Jackson	5	–	Wilson	33	6
Van Buren	–	–	Harding	5	–
W. H. Harrison	–	–	Coolidge	20	4
Tyler	6	1	Hoover	21	3
Polk	2	–	F.D. Roosevelt	372	9
Taylor	–	–	Truman	180	12
Fillmore	–	–	Eisenhower	73	2
Pierce	9	5	Kennedy	12	–
Buchanan	4	–	L.B. Johnson	16	–
Lincoln	2	–	Nixon	26	7
A. Johnson	21	15	Ford	48	12
Grant	45	4	Carter	13	2
Hayes	12	1	Reagan	39	9
Garfield	–	–	Bush	29	1
Arthur	4	1	Clinton	36	2
Cleveland (1st term)	304	2	**Totals**	**1484**	**106**

President Clinton's Vetoes

Of the 37 vetoes exercised by President Clinton, all but 1 have been regular vetoes, which have been returned to Congress and subject to congressional override votes. Table 2 provides information about the Clinton vetoes.

2. President Clinton's Vetoes

Bill Number	Date of Veto	Title	Override Attempt
H.R. 1158	06/07/95	Second Supplemental Appropriations and Rescissions Act for FY1995	No attempt.
S. 21	08/11/95	Bosnia and Herzegovina Self-Defense Act of 1995	No attempt.
H.R. 1854	10/03/95	Legislative Branch Appropriations for FY1996	No attempt.
H.R. 2586	11/13/95	Increase in the Statutory Debt Limit	No attempt.
H.J. Res. 115	11/14/95	Second Continuing Resolution for FY1996	No attempt.
H.R. 2491	12/06/95	Budget Reconciliation	No attempt.
H.R. 1977	12/18/95	Interior Appropriations for FY1996	House sustained 01/04/96 by 239-177.
H.R. 2099	12/18/95	Veterans Affairs and Housing and Urban Development Appropriations for FY1996	No attempt.
H.R. 2076	12/19/95	Commerce, Justice, and State Appropriations for FY1996	House sustained 01/03/96 by 240-159.
H.R. 1058	12/19/95	Securities Litigation Reform Act	House overrode 12/20/95 by 319-100. Senate overrode 12/22/95 by 68-30. Public Law 104-67.
H.R. 1530	12/28/95	Defense Authorizations for FY1996	House sustained 01/03/96 by 240-156.
H.R. 4	01/09/96	Welfare Reform Act	No attempt.
H.R. 1833	04/10/96	Partial-Birth Abortion Ban Act of 1995	House overrode 09/19/96 by 285-188.
H.R. 1561	04/12/96	American Overseas Interest Act of 1996	House sustained 04/30/96 by 234-188.
H.R. 956	05/02/96	Common Sense Product Liability Legal Reform Act of 1996	House sustained 05/09/96 by 258-163.
H.R. 743	06/30/96	Teamwork for Employees and Managers Act of 1996	No attempt.
H.R. 2909	10/02/96	Amends Silvio O. Conte National Fish and Wildlife Refuge Act	No attempt.
H.R. 1469	06/09/97	Flood Relief Bill	No attempt.
H.R. 1122	10/10/97	Partial Birth Abortion	House overrode 07/23/98 by 296-132. Senate sustained 09/18/98 by 64-36.
H.R. 2631	11/13/97	Disapproving Cancellations	House overrode 02/05/98 by 347-69. Senate overrode 02/25/98 by 78-20. P.L. 105-159.
S. 1502	05/20/98	D.C. Student Vouchers	No attempt.
H.R. 2709	06/23/98	Iran Sanctions bill	No attempt.
H.R. 2646	07/21/98	Education Savings Account	No attempt.

Bill Number	Date of Veto	Title	Override Attempt
H.R. 4101	10/07/98	FY1999 Agriculture Appropriations	No attempt.
H.R. 1757	10/21/98	Foreign Affairs Reform	No attempt.
H.R. 2488	09/23/99	Tax Relief Bill	No attempt.
H.R. 2587	09/28/99	D.C. Appropriations, FY2000	No attempt.
H.R. 2606	10/18/99	FY00 Foreign Operations Spending	No attempt.
H.R. 2670	10/26/99	Commerce, Justice, and State Appropriations, FY00	No attempt.
H.R. 3064	11/03/99	District of Columbia Appropriations, FY2000	No attempt.
S. 1287	04/25/00	Nuclear Waste Policy Amendments of 2000	Senate sustained 05/3/00 by 64-35.
H.R. 4810	08/05/00	Marriage Tax Relief Bill	House sustained 09/13/00 by 270-158.
H.R. 8	08/31/00	Estate Tax Elimination Act	House sustained 09/07/00 by 274-157.
H.R. 4733	10/07/00	Energy and Water Development Appropriations	House overrode 10/11/00 by 315-98. Senate referred veto to committee.
H.R. 4516	10/30/00	Legislative Branch and Treasury Appropriations	No attempt.
H.R. 4392	11/04/00	Intelligence Reauthorization Bill	No attempt.
H.R. 2415	12/19/00	Consumer Bankruptcy Overhaul Act	Pocket veto.

REFERENCES

U.S. Congress, Secretary of the Senate, *Presidential Vetoes, 1789-1988* (Washington: GPO, 1992), 595 pp. S. Pub. 102-12.

U.S. Congress, Secretary of the Senate, *Presidential Vetoes, 1989-1991* (Washington: GPO, 1992), 12 pp. S. Pub. 102-13.

CRS REPORTS

CRS Report 98-156. *The Presidential Veto and Congressional Procedure*, by Gary L. Galemore.

CRS Report 98-148, *Presidential Vetoes, 1789-Present: A Summary Overview*, by Gary L. Galemore.

CRS Report 98-147. *President Clinton's Vetoes*, by Gary L. Galemore.

Challenges to Presidential Vetoes

Gary L. Galemore

Background

The President's veto authority is among the Chief Executive's most significant tools in legislative dealings with Congress. It not only is effective in sometimes blocking legislation undesirable to the President, but also it can be used by the President as a threat to persuade Congress to modify legislation before final passage.

The President

When presented with legislation passed by both houses of Congress, the President may sign it into law within the 10-day period prescribed in the Constitution, let it become law without his signature, or veto it. (All bills and joint resolutions, except those proposing amendments to the Constitution, must be presented to the President. Amendments to the Constitution, which require a two-thirds vote in each house, are sent directly to the states for approval.)

Generally, if Congress has adjourned, preventing the return of a bill, the President may withhold his signature beyond the 10-day period prescribed in the Constitution and the bill neither becomes law nor is required to be returned to Congress for further action. This latter practice, which has been subject to considerable legal discussion, has been dubbed the "pocket veto."

Unlike the situation when a vetoed bill is returned, Congress does not have an opportunity or constitutional authority to override a pocket veto.

Historically, the veto power granted the President by the Constitution has proven to be an effective tool for the Chief Executive in his dealings with Congress. Article I, Section 7 of the Constitution provides, in effect, that the President needs the vote of only one more than one-third of a quorum in either the House of Representatives or the Senate to sustain a veto.

Of the 2,538 total vetoes cast by Presidents, only, 1,471 have been "regular" vetoes (returned bills), subject to congressional override. The other 1,067 have been "pocket vetoes," not constitutionally subject to congressional reversal attempts. Congress has attempted overrides 307 times. Of those attempts, Congress has successfully overridden only 105, or 7.2%, of all regular vetoes. Presidential vetoes are, on average, sustained 92.8% of the time. If pocket vetoes are included, the chance of any President's veto standing rises to 95.8%. However, Presidents, on average, have only vetoed about 2% to 3% of all the legislation presented to them for their signature.

CONGRESSIONAL PROCEDURE

The Constitution provides that, when a President vetoes a bill, "he shall return it with his objections to the house in which it shall have originated." The returned bill then becomes a question of "high privilege" or, in other words, takes precedence over other pending business before Congress. Neither house, however, is under any legal, constitutional, or procedural obligation to schedule immediately a vote to override, but may do so anytime during a Congress. It is not unusual for Congress to ignore a President's veto if party leaders feel they do not have sufficient votes to override. In other cases, vetoes have been challenged and sustained in one house, eliminating the need for a vote in the other chamber. On nine occasions, one house has overridden the President's veto only to have the other chamber let the veto go unchallenged.

Although a bill may have passed originally by a large majority vote in both houses, the required two-thirds vote to override has posed serious problems for Congress. Prior to 1969, Congress overrode approximately one of every 18 regular vetoes. Since 1969, Congress has overridden about one out of every five regular vetoes. During the past quarter century, a returned veto has been either unchallenged or sustained 80% of the time while, prior to 1969, vetoes were unchallenged or sustained 95% of the time. It can be argued that the difficulty faced by the legislature in meeting the two-thirds requirement in both houses has encouraged Congress to pass omnibus legislation, strengthened the hand of the minority in Congress, and made the Chief Executive a more active player in the legislative process. It has also seemingly made Congress more reticent at times to attempt overrides of less significant legislation.

Congressional procedure for reconsidering vetoed legislation is similar in both the House and the Senate. Congressional action on a vetoed measure begins when the President returns the bill to the house of origin along with a veto message indicating his objections. Once the vetoed legislation has been received by the originating chamber, that chamber is constitutionally required "to reconsider" the vetoed bill. The Constitution is silent, however, on the definition of reconsideration. In lieu of constitutional direction, House and Senate procedures and tradition have governed the treatment of vetoed bills returned by the President. In either house, on receipt of the vetoed bill, the President's message is read into the journal of the receiving house. After entering the message into the journal, the House or the Senate complies with the constitutional requirement "to reconsider" by laying the measure on the table, referring the bill back to committee, postponing consideration to a certain day, or immediately voting on override.

Congressional procedures, tradition, and judicial ruling (*Missouri Pacific Ry. Co. v. Kansas*, 248 U.S. 276 (1919)) have determined that the vote required to pass a bill over a veto means two-thirds of a quorum. If both chambers satisfy the two-thirds requirement, the bill becomes law over the President's objections. This has occurred on 105 occasions out of 307 override attempts. If either house does not vote on reconsideration or fails to produce a two-thirds majority to override, the veto is sustained. When one house fails to override, the other house need not attempt to override, even if the votes are available to succeed. Moreover, because vetoes are difficult to override, they have been challenged in only 21% of the 1,471 "regular" vetoes cast.

The Senate and House may vote to override a veto at any time during a Congress. To provide a more accurate calculation of elapsed time between the veto and final congressional vote, it is necessary to subtract the days Congress was adjourned. This is particularly critical for Congresses prior to 1940, since those Congresses were often divided into three separate sessions. Since it is not uncommon for Congress to pass and present bills to the President late in a session, these earlier Congresses often adjourned and did not act on the veto until they returned for the next consecutive session.

An analysis of the time intervals or number of days it takes Congress to attempt an override of a presidential veto revealed the following performance. Historically, 67% of all congressional override attempts occurred in seven days or less. In fact, almost 18% occurred on the same day the veto was received, and 34% took place within one day of receiving the veto. Override attempts which occurred within 100 days or less of the veto make up 96% of all attempted overrides. Only 4% of veto override attempts took place after 100 days, or 15 of the 307 total. In one case, Congress took 195 days before voting to override, the longest elapsed time between receiving a veto and the vote to override. (See Table 1 on page 82 for more details.)

The list of congressional override attempts in this report provides individual veto profile details on the President, Congress, bill number, short title, veto date, and House and Senate override dates. The "yeas" and "nays" are also listed, with the "yeas" appearing first. A "yea" vote is a vote to override. It also includes a number for the total days elapsed between the date of the veto and the date Congress voted to override. The term "total days" includes days between sessions when Congress was adjourned. "Adjournment days" were subtracted from "total days" to determine the number of days Congress was in session. The "in session days" were then used to determine the elapsed time that expired before Congress took action in the form of an override vote.

Listing of Veto Override Attempts

Gary L. Galemore

George Washington

2nd Congress, 1st Session

H.R. 163—Apportionment of Representatives, vetoed April 5, 1792. House sustained April 6, 1792, 28-33.

Total Days:	1
Adjournment Days:	0
In Session Days:	1

4th Congress, 2nd Session

H.R. 219—To Amend the Military Establishment Act, vetoed February 28, 1797. House sustained March 1, 1797, 55-36.

Total Days:	1
Adjournment Days:	0
In Session Days:	1

JAMES MADISON

11th Congress, 3rd Session

H.R. 155—An Act incorporating the Protestant Episcopal Church, vetoed February 21, 1811. House sustained February 23, 1811, 29-74.

Total Days:	2
Adjournment Days:	0
In Session Days:	2

H.R. 170—For the relief of a Baptist Church, vetoed February 28, 1811. House sustained March 2, 1811, 33-55.

Total Days:	2
Adjournment Days:	0
In Session Days:	2

12th Congress, 1st Session

H.R. 81—An Act affecting district courts of the United States, vetoed April 3, 1812. House sustained April 8, 1812, 26-70.

Total Days:	5
Adjournment Days:	0
In Session Days:	5

13th Congress, 3rd Session

S. 67—An Act incorporating the Bank of the United States of America, vetoed January 30, 1815. Senate sustained February 2, 1815, 15-19.

Total Days:	3
Adjournment Days:	0
In Session Days:	3

14th Congress, 2nd Session

H.R. 29—An Act funding internal improvements, vetoed March 3, 1817. House sustained March 3, 1817, 60-56.

Total Days:	Same Day
Adjournment Days:	0
In Session Days:	Same Day

JAMES MONROE

17th Congress, 1st Session

H.R. 50—To repair the Cumberland Road, vetoed May 4, 1822. House sustained May 6, 1822, 68-72.

Total Days:	2
Adjournment Days:	0
In Session Days:	2

ANDREW JACKSON

21st Congress, 1st Session

S. 27—To authorize stock in the Washington Turnpike Road Company, vetoed May 31, 1830. Senate sustained May 31, 1830, 21-17.

Total Days:	Same Day
Adjournment Days:	0
In Session Days:	Same Day

H.R. 285--To authorize stock in the Maysville, Washington, Paris, and Lexington turnpikes, vetoed May 27, 1830. House sustained May 28, 1830, 96-92.

Total Days:	1
Adjournment Days:	0
In Session Days:	1

22nd Congress, 1st Session

S. 147—Amends an Act to incorporate the Bank of the United States, vetoed July 10, 1832. Senate sustained July 13, 1832, 22-19.

Total Days:	3
Adjournment Days:	0
In Session Days:	3

24th Congress, 1st Session

S.141—To appoint a day for the annual meeting of Congress, vetoed June 10, 1836. Senate sustained June 27, 1836, 16-23.

Total Days:	17
Adjournment Days:	0
In Session Days:	17

JOHN TYLER

27th Congress, 1st Session

S. 5—To incorporate the Fiscal Bank of the United States, vetoed August 16, 1841. Senate sustained August 18, 1841, 25-24.

Total Days:	3
Adjournment Days:	0
In Session Days:	3

H.R. 14—Establishes the Fiscal Corporation of the United States, vetoed September 9, 1841. House sustained September 10, 1841, 92-87.

Total Days:	1
Adjournment Days:	0
In Session Days:	1

27th Congress, 2nd Session

H.R. 472—To modify laws affecting the collection of duties on imports, vetoed August 9, 1842. House sustained August 17, 1842, 92-87.

Total Days:	8
Adjournment Days:	0
In Session Days:	8

H.R. 480—To extend laws on the collection of duties on imports, vetoed June 29, 1842. House sustained July 4, 1842, 114-97.

Total Days:	5
Adjournment Days:	0
In Session Days:	5

28th Congress, 1st Session

H.R. 203—Appropriations for harbors and rivers, vetoed June 11, 1844. House sustained June 11, 1844, 104-84.

Total Days:	Same Day
Adjournment Days:	0
In Session Days:	Same Day

28th Congress, 2nd Session

S. 66—An Act relating to revenue cutters and steamers, vetoed February 20, 1845. Senate overrode March 3, 1945, 41-1. House overrode March 3, 1845, 127-30.

Total Days:	11
Adjournment Days:	0
In Session Days:	11

JAMES POLK

29th Congress, 1st Session

S. 68—To settle claims against the French, vetoed August 8, 1846. Senate sustained August 10, 1846, 27-15.

Total Days:	2
Adjournment Days:	0
In Session Days:	2

H.R. 18—Appropriations for rivers and harbors, vetoed August 3, 1846. House sustained August 4, 1846, 97-91.

Total Days:	1
Adjournment Days:	0
In Session Days:	1

FRANKLIN PIERCE

33rd Congress, 1st Session

S. 44—Granting public lands, vetoed May 3, 1854. Senate sustained July 6, 1854, 21-26.

Total Days:	64
Adjournment Days:	0
In Session Days:	64

H.R. 117—To settle claims against the French, vetoed February 17, 1855. House sustained February 19, 1855, 113-86.

Total Days:	2
Adjournment Days:	0
In Session Days:	2

H.R. 392—Appropriations for public works, vetoed August 4, 1854. House sustained December 6, 1854. 95-80.

Total Days:	124
Adjournment Days:	119
In Session Days:	5

33rd Congress, 2nd Session

H.R. 595—Appropriations for transporting the United States mail, vetoed March 3, 1855. House sustained March 3, 1855, 79-99.

Total Days:	Same Day
Adjournment Days:	0
In Session Days:	Same Day

34th Congress, 1st Session

S. 1—Appropriations for deepening a channel construction, vetoed May 19, 1856. Senate overrode July 7, 1856, 28-8. House overrode July 8, 1856, 139-55.

Total Days:	50
Adjournment Days:	0
In Session Days:	50

S. 2—Appropriations for deepening a channel construction, vetoed May 22, 1856. Senate overrode July 7, 1856, 28-10. House overrode July 8, 1856, 136-54.

Total Days:	47
Adjournment Days:	0
In Session Days:	47

S.14—To remove navigational obstructions, vetoed May 19, 1856. Senate overrode July 7, 1856, 31-12. House overrode July 8, 1856, 143-55.

Total Days:	50
Adjournment Days:	0
In Session Days:	50

S. 53—To improve navigation at ports, vetoed August 14, 1856. Senate overrode August 16, 1856, 31-14. House overrode August 16, 1856, 127-47.

Total Days:	2
Adjournment Days:	0
In Session Days:	2

H.R. 12—To improve the Des Moines Rapids, vetoed August 11, 1856. House overrode August 11, 1856, 130-54. Senate overrode August 16, 1856, 30-14.

Total Days:	5
Adjournment Days:	0
In Session Days:	5

JAMES BUCHANAN

35th Congress, 2nd Session

H.R. 2—To donate public lands, vetoed February 24, 1859. House sustained February 26, 1859, 105-96.

Total Days:	2
Adjournment Days:	0
In Session Days:	2

36th Congress, 1st Session

S. 29—For the relief of Arthur Edwards, vetoed April 17, 1860. Senate sustained June 7, 1860, 22-30.

Total Days:	50
Adjournment Days:	0
In Session Days:	50

S. 416—To secure homelands, vetoed June 22, 1860. Senate sustained June 23, 1860, 28-18.

Total Days:	1
Adjournment Days:	0
In Session Days:	1

36th Congress, 2nd Session

H.R. 915—For the relief of Hockaday and Leggit, vetoed January 25, 1861. House sustained January 26, 1861, 81-67.

Total Days:	1
Adjournment Days:	0
In Session Days:	1

ABRAHAM LINCOLN

37th Congress, 2nd Session

S. 343—To provide additional medical officers, vetoed July 2, 1862. Senate sustained July 2, 1862, 0-37.

Total Days:	Same Day
Adjournment Days:	0
In Session Days:	Same Day

ANDREW JOHNSON

39th Congress, 1st Session

S. 60—To establish a Freedmen's Bureau, vetoed February 19, 1866. Senate sustained February 20, 1866, 30-18.

Total Days:	1
Adjournment Days:	0
In Session Days:	1

S. 61—To protect civil rights, vetoed March 27, 1866. Senate overrode April 6, 1866, 33-15. House overrode April 9, 1866, 122-41.

Total Days:	14
Adjournment Days:	0
In Session Days:	14

H.R. 613—To amend the Freedmen's Bureau Act, vetoed July 16, 1866. House overrode July 16, 1866, 103-33. Senate overrode July 16, 1866, 33-12.

Total Days:	Same Day
Adjournment Days:	0
In Session Days:	Same Day

39th Congress, 2nd Session

S. 1—To regulate voting in the District of Columbia, vetoed January 5, 1967. Senate overrode January 7, 1867, 29-10. House overrode January 8, 1867, 112-38.

Total Days:	3
Adjournment Days:	0
In Session Days:	3

S. 453—Regulating the tenure of civil offices, vetoed March 2, 1867. Senate overrode March 2, 1867, 35-11. House overrode March 2, 1867, 138-40.

Total Days:	Same Day
Adjournment Days:	0
In Session Days:	Same Day

S. 456—Admitting the State of Nebraska, vetoed January 29, 1867. Senate overrode February 8, 1867, 31-9. House overrode February 9, 1867, 120-44.

Total Days:	11
Adjournment Days:	0
In Session Days:	11

S. 462—To admit the State of Colorado, vetoed January 28, 1867. Senate sustained March 1, 1867, 29-19.

Total Days:	32
Adjournment Days:	0
In Session Days:	32

H.R. 1143—To govern the rebel states, vetoed March 2, 1867. House overrode March 2, 1867, 138-51. Senate overrode March 2, 1867, 38-10.

Total Days:	Same Day
Adjournment Days:	0
In Session Days:	Same Day

40th Congress, 1st Session

H.R. 33—To amend the Rebel States Governance Act, vetoed March 23, 1867. House overrode March 23, 1867, 114-25. Senate overrode March 23, 1867, 40-7.

Total Days:	Same Day
Adjournment Days:	0
In Session Days:	Same Day

H.R. 123—Amends an Act to provide more efficient government for the rebel states, vetoed July 19, 1867. House overrode July 19, 1867, 109-25. Senate overrode July 19, 1867, 30-6.

Total Days:	Same Day
Adjournment Days:	0
In Session Days:	Same Day

H.J. Res. 71—To govern the rebel states, vetoed July 19, 1867. House overrode July 19, 1867, 99-22. Senate overrode July 19, 1867, 32-4.

Total Days:	Same Day
Adjournment Days:	0
In Session Days:	Same Day

40th Congress, 2nd Session

S. 213—To amend the Judiciary Act, vetoed March 25, 1868. Senate overrode March 26, 1868, 33-9. House overrode March 27, 1868, 115-34.

Total Days:	2
Adjournment Days:	0
In Session Days:	2

S. 567—To discontinue the Freedmen's Bureau, vetoed July 25, 1868. Senate overrode July 25, 1868, 42-5. House overrode July 25, 1868, 115-23.

Total Days:	Same Day
Adjournment Days:	0
In Session Days:	Same Day

S. J. Res. 139—Electoral Reform, vetoed July 20, 1868. Senate overrode July 20, 1868, 45-8. House overrode July 20, 1868, 134-36.

Total Days:	Same Day
Adjournment Days:	0
In Session Days:	Same Day

H.R. 1039—To admit the State of Arkansas, vetoed June 20, 1868. House overrode June 20, 1868, 111-31. Senate overrode June 22, 1868, 30-7.

Total Days:	2
Adjournment Days:	0
In Session Days:	2

H.R. 1058—To admit North Carolina, South Carolina, Louisiana, Georgia, Alabama, and Florida, to representation in Congress, vetoed June 25, 1868. House overrode June 25, 1868, 108-32. Senate overrode June 25, 1868, 35-8.

Total Days:	Same Day
Adjournment Days:	0
In Session Days:	Same Day

H.R. 1460—Regulating imported copper, vetoed February 22, 1869. House overrode February 23, 1869, 115-56. Senate overrode February 24, 1869, 38-12.

Total Days:	2
Adjournment Days:	0
In Session Days:	2

ULYSSES S. GRANT

41st Congress, 2nd Session

S. 273—For the relief of Rollin White, vetoed January 11, 1870. Senate overrode May 31, 1870, 41-13. House sustained June 22, 1870, 12-168.

Total Days:	162
Adjournment Days:	0
In Session Days:	162

41st Congress, 3rd Session

S.J. Res. 92—For relief of ship contractors, vetoed February 7, 1871. Senate sustained February 16, 1871, 2-57.

Total Days:	9
Adjournment Days:	0
In Session Days:	9

42nd Congress, 2nd Session

S. 955—Granting a pension to Mary Ann Montgomery, vetoed May 14, 1872. Senate overrode May 17, 1872, 44-1. House overrode June 7, 1872, 101-44.

Total Days:	24
Adjournment Days:	0
In Session Days:	24

43rd Congress, 1st Session

S. 617—To fix the amount of United States notes and their circulation to national banks, vetoed April 22, 1874. Senate sustained April 28, 1874, 34-30.

Total Days:	5
Adjournment Days:	0
In Session Days:	5

44th Congress, 1st Session

S. 489—For the relief of G. B. Tyler and E. H. Luckett, vetoed March 31, 1876. Senate overrode May 20, 1876, 46-0. House overrode May 26, 1876, 181-14.

Total Days:	56
Adjournment Days:	0
In Session Days:	56

S. 779—To sell Indian reservation lands in the states of Kansas and Nebraska, vetoed August 15, 1876. Senate overrode August 15, 1876, 36-0. House overrode August 15, 1876, 120-18.

Total Days:	Same Day
Adjournment Days:	0
In Session Days:	Same Day

H.R. 1337—To provide for the relief of Nelson Tiffany, vetoed July 11, 1876. House overrode July 28, 1876, 177-1. Senate overrode July 31, 1876, 40-0.

Total Days:	20
Adjournment Days:	0
In Session Days:	20

H.R. 3156—To perfect the revision of the Statutes of the United States, vetoed February 14, 1877. House sustained February 15, 1877, 1-211.

Total Days:	1
Adjournment Days:	0
In Session Days:	1

H.R. 4350—To abolish the Board of Commissions from the District of Columbia Police Department, vetoed January 23, 1877. House overrode January 30, 1877, 159-78. Senate sustained February 6, 1877, 33-22.

Total Days:	14
Adjournment Days:	0
In Session Days:	14

RUTHERFORD B. HAYES

45th Congress, 2nd Session

H.R. 1093—To coin silver dollars, vetoed February 28, 1878. House overrode February 28, 1878, 196-73. Senate overrode February 28, 1878, 46-19.

Total Days:	Same Day
Adjournment Days:	0
In Session Days:	Same Day

45th Congress, 3rd Session

H.R. 2423—To restrict Chinese immigration, vetoed March 1, 1879. House sustained March 1, 1879, 110-96.

Total Days:	Same Day
Adjournment Days:	0
In Session Days:	Same Day

46th Congress, 1st Session

H.R. 1—To make appropriations for the Army, vetoed April 29, 1879. House sustained May 1, 1879, 121-110.

Total Days:	2
Adjournment Days:	0
In Session Days:	2

H.R. 2—To make appropriations for the legislative, executive, and judicial expenses of the government, vetoed May 29, 1879. House sustained May 29, 1879, 114-93.

Total Days:	Same Day
Adjournment Days:	0
In Session Days:	Same Day

H.R. 1382—To prohibit military interference at elections, vetoed May 12, 1879. House sustained May 13, 1879, 128-97.

Total Days:	1
Adjournment Days:	0
In Session Days:	1

H.R. 2252—Making appropriations for certain judicial expenses, vetoed June 23, 1879. House sustained June 23, 1879, 102-78.

Total Days:	Same Day
Adjournment Days:	0
In Session Days:	Same Day

H.R. 2382—Making appropriations for U.S. Marshals, vetoed June 30, 1879. House sustained June 30, 1879, 85-63.

Total Days:	Same Day
Adjournment Days:	0
In Session Days:	Same Day

CHESTER A. ARTHUR

47th Congress, 1st Session

S. 71—To execute certain treaty stipulations relating to the Chinese, vetoed April 4, 1882. Senate sustained April 5, 1882, 29-21.

Total Days:	1
Adjournment Days:	0
In Session Days:	1

H. R. 6242—Making appropriations for rivers and harbors, vetoed August 1, 1882. House overrode August 2, 1882, 122-59. Senate overrode August 2, 1882, 41-16.

Total Days:	1
Adjournment Days:	0
In Session Days:	1

48th Congress, 1st Session

H.R. 1015—To provide for the relief of Fitz-John Porter, vetoed July 2, 1884. House overrode July 2, 1884, 168-78. Senate sustained July 3, 1884, 27-27.

Total Days:	1
Adjournment Days:	0
In Session Days:	1

GROVER CLEVELAND

49th Congress, 1st Session

S. 150—To quiet title of settlers on the Des Moines River lands in the State of Iowa, vetoed March 11, 1886. Senate overrode June 29, 1886, 34-15. House sustained July 1, 1886, 161-93.

Total Days:	112
Adjournment Days:	0
In Session Days:	112

S. 183—For the relief of Thomas S. Hopkins, vetoed June 19, 1886. Senate overrode February 23, 1887, 55-7. House sustained March 3, 1887, 153-95.

Total Days:	257
Adjournment Days:	123
In Session Days:	134

S.349—For the promotion of anatomical science and to prevent the desecration of graves, vetoed April 26, 1886. Senate sustained April 30, 1886, 6-48.

Total Days: 4
Adjournment Days: 0
In Session Days: 4

S. 763—For the erection of a public building at Sioux City, Iowa, vetoed June 19, 1886. Senate overrode March 3, 1887, 38-19. House sustained March 3, 1887, 107-77.

Total Days: 257
Adjournment Days: 123
In Session Days: 134

S. 789—Granting a pension to John S. Williams, vetoed June 2, 1886. Senate sustained August 4, 1886, 19-15.

Total Days: 63
Adjournment Days: 0
In Session Days: 63

S 856—To provide for the erection of a public building at Dayton, Ohio, vetoed July 9, 1886. Senate overrode March 3, 1887, 39-18. House overrode March 3, 1887, 133-64.

Total Days: 237
Adjournment Days: 123
In Session Days: 114

S. 2005—Granting a pension to Mary J. Nottage, vetoed June 22, 1886. Senate sustained August 3, 1886, 26-19.

Total Days: 42
Adjournment Days: 0
In Session Days: 42

H.R. 1059—Granting a pension to Joseph Romiser, vetoed July 5, 1886. House overrode July 16, 1886, 175-38. Senate overrode August 3, 1886, 50-0.

Total Days:	29
Adjournment Days:	0
In Session Days:	29

H.R. 4002—Granting a pension to Carter W. Tiller, vetoed June 19, 1886. House sustained February 2, 1887, 135-107.

Total Days:	228
Adjournment Days:	123
In Session Days:	105

H.R. 5394—Granting a pension to Sally Ann Bradley, vetoed July 6, 1886. House sustained March 3, 1887, 123-122.

Total Days:	240
Adjournment Days:	123
In Session Days:	117

H.R. 5603—Granting a pension to Catherine McCarty, vetoed July 6, 1886. House sustained July 16, 1886, 124-97.

Total Days:	10
Adjournment Days:	0
In Session Days:	10

H.R. 5997—Granting a pension to Elizabeth Luce, vetoed June 19, 1886. House sustained July 16, 1886, 116-124.

Total Days:	27
Adjournment Days:	0
In Session Days:	27

H.R. 6136—Granting a pension to John W. Farris, vetoed June 21, 1886. House sustained February 22, 1887, 131-94.

Total Days:	246
Adjournment Days:	123
In Session Days:	123

H.R. 7109—Granting a pension to Andrew J. Wilson, vetoed June 23, 1886. House sustained July 29, 1886, 106-85.

Total Days:	36
Adjournment Days:	0
In Session Days:	36

H.R. 7167—Granting a pension to Maria Hunter, vetoed June 23, 1886. House sustained July 30, 1886, 111-108.

Total Days:	37
Adjournment Days:	0
In Session Days:	37

H.R. 7436—Granting a pension to Mary Anderson, vetoed June 23, 1886. House sustained July 30, 1886, 120-95.

Total Days:	37
Adjournment Days:	0
In Session Days:	37

49th Congress, 2nd Session

S. 1162—To erect a post-office building, vetoed February 25, 1887. Senate overrode March 3, 1887, 36-15.

Total Days:	6
Adjournment Days:	0
In Session Days:	6

H.R. 10203—Making appropriations for seed distribution in Texas, vetoed February 16, 1887. House sustained February 17, 1887, 83-159.

Total Days:	1
Adjournment Days:	0
In Session Days:	1

H.R. 10457—For the relief of dependent children of discharged and disabled soldiers and sailors, vetoed February 11, 1887. House sustained February 24, 1887, 175-125.

Total Days:	13
Adjournment Days:	0
In Session Days:	13

50th Congress, 1st Session

H.R. 4357—To erect a public building at Allentown, Pennsylvania, vetoed May 9, 1888. House sustained July 19, 1888, 140-82.

Total Days:	71
Adjournment Days:	0
In Session Days:	71

50th Congress, 2nd Session

S. 139—To credit and pay to the several states and territories and the District of Columbia all moneys collected under the direct tax levied by the Act of Congress approved August 5, 1861, vetoed March 2, 1889. Senate overrode March 2, 1889, 45-9. House did not challenge veto.

Total Days:	Same Day
Adjournment Days:	0
In Session Days:	Same Day

S. 3646—For the relief of William R. Wheaton and Charles H. Chamberlain of California, vetoed January 17, 1889. Senate overrode February 26, 1889, 35-8. House did not challenge veto.

Total Days:	40
Adjournment Days:	0
In Session Days:	40

H.R. 1368—To quiet title of settlers on the Des Moines River in the State of Iowa, vetoed February 21, 1889. House sustained March 1, 1889, 147-104.

Total Days:	8
Adjournment Days:	0
In Session Days:	8

BENJAMIN HARRISON

51st Congress, 1st Session

H.R. 848—To authorize the construction of an addition to the public building at Dallas, Texas, vetoed April 29, 1890. House overrode February 10, 1891, 143-69. Senate did not challenge veto.

Total Days:	256
Adjournment Days:	61
In Session Days:	195

52nd Congress, 1st Session

S. 1958—To submit to the Court of Claims the title of William McGarrahan to the Ranch Panoche Grande, in the State of California, vetoed July 29, 1892. Senate sustained January 17, 1893, 29-18.

Total Days:	172
Adjournment Days:	92
In Session Days:	80

52nd Congress, 2nd Session

H.R. 9612—To prescribe the number of district attorneys and marshals in the State of Alabama, vetoed February 27, 1893. House overrode March 2, 1893, 184-55. Senate overrode Mach 3, 1893, 58-1.

Total Days:	4
Adjournment Days:	0
In Session Days:	4

GROVER CLEVELAND

53rd Congress, 2nd Session

H.R. 4956—Directing the coinage of silver bullion, vetoed March 29, 1894. House sustained April 4, 1894, 144-114.

Total Days:	6
Adjournment Days:	0
In Session Days:	6

53rd Congress, 3rd Session

H.R. 4658—Granting a pension to Hiram R. Rhea, vetoed February 23, 1895. House sustained February 28, 1895, 97-144.

Total Days:	5
Adjournment Days:	0
In Session Days:	5

54th Congress, 1st Session

H.R. 577—Granting a pension to Lydia A. Taft, vetoed May 20, 1896. House sustained December 14, 1896, 98-85.

Total Days:	208
Adjournment Days:	179
In Session Days:	29

H.R. 1094—Granting a pension to Francis E. Hoover, vetoed April 25, 1896. House overrode May 21, 1896, 196-47. Senate overrode June 10, 1896, 36-9.

Total Days:	26
Adjournment Days:	0
In Session Days:	26

H.R. 1139—Granting a pension to Caroline D. Mowatt, vetoed May 19, 1896. House overrode February 9, 1897, 143-55. Senate overrode March 3, 1897, 39-7.

Total Days:	288
Adjournment Days:	179
In Session Days:	109

H.R. 2769—To authorize the leasing of land for educational purposes in Arizona, vetoed February 28, 1896. House overrode February 29, 1896, 199-38. Senate did not challenge veto.

Total Days:	1
Adjournment Days:	0
In Session Days:	1

H.R. 4526—Granting a pension to Jonathan Scott, vetoed May 30, 1896. House overrode January 26, 1897, 137-53. Senate did not challenge veto.

Total Days:	241
Adjournment Days:	179
In Session Days:	62

H.R. 7977—Making appropriations for public works on rivers and harbors, vetoed May 29, 1896. House overrode June 2, 1896, 219-61. Senate overrode June 2, 1896, 56-5.

Total Days:	4
Adjournment Days:	0
In Session Days:	4

H.R. 8293—Making appropriations to supply deficiencies, vetoed June 6, 1896. House sustained June 6, 1896, 39-171.

Total Days:	Same Day
Adjournment Days:	0
In Session Days:	Same Day

54th Congress, 2nd Session

H.R. 1185—Granting a pension to Rachel Patton, vetoed May 21, 1896. House overrode February 9, 1897, 137-60. Senate overrode March 3, 1897, 37-10.

Total Days:	286
Adjournment Days:	179
In Session Days:	107

H.R. 7864—To amend the immigration laws, vetoed March 2, 1897. House overrode March 3, 1897, 195-37. Senate did not challenge veto.

Total Days:	1
Adjournment Days:	0
In Session Days:	1

H.R. 9469—To reorganize judicial districts in the State of Texas, vetoed January 14, 1897. House overrode January 22, 1897, 144-68. Senate overrode February 8, 1897, 57-1.

Total Days:	25
Adjournment Days:	0
In Session Days:	25

WILLIAM MCKINLEY

55th Congress, 2nd Session

H.R. 2219—For the relief of the administrators of the estate of Issac Tice, vetoed May 16, 1898. House sustained May 16, 1898, 0-189.

Total Days: Same Day
Adjournment Days: 0
In Session Days: Same Day

THEODORE ROOSEVELT

60th Congress, 1st Session

H.R. 4763—Transferring Commander William Wilmot White from the retired list to the active list of the Navy, vetoed April 7, 1908. House sustained April 8, 1908, 0-258.

Total Days: 1
Adjournment Days: 0
In Session Days: 1

H.R. 15444—Extending the time for construction of a dam across the Rainy River, vetoed April 13, 1908. House overrode May 23, 1908, 240-5. Senate overrode May 23, 1908, 49-0.

Total Days: 40
Adjournment Days: 0
In Session Days: 40

WILLIAM HOWARD TAFT

62nd Congress, 1st Session

H.R. 4413—To place on the free list various agricultural and textile products, vetoed August 18, 1911. House sustained August 18, 1911, 227-126.

Total Days: Same Day
Adjournment Days: 0
In Session Days: Same Day

H.R. 11019—To reduce the duties on wool and manufactures of wool, vetoed August 17, 1911. House sustained August 18, 1911, 227-129.

Total Days:	1
Adjournment Days:	0
In Session Days:	1

62nd Congress, 2nd Session

S. 4862—For the relief of persons who supplied labor and materials for the construction of Corbett Tunnel, vetoed July 18, 1912. Senate overrode July 31, 1912, 42-17. House sustained August 16, 1912, 138-77.

Total Days:	29
Adjournment Days:	0
In Session Days:	29

H.R. 18642—Amends an Act to provide revenue, equalize duties, and encourage the industries of the United States, vetoed August 14, 1912. House overrode August 14, 1912, 174-83. Senate sustained August 16, 1912, 32-39.

Total Days:	2
Adjournment Days:	0
In Session Days:	2

H.R. 22195—To reduce duties on wool and wool industries, vetoed August 9, 1912. House overrode August 13, 1912, 174-80. Senate sustained August 16, 1912, 39-36.

Total Days:	7
Adjournment Days:	0
In Session Days:	7

H.R. 24023—Making appropriations for the legislative, executive, and judicial expenses of the government, vetoed August 15, 1912. House sustained August 15, 1912, 147-107.

Total Days:	Same Day
Adjournment Days:	0
In Session Days:	Same Day

H.R. 26321—Making appropriations for the legislative, executive, and judicial expenses of the government, vetoed August 21, 1912. House overrode August 21, 1912, 154-53. Senate sustained August 21, 1912, 34-27.

Total Days:	Same Day
Adjournment Days:	0
In Session Days:	Same Day

62nd Congress, 3rd Session

S. 3175—To regulate the immigration of aliens, vetoed February 14, 1913. Senate overrode February 18, 1913, 72-18. House sustained February 19, 1913, 213-114.

Total Days:	5
Adjournment Days:	0
In Session Days:	5

H.R. 28775—Making appropriations for civil expenses of the government, vetoed March 4, 1913. House overrode March 4, 1913, 264-48. Senate did not challenge veto.

Total Days:	Same Day
Adjournment Days:	0
In Session Days:	Same Day

WOODROW WILSON

63rd Congress, 3rd Session

H.R. 6060—To regulate immigration, vetoed January 28, 1915. House sustained February 4, 1915, 261-136.

Total Days:	7
Adjournment Days:	0
In Session Days:	7

64th Congress, 2nd Session

H.R. 10384—To regulate immigration, vetoed January 29, 1917. House overrode February 1, 1917, 287-106. Senate overrode February 5, 1917, 62-19.

Total Days:	7
Adjournment Days:	0
In Session Days:	7

65th Congress, 2nd Session

H.R. 7237—Making appropriations for the Post Office Department, vetoed June 29, 1918. House sustained June 29, 1918, 114-186.

Total Days:	Same Day
Adjournment Days:	0
In Session Days:	Same Day

H.R. 9054—Making appropriations for the Department of Agriculture, vetoed, July 12, 1918. House sustained July 13, 1918, 73-173.

Total Days:	1
Adjournment Days:	0
In Session Days:	1

H.R. 10358—Making appropriations for the legislative, executive, and judicial expenses of government, vetoed July 1, 1918. House sustained July 1, 1918, 50-248.

Total Days:	Same Day
Adjournment Days:	0
In Session Days:	Same Day

66th Congress, 1st Session

H.R. 3157—Making appropriations for the Department of Agriculture, vetoed July 11, 1919. House sustained July 12, 1919, 248-135.

Total Days:	1
Adjournment Days:	0
In Session Days:	1

H.R. 3854—To repeal the daylight saving law, vetoed August 15, 1919. House overrode August 19, 1919, 223-101. Senate overrode August 20, 1919, 57-19.

Total Days:	5
Adjournment Days:	0
In Session Days:	5

H.R. 6810—To regulate intoxicating beverages, vetoed October 27, 1919. House overrode October 27, 1919, 175-55. Senate overrode October 28, 1919, 65-20.

Total Days:	1
Adjournment Days:	0
In Session Days:	1

66th Congress, 2nd Session

H.R. 9783—To provide for a national budget system and government audit, vetoed June 4, 1920. House sustained June 4, 1920, 178-103.

Total Days:	Same Day
Adjournment Days:	0
In Session Days:	Same Day

H.R. 12610—Making appropriations for the legislative, executive, and judicial expenses of the government, vetoed May 13, 1920. House sustained May 14, 1920, 170-127.

Total Days:	1
Adjournment Days:	0
In Session Days:	1

H.J. Res. 327—Terminating the state of war between the United States and the Imperial German Government, vetoed May 27, 1920. House sustained May 28, 1920, 220-152.

Total Days:	1
Adjournment Days:	0
In Session Days:	1

66th Congress, 3rd Session

S. 793—Authorizing the issuance of a patent to the Milk River Valley Gun Club, vetoed February 3, 1921. Senate sustained February 7, 1921, 9-47.

Total Days:	5
Adjournment Days:	0
In Session Days:	5

S.J. Res. 212—To provide relief to certain agriculture sections of the country, vetoed January 3, 1921. Senate overrode January 3, 1921, 53-5. House overrode January 4, 1921, 250-66.

Total Days: 1
Adjournment Days: 0
In Session Days: 1

H.R. 517—Amends an Act providing for drainage on Indians lands, vetoed February 15, 1921. House overrode February 24, 1921, 323-18. Senate overrode March 2, 1921, 67-5.

Total Days: 15
Adjournment Days: 0
In Session Days: 15

H.R. 15275—Imposing temporary duties of agricultural products, vetoed March 3, 1921. House sustained March 3, 1921, 201-132.

Total Days: Same Day
Adjournment Days: 0
In Session Days: Same Day

H.J. Res. 440—Directing the Secretary of War to cease enlisting men in the Regular Army, vetoed February 5, 1921. House overrode February 5, 1921, 271-16. Senate overrode February 7, 1921, 67-1.

Total Days: 2
Adjournment Days: 0
In Session Days: 2

WARREN G. HARDING

67th Congress, 2nd Session

H.R. 10874—To provide adjusted compensation for veterans, vetoed September 19, 1922. House overrode September 20, 1922, 258-54. Senate sustained September 20, 1922, 44-28.

Total Days: 1
Adjournment Days: 0
In Session Days: 1

CALVIN COOLIDGE

68th Congress, 1st Session

S. 5—Granting pensions to soldiers and sailors, vetoed May 3, 1924. Senate sustained May 13, 1924, 53-28.

Total Days:	10
Adjournment Days:	0
In Session Days:	10

H.R. 7959—To provide adjusted compensation for veterans, vetoed May 15, 1924. House overrode May 17, 1924, 313-78. Senate overrode May 19, 1924, 59-26.

Total Days:	4
Adjournment Days:	0
In Session Days:	4

70th Congress, 1st Session

S. 750—To amend National Defense Act, vetoed May 22, 1928. Senate sustained May 24, 1928, 44-32.

Total Days:	2
Adjournment Days:	0
In Session Days:	2

S. 777—Making retirement available to Army officers, vetoed May 22, 1928. Senate overrode May 24, 1928, 66-14. House overrode May 24, 1928, 245-101.

Total Days:	2
Adjournment Days:	0
In Session Days:	2

S. 3555—To establish a Federal Farm Board, vetoed May 23, 1928. Senate sustained May 25, 1928, 50-31.

Total Days:	2
Adjournment Days:	0
In Session Days:	2

S. 3674—Amend Act to provide rural postal roads, vetoed May 18, 1928. Senate overrode May 24, 1928, 57-22. House sustained May 25, 1928, 161-182.

Total Days:	7
Adjournment Days:	0
In Session Days:	7

H.R. 5681—To amend Act fixing compensation of postal employees, vetoed May 18, 1928. House overrode May 22, 1928, 320-42. Senate overrode May 24, 1928, 70-9.

Total Days:	6
Adjournment Days:	0
In Session Days:	6

H.R. 7900—Granting allowance to postmasters, vetoed May 18, 1928. House overrode May 22, 1928, 318-46. Senate overrode May 24, 1928, 63-17.

Total Days:	6
Adjournment Days:	0
In Session Days:	6

HERBERT HOOVER

71st Congress, 2nd Session

S. 476—Granting pensions for soldiers and sailors, vetoed May 28, 1930. Senate overrode June 2, 1930, 61-18. House overrode June 2, 1930, 299-14.

Total Days:	5
Adjournment Days:	0
In Session Days:	5

H.R. 2029—To coin silver pieces, vetoed April 21, 1930. House sustained April 22, 1930, 96-244.

Total Days:	1
Adjournment Days:	0
In Session Days:	1

H.R. 10381—To amend World War Veterans Act, vetoed June 26, 1930. House sustained June 26, 1930, 182-188.

Total Days:	Same Day
Adjournment Days:	0
In Session Days:	Same Day

71st Congress, 3rd Session

S.J. Res. 49—To create a corporation for operation of government properties in the State of Alabama, vetoed March 3, 1931. Senate sustained March 3, 1931, 49-34.

Total Days:	Same Day
Adjournment Days:	0
In Session Days:	Same Day

H.R. 1036—For the relief of Homer N. Horine, vetoed February 7, 1931. House sustained February 7, 1931, 10-278.

Total Days:	Same Day
Adjournment Days:	0
In Session Days:	Same Day

H.R. 17054—To increase the loan basis of adjusted-service certificates, vetoed February 26, 1931. House overrode February 26, 1931, 328-79. Senate overrode February 27, 1931, 76-17.

Total Days:	1
Adjournment Days:	0
In Session Days:	1

H.R. 6662—To amend the Tariff Act of 1930, vetoed May 11, 1932. House sustained May 11, 1932, 178-166.

Total Days:	Same Day
Adjournment Days:	0
In Session Days:	Same Day

72nd Congress, 2nd Session

H.R. 7233—To provide for the independence of the Philippines, vetoed January 13, 1933. House overrode January 13, 1933, 274-94. Senate overrode January 17, 1933, 66-26.

Total Days:	5
Adjournment Days:	0
In Session Days:	5

H.R. 13975—Making appropriations for deficiencies in certain appropriations, vetoed January 24, 1933. House sustained January 24, 1933, 193-158.

Total Days:	Same Day
Adjournment Days:	0
In Session Days:	Same Day

FRANKLIN D. ROOSEVELT

73rd Congress, 2nd Session

H.R. 6663—Making appropriations for the executive office and independent agencies, vetoed March 27, 1934. House overrode March 27, 1934, 310-72. Senate overrode March 28, 1934, 63-27.

Total Days: 1
Adjournment Days: 0
In Session Days: 1

74th Congress, 1st Session

H.R. 3896—To provide for payment to veterans, vetoed May 22, 1935. House overrode May 22, 1935, 322-98. Senate sustained May 23, 1935, 54-40.

Total Days: 1
Adjournment Days: 0
In Session Days: 1

75th Congress, 1st Session

H.R. 5478—To amend law to provide for the renewal of expiring 5-year level premium term policies for another 5-year period for ex-servicemen, vetoed May 28, 1937. House overrode June 1, 1937, 372-13. Senate overrode June 1, 1937, 69-12.

Total Days: 4
Adjournment Days: 0
In Session Days: 4

H.R. 6763—To extend for 1 year the interest rate on certain federal land-bank loans, vetoed June 9, 1937. House overrode July 13, 1937, 260-98. Senate overrode July 22, 1937, 71-19.

Total Days: 43
Adjournment Days: 0
In Session Days: 43

75th Congress, 3rd Session

H.R. 10530—To extend for 2 years the interest on certain federal land-bank loans, vetoed June 15, 1938. House overrode June 15, 1938, 244-88. Senate overrode June 16, 1938, 57-18.

Total Days:	1
Adjournment Days:	0
In Session Days:	1

76th Congress, 3rd Session

H.R. 3233—To repeal certain acts of Congress, vetoed June 11, 1940. House sustained August 5, 1940, 185-105.

Total Days:	55
Adjournment Days:	0
In Session Days:	55

H.R. 3840—To provide for national defense, vetoed June 24, 1940. House sustained September 25, 1940, 197-114.

Total Days:	93
Adjournment Days:	0
In Session Days:	93

H.R. 5118—For relief of the State of Ohio, vetoed January 24, 1940. House sustained January 24, 1940, 171-152.

Total Days:	Same Day
Adjournment Days:	0
In Session Days:	Same Day

H.R. 6324—To provide for more expeditious settlement of disputes with the United States, vetoed December 18, 1940. House sustained December 18, 1940, 153-127.

Total Days: Same Day
Adjournment Days: 0
In Session Days: Same Day

H.R. 6901—Granting increase in pensions to certain widows of veterans of the Civil War, vetoed April 25, 1940. House sustained April 26, 1940, 218-142.

Total Days: 1
Adjournment Days: 0
In Session Days: 1

H.R. 7737—To amend the judicial code, vetoed June 10, 1940. House overrode August 5, 1940, 254-46. Senate did not challenge veto.

Total Days: 56
Adjournment Days: 0
In Session Days: 56

H.R. 9381—To provide for the alteration of certain bridges, vetoed June 10, 1940. House overrode June 19, 1940, 324-68. Senate overrode June 21, 1940, 65-17.

Total Days: 11
Adjournment Days: 0
In Session Days: 11

77th Congress, 1st Session

S. 1580—To supplement the Federal Aid Road Act, vetoed August 2, 1941. Senate overrode August 6, 1941, 57-19. House sustained August 7, 1941, 251-128.

Total Days: 5
Adjournment Days: 0
In Session Days: 5

78th Congress, 1st Session

S. 514—For the relief of Blanch H. Karsch, vetoed October 28, 1943. Senate overrode November 18, 1943, 65-4. House did not challenge veto.

Total Days:	21
Adjournment Days:	0
In Session Days:	21

S. 796—To prevent strikes at facilities used in the prosecution of war, vetoed June 25, 1943. Senate overrode June 25, 1943, 56-25. House overrode June 25, 1943, 244-108.

Total Days:	Same Day
Adjournment Days:	0
In Session Days:	Same Day

H.R. 2869—To continue the Commodity Credit Corporation, vetoed July 2, 1943. House sustained July 2, 1943, 228-154.

Total Days:	Same Day
Adjournment Days:	0
In Session Days:	Same Day

78th Congress, 2nd Session

H.R. 3477—To continue the Commodity Credit Corporation, vetoed February 18, 1944. House sustained February 18, 1944, 266-151.

Total Days:	Same Day
Adjournment Days:	0
In Session Days:	Same Day

H.R. 3687—To provide revenue through the Revenue Act of 1943, vetoed February 22, 1944. House overrode February 24, 1944, 299-95. Senate overrode February 25, 1944, 72-14.

Total Days:	3
Adjournment Days:	0
In Session Days:	3

HARRY S. TRUMAN

79th Congress, 2nd Session

H.J. Res. 106—To amend the Selective Training and Service Act, vetoed May 3, 1945. House sustained May 3, 1945, 186-177.

Total Days:	Same Day
Adjournment Days:	0
In Session Days:	Same Day

H.R. 4908—To provide for the appointment of boards to investigate labor disputes, vetoed June 11, 1946. House sustained June 11, 1946, 255-135.

Total Days:	Same Day
Adjournment Days:	0
In Session Days:	Same Day

H.R. 6042—To amend the Emergency Price Control Act of 1942, vetoed June 29, 1946. House sustained June 19, 1946, 173-142.

Total Days:	Same Day
Adjournment Days:	0
In Session Days:	Same Day

H.J. Res. 225—To quiet the titles applying to navigable waters in certain states, vetoed August 1, 1946. House sustained August 2, 1946, 139-95.

Total Days:	1
Adjournment Days:	0
In Session Days:	1

80th Congress, 1st Session

H.R. 1—To reduce individual income-tax payments, vetoed June 16, 1947. House sustained June 17, 1947, 268-137.

Total Days:	1
Adjournment Days:	0
In Session Days:	1

H.R. 3020—Labor-Management Relations Act of 1947, vetoed June 20, 1947. House overrode June 20, 1947, 331-83. Senate overrode June 23, 1947, 68-25.

Total Days:	3
Adjournment Days:	0
In Session Days:	3

H.R. 3950—To reduce individual income-tax payments, vetoed July 18, 1947. House overrode July 18, 1947, 299-108. Senate sustained July 18, 1947, 57-36.

Total Days:	Same Day
Adjournment Days:	0
In Session Days:	Same Day

80th Congress, 2nd Session

S. 110—To amend the Interstate Commerce Act, vetoed June 10, 1948. Senate overrode June 16, 1948, 63-25. House overrode June 17, 1948, 297-102.

Total Days:	7
Adjournment Days:	0
In Session Days:	7

S.1004—To amend the Atomic Energy Act of 1946, vetoed May 15, 1948. Senate sustained May 21, 1948, 47-29

Total Days:	6
Adjournment Days:	0
In Session Days:	6

H.R. 4790—To reduce individual income-tax payments, vetoed April 1, 1948. House overrode April 2, 1948, 311-88. Senate overrode April 2, 1948, 77-10.

Total Days:	1
Adjournment Days:	0
In Session Days:	1

H.R. 5052—To exclude vendors of newspapers from the Social Security Act, vetoed April 5, 1948. House overrode April 14, 1948, 308-28. Senate overrode April 20, 1948, 77-7.

Total Days:	15
Adjournment Days:	0
In Session Days:	15

H.R. 6355—Making supplemental appropriations for the Federal Security Agency, vetoed June 14, 1948. House overrode June 16, 1948, 288-115. Senate overrode June 16, 1948, 72-17.

Total Days:	2
Adjournment Days:	0
In Session Days:	2

H.J. Res. 296—To maintain the status quo in respect of certain employment taxes and social security benefits pending action by the Congress on extended social security coverage, vetoed June 14, 1948. House overrode June 14, 1948, 298-75. Senate overrode June 14, 1948, 65-12.

Total Days:	Same Day
Adjournment Days:	0
In Session Days:	Same Day

81st Congress, 1st Session

H.R. 1036—For the relief of R. C. Owen, Jr. and Ray Owen, vetoed April 21, 1949. House overrode May 18, 1949, 318-49. Senate overrode September 15, 1949, 45-6.

Total Days:	145
Adjournment Days:	0
In Session Days:	145

81st Congress, 2nd Session

S. 3906—To amend the War Contractors Relief Act, vetoed August 21, 1950. Senate sustained September 13, 1950, 30-39.

Total Days:	23
Adjournment Days:	0
In Session Days:	23

H.R. 87—Promotion of veterans of World War II in field service of the Post Office Department, vetoed June 23, 1950. House overrode June 26, 1950, 213-72. Senate sustained August 31, 1950, 48-29.

Total Days:	70
Adjournment Days:	0
In Session Days:	70

H.R. 6217—To provide security for veterans of the Spanish-American War, vetoed September 6, 1950. House overrode September 14, 1950, 321-12. Senate overrode September 19, 1950, 58-3.

Total Days:	13
Adjournment Days:	0
In Session Days:	13

H.R. 9490—To protect the United States against certain un-American and subversive activities, vetoed September 22, 1950. House overrode September 22, 1950, 286-48. Senate overrode September 23, 1950, 57-10.

Total Days:	1
Adjournment Days:	0
In Session Days:	1

H.J. Res. 238—To amend the Nationality Act of 1940, vetoed September 9, 1950. House overrode September 14, 1950, 307-14. Senate did not challenge veto.

Total Days:	5
Adjournment Days:	0
In Session Days:	5

82nd Congress, 1st Session

S. 1864—To authorize payments by the Administrator of Veteran's Affairs, vetoed October 18, 1951. Senate overrode October 18, 1951, 55-10. House overrode October 20, 1951, 223-53.

Total Days:	2
Adjournment Days:	0
In Session Days:	2

H.R. 3096—To acquire land for the departments of the military services and the Federal Civil Defense Administration, vetoed May 15, 1951. House overrode May 17, 1951, 312-68. Senate did not challenge veto.

Total Days:	2
Adjournment Days:	0
In Session Days:	2

H.R. 3193—To establish a rate of pension for veterans, vetoed August 6, 1951. House overrode August 17, 1951, 318-45. Senate overrode September 18, 1951, 69-9.

Total Days: 43
Adjournment Days: 0
In Session Days: 43

H.R. 5678—To revise the laws relating to immigration, vetoed June 25, 1952. House overrode June 26, 1952, 278-112. Senate overrode June 27, 1952, 57-26.

Total Days: 1
Adjournment Days: 0
In Session Days: 1

DWIGHT D. EISENHOWER

84th Congress, 1st Session

S. 1—To increase compensation of employees of the Post Office Department, vetoed May 19, 1955. Senate sustained May 24, 1955, 54-39.

Total Days: 5
Adjournment Days: 0
In Session Days: 5

84th Congress, 2nd Session

H.R. 12—To amend the Agriculture Act of 1949, vetoed April 16, 1956. House sustained April 18, 1956, 202-211.

Total Days: 2
Adjournment Days: 0
In Session Days: 2

85th Congress, 2nd Session

S. 2266—To provide a method for fixing wage rates at the Portsmouth Naval Shipyard, vetoed August 4, 1958. Senate overrode August 12, 1958, 69-20. House sustained August 13, 1958, 202-180.

Total Days:	11
Adjournment Days:	0
In Session Days:	11

86th Congress, 1st Session

S. 57—To improve urban communities, vetoed July 7, 1959. Senate sustained August 12, 1959, 55-40.

Total Days:	36
Adjournment Days:	0
In Session Days:	36

S. 144—To amend Reorganization Plan No. 2 of 1953, vetoed April 27, 1959. Senate overrode April 28, 1959. House sustained April 30, 1959, 280-146.

Total Days:	3
Adjournment Days:	0
In Session Days:	3

S. 2539—To improve urban communities, vetoed September 3, 1959. Senate sustained September 4, 1959, 58-36.

Total Days:	1
Adjournment Days:	0
In Session Days:	1

H.R. 7509—To make appropriations for the civil functions of the Department of the Army, vetoed August 26, 1959. House sustained September 2, 1959, 274-138.

Total Days:	7
Adjournment Days:	0
In Session Days:	7

H.R. 9105—Making appropriations for the civil functions of the Department of the Army, vetoed September 9, 1959. House overrode September 10, 1959, 280-121. Senate overrode September 10, 1959, 72-23.

Total Days:	1
Adjournment Days:	0
In Session Days:	1

86th Congress, 2nd Session

S. 722—To establish an effective program to alleviate conditions of unemployment, vetoed May 13, 1960. Senate sustained May 24, 1960, 45-39.

Total Days:	11
Adjournment Days:	0
In Session Days:	11

H.R. 3610—To amend the Federal Water Pollution Act, vetoed February 22, 1960. House sustained February 25, 1960, 249-157.

Total Days:	3
Adjournment Days:	0
In Session Days:	3

H.R. 9883—To adjust compensation for employees of the federal government, vetoed June 30, 1960. House overrode July 1, 1960, 345-69. Senate overrode July 1, 1960, 74-24.

Total Days:	1
Adjournment Days:	0
In Session Days:	1

Richard M. Nixon

91st Congress, 2nd Session

S. 3637—To revise the provisions of the Communications Act of 1934, vetoed October 12, 1970. Senate sustained November 23, 1970, 58-34.

Total Days:	42
Adjournment Days:	0
In Session Days:	42

S. 3867—To assure opportunities for employment and training to unemployed persons, vetoed December 16, 1970. Senate sustained December 21, 1970, 48-35.

Total Days:	5
Adjournment Days:	0
In Session Days:	5

H.R. 11102—To amend the provisions of the Public Health Service Act, vetoed June 22, 1970. House overrode June 25, 1970, 279-98. Senate overrode June 30, 1970, 76-19.

Total Days:	7
Adjournment Days:	0
In Session Days:	7

H.R. 13111—Making appropriations for the Departments of Labor and Health, Education, and Welfare, vetoed January 26, 1970. House sustained January 28, 1970, 226-191.

Total Days:	2
Adjournment Days:	0
In Session Days:	2

H.R. 16916—Making appropriations for the Office of Education, vetoed August 11, 1970. House overrode August 13, 1970, 289-114. Senate overrode August 18, 1970, 77-16.

Total Days: 7
Adjournment Days: 0
In Session Days: 7

H.R. 17548—Making appropriations for sundry independent agencies and the Department of Housing and Urban Development, vetoed August 11, 1970. House sustained August 13, 1970, 203-195.

Total Days: 2
Adjournment Days: 0
In Session Days: 2

92nd Congress, 1st Session

S. 575—To carry out the Appalachian Development Act of 1965, vetoed June 29, 1971. Senate sustained July 14, 1971, 57-36.

Total Days: 15
Adjournment Days: 0
In Session Days: 15

S. 2007—To continue authorized programs under the Economic Opportunity Act of 1964, vetoed December 9, 1971. Senate sustained December 10, 1971, 51-36.

Total Days: 1
Adjournment Days: 0
In Session Days: 1

92nd Congress, 2nd Session

S. 2770—To amend the Federal Water Pollution Control Act, vetoed October 17, 1972. Senate overrode October 17, 1972, 52-12. House overrode October 18, 1972, 247-23.

Total Days:	1
Adjournment Days:	0
In Session Days:	1

H.R. 15417—Making appropriations for the Departments of Labor, and Health, Education, and Welfare, vetoed August 16, 1972. House sustained August 16, 1972, 203-171.

Total Days:	Same Day
Adjournment Days:	0
In Session Days:	Same Day

H.R. 15927—To amend the Railroad Retirement Act of 1937, vetoed October 4, 1972. House overrode October 4, 1972, 353-29. Senate overrode October 4, 1972, 76-5.

Total Days:	Same Day
Adjournment Days:	0
In Session Days:	Same Day

93rd Congress, 1st Session

S. 7—To amend the Vocational Rehabilitation Act, vetoed March 27, 1973. Senate sustained April 3, 1973, 60-36.

Total Days:	7
Adjournment Days:	0
In Session Days:	7

S. 504—To amend the Public Health Service Act, vetoed August 1, 1973. Senate overrode August 2, 1973, 77-16. House sustained September 12, 1973, 273-144.

Total Days:	42
Adjournment Days:	0
In Session Days:	42

S. 518—To abolish the offices of Director and Deputy Director of the Office of Management and Budget, vetoed May 18, 1973. Senate overrode May 22, 1973, 62-22. House sustained May 23, 1973, 236-178.

Total Days:	5
Adjournment Days:	0
In Session Days:	5

S. 1317—To authorize appropriations for the United States Information Agency, vetoed October 23, 1973. Senate sustained October 30, 1973, 54-42.

Total Days:	7
Adjournment Days:	0
In Session Days:	7

S. 1672—To amend the Small Business Act, vetoed September 22, 1973. Senate sustained September 25, 1973, 59-36.

Total Days:	3
Adjournment Days:	0
In Session Days:	3

H.R. 3298—To restore rural water and sewer grant programs, vetoed April 5, 1973. House sustained April 10, 1973, 225-189.

Total Days:	5
Adjournment Days:	0
In Session Days:	5

H.R. 7447—Making supplemental appropriations for fiscal year ending June 30, 1973, vetoed June 27, 1973. House sustained June 27, 1973, 241-173.

Total Days:	Same Day
Adjournment Days:	0
In Session Days:	Same Day

H.R. 7935—To amend the Fair Labor Standards Act of 1938 to increase the minimum wage rates under the Act, vetoed September 6, 1973. House sustained September 19, 1973, 259-164.

Total Days:	13
Adjournment Days:	0
In Session Days:	13

H.J. Res. 542—Amending the War Powers Act, vetoed October 24, 1973. House overrode November 7, 1973, 284-135. Senate overrode November 7, 1973, 75-18.

Total Days:	14
Adjournment Days:	0
In Session Days:	14

93rd Congress, 2nd Session

S. 2589—To direct the development of contingency plans for reducing petroleum consumption, vetoed March 6, 1974. Senate sustained March 6, 1974, 58-40.

Total Days:	Same Day
Adjournment Days:	0
In Session Days:	Same Day

93rd Congress, 2nd Session

H.R. 6191—To amend the Tariff Schedules of the United States, vetoed November 26, 1974. House sustained December 3, 1974, 249-150.

Total Days:	7
Adjournment Days:	0
In Session Days:	7

H.R. 6624—For the relief of Alvin W. Burt, Jr., Eileen Wallace Kennedy Pope, and David Douglas Kennedy, vetoed October 29, 1974. House sustained November 20, 1974, 236-163.

Total Days:	23
Adjournment Days:	0
In Session Days:	23

H.R. 12471—To amend section 552 of Title 5, United States Code, vetoed October 17, 1974. House overrode November 21, 1974, 371-31. Senate overrode November 21, 1974, 65-27.

Total Days:	35
Adjournment Days:	0
In Session Days:	35

H.R. 12628—To amend Title 38, United States Code, vetoed November 26, 1974. House overrode December 3, 1974, 394-10. Senate overrode December 3, 1974, 90-1.

Total Days:	7
Adjournment Days:	0
In Session Days:	7

H.R. 14225—To amend the Rehabilitation Act of 1973, vetoed October 29, 1974. House overrode November 20, 1974, 398-7. Senate overrode November 21, 1974, 90-1.

Total Days:	23
Adjournment Days:	0
In Session Days:	23

H.R. 15301—To amend the Railroad Retirement Act of 1937, vetoed October 12, 1974. House overrode October 15, 1974, 360-12. Senate overrode October 16, 1974, 72-1.

Total Days:	4
Adjournment Days:	0
In Session Days:	4

H.J. Res. 1131—Making further appropriations for the fiscal year 1975, vetoed October 14, 1974. House sustained October 15, 1974, 223-135.

Total Days:	1
Adjournment Days:	0
In Session Days:	1

H.J. Res. 1163—Making further appropriations for the fiscal year 1975, vetoed October 17, 1974. House sustained October 17, 1974, 161-83.

Total Days:	Same Day
Adjournment Days:	0
In Session Days:	Same Day

94th Congress, 1st Session

S. 66—To amend Title III of the Public Health Service Act, vetoed July 26, 1975. Senate overrode July 26, 1975, 67-15. House overrode July 29, 1975, 384-43.

Total Days:	3
Adjournment Days:	0
In Session Days:	3

S. 1849—To extend the Emergency Petroleum Allocation Act, vetoed September 9, 1975. Senate sustained September 10, 1975, 61-39.

Total Days:	1
Adjournment Days:	0
In Session Days:	1

H.R. 25—To regulate surface coal mining operations, vetoed May 20, 1975. House sustained June 10, 1975, 278-143.

Total Days:	21
Adjournment Days:	0
In Session Days:	21

H.R. 4222—To amend the National School Lunch and Child Nutrition Acts, vetoed October 3, 1975. House overrode October 7, 1975, 397-18. Senate overrode October 7, 1975, 79-13.

Total Days:	4
Adjournment Days:	0
In Session Days:	4

H.R. 4296—To adjust target prices of various 1975 crops, vetoed May 1, 1975. House sustained May 3, 1975, 254-182.

Total Days:	2
Adjournment Days:	0
In Session Days:	2

H.R. 4481—Emergency Employment Appropriations Act, vetoed May 28, 1975. House sustained June 4, 1975, 277-145.

Total Days:	7
Adjournment Days:	0
In Session Days:	7

H.R. 4485—To provide for greater home ownership opportunities, vetoed June 24, 1975. House sustained June 25, 1975, 268-157.

Total Days:	1
Adjournment Days:	0
In Session Days:	1

H.R. 5559—To amend section 883(a) of the Internal Revenue Code, vetoed December 17, 1975. House sustained December 18, 1975, 265-157.

Total Days:	1
Adjournment Days:	0
In Session Days:	1

H.R. 5901—Appropriations for education divisions for the fiscal year ending June 20, 1976, vetoed July 25, 1975. House overrode September 9, 1975, 379-41. Senate overrode September 10, 1975, 88-12.

Total Days:	47
Adjournment Days:	0
In Session Days:	47

H.R. 8069—Making appropriations for the Departments of Labor, and Health, Education, and Welfare, vetoed December 19, 1975. House overrode January 27, 1976, 310-113. Senate overrode January 28, 1976, 70-24.

Total Days:	40
Adjournment Days:	0
In Session Days:	40

94th Congress, 2nd Session

S. 391—To amend the Mineral Leasing Act of 1920, vetoed July 3, 1976. Senate overrode August 3, 1976, 75-17. House overrode August 4, 1976, 316-85.

Total Days:	32
Adjournment Days:	0
In Session Days:	32

S. 2350—To amend the National Security Act of 1947, vetoed December 31, 1975. Senate overrode January 22, 1976, 72-16. House did not challenge veto.

Total Days:	22
Adjournment Days:	0
In Session Days:	22

S. 3201—To amend the Public Works and Economic Development Act of 1965, vetoed July 6, 1976. Senate overrode July 21, 1976, 73-24. House overrode July 22, 1976, 310-96.

Total Days:	1
Adjournment Days:	0
In Session Days:	1

S.J. Res. 121—To provide quarterly adjustments in the support price for milk, vetoed January 30, 1976. Senate sustained February 4, 1976, 37-51.

Total Days:	5
Adjournment Days:	0
In Session Days:	5

H.R. 5247—To authorize local public works, vetoed February 13, 1976. House overrode February 19, 1976, 319-98. Senate sustained February 19, 1976, 63-35.

Total Days:	6
Adjournment Days:	0
In Session Days:	6

H.R. 8617—To allow federal employees to participate in the political process, vetoed April 12, 1976. House sustained April 29, 1976, 253-160.

Total Days:	17
Adjournment Days:	0
In Session Days:	17

H.R. 8800—To promote electric vehicle technologies, vetoed September 13, 1976. House overrode September 16, 1976, 307-101. Senate overrode September 17, 1976, 53-20.

Total Days:	4
Adjournment Days:	0
In Session Days:	4

H.R. 9803—Setting time tables for payments to child care centers, vetoed April 6, 1976. House overrode May 4, 1976, 301-101. Senate sustained May 5, 1976, 60-34.

Total Days:	29
Adjournment Days:	0
In Session Days:	29

H.R. 12384—To authorize certain construction at military installations, vetoed July 2, 1976. House overrode July 22, 1976, 270-131. Senate sustained July 22, 1976, 51-42.

Total Days:	20
Adjournment Days:	0
In Session Days:	20

H.R. 13655—To research advanced automobile propulsion systems, vetoed September 24, 1976. House overrode September 29, 1976, 293-102. Senate sustained September 29, 1976, 41-35.

Total Days:	5
Adjournment Days:	0
In Session Days:	5

H.R. 14232—Making appropriations for the Departments of Labor and Health, Education, and Welfare, vetoed September 29, 1976. House overrode September 30, 1976, 312-93. Senate overrode September 30, 1976, 67-15.

Total Days:	1
Adjournment Days:	0
In Session Days:	1

JIMMY CARTER

95th Congress, 2nd Session

H.R. 10929—To authorize appropriations for the Department of Defense, vetoed August 17, 1978. House sustained September 7, 1978, 191-206.

Total Days:	21
Adjournment Days:	0
In Session Days:	21

H.R. 19828—Energy and Water Development Appropriations Act, vetoed October 5, 1978. House sustained October 5, 1978, 223-190.

Total Days:	Same Day
Adjournment Days:	0
In Session Days:	Same Day

96th Congress, 2nd Session

H.R. 7102—To promote the recruitment of health care personnel, vetoed August 22, 1980. House overrode August 26, 1980, 401-5. Senate overrode August 26, 1980, 85-0.

Total Days:	4
Adjournment Days:	0
In Session Days:	4

H.R. 7428—To extend the public debt limit through June 30, 1980, vetoed June 5, 1980. House overrode June 5, 1980, 335-34. Senate overrode June 6, 1980, 68-10.

Total Days:	1
Adjournment Days:	0
In Session Days:	1

RONALD W. REAGAN

97th Congress, 2nd Session

S. 1503—Standby Petroleum Allocation Act of 1982, vetoed March 20, 1982. Senate sustained March 24, 1982, 58-36.

Total Days:	4
Adjournment Days:	0
In Session Days:	4

H.R. 5922—Making urgent supplemental appropriations, vetoed June 24, 1982. House sustained June 24, 1982, 253-151.

Total Days:	Same Day
Adjournment Days:	0
In Session Days:	Same Day

H.R. 6198—To amend the manufacturing clause of the Copyright Law, vetoed July 8, 1982. House overrode July 13, 1982, 324-86. Senate overrode July 13, 1982, 84-9.

Total Days:	5
Adjournment Days:	0
In Session Days:	5

H.R. 6682—Urgent supplemental appropriations for the fiscal year ending September 30, 1982, vetoed June 25, 1982. House sustained July 13, 1982, 242-169.

Total Days:	18
Adjournment Days:	0
In Session Days:	18

H.R. 6863—Supplemental appropriations for the fiscal year ending September 30, 1982, vetoed August 28, 1982. House overrode September 9, 1982, 301-117. Senate overrode September 10, 1982, 60-30.

Total Days:	13
Adjournment Days:	0
In Session Days:	13

98th Congress, 1st Session

H.R. 1062—To convey certain lands in Lane County, Oregon, vetoed October 19, 1983. House overrode October 25, 1983, 297-125. Senate overrode October 25, 1983, 95-0.

Total Days:	6
Adjournment Days:	0
In Session Days:	6

98th Congress, 2nd Session

S. 684—To authorize an ongoing program of water resources research, vetoed February 21, 1984. Senate overrode March 21, 1984, 86-12. House overrode March 22, 1984, 309-81.

Total Days:	29
Adjournment Days:	0
In Session Days:	29

99th Congress, 1st Session

H.R. 1562—To promote the economic recovery of the United States textile industry, vetoed December 17, 1985. House sustained August 6, 1986, 276-149.

Total Days:	232
Adjournment Days:	33
In Session Days:	199

H.R. 2409—To amend the Public Health Service Act, vetoed November 8, 1985. House overrode November 12, 1985, 380-32. Senate overrode November 20, 1985, 89-7.

Total Days:	12
Adjournment Days:	0
In Session Days:	12

99th Congress, 2nd Session

S.J. Res. 316—To prohibit the sale of defense articles to Saudi Arabia, vetoed May 21, 1986. Senate sustained June 5, 1986, 66-34.

Total Days:	15
Adjournment Days:	0
In Session Days:	15

H.R. 4686—To prohibit loans to South Africa, vetoed September 26, 1986. House overrode September 29, 1986, 313-83. Senate overrode October 2, 1986, 78-21.

Total Days:	6
Adjournment Days:	0
In Session Days:	6

100th Congress, 1st Session

H.R. 1—To amend the Federal Water Pollution Control Act, vetoed January 30, 1987. House overrode February 3, 1987, 401-26. Senate overrode February 4, 1987, 86-14.

Total Days:	5
Adjournment Days:	0
In Session Days:	5

H.R. 2—To authorize funds for highways and mass transportation, vetoed March 27, 1987. House overrode March 31, 1987, 350-73. Senate sustained April 1, 1987, 65-35. Upon reconsideration the Senate overrode April 2, 1987, 67-33.

Total Days:	6
Adjournment Days:	0
In Session Days:	6

100th Congress, 2nd Session

S. 557—To amend Title IX of the Education Amendments of 1972, vetoed March 16, 1988. Senate overrode March 22, 1988, 73-24. House overrode March 22, 1988, 292-133.

Total Days:	6
Adjournment Days:	0
In Session Days:	6

H.R. 3—To enhance the competitiveness of American industry, vetoed May 24, 1988. House overrode May 24, 1988, 308-113. Senate sustained June 8, 1988, 61-37.

Total Days:	15
Adjournment Days:	0
In Session Days:	15

H.R. 1154—To remedy injury to the United States textile industry, vetoed September 28, 1988. House sustained October 4, 1988, 272-152.

Total Days:	6
Adjournment Days:	0
In Session Days:	6

GEORGE BUSH

101st Congress, 1st Session

S.J. Res. 113—To prohibit co-development of the FS-X aircraft with Japan, vetoed July 31, 1989. Senate sustained September 13, 1989, 66-34.

Total Days:	44
Adjournment Days:	0
In Session Days:	44

H.R. 2—To amend the Fair Labor Standards Act of 1938, vetoed June 13, 1989. House sustained June 14, 1989, 247-178.

Total Days:	1
Adjournment Days:	0
In Session Days:	1

H.R. 1231—To establish a commission to investigate the dispute between Eastern Airlines and collective bargaining units, vetoed November 21, 1989. House sustained March 7, 1990, 261-160.

Total Days: 106
Adjournment Days: 35
In Session Days: 71

H.R. 2712—To waive the two year residence requirement for Chinese nationals in this country, vetoed November 30, 1989. House overrode January 24, 1990, 390-25. Senate sustained January 25, 1990, 62-37.

Total Days: 56
Adjournment Days: 30
In Session Days: 16

H.R. 2990—Making appropriations for the Departments of Labor, Health and Human Services, and Education, vetoed October 21, 1989. House sustained October 25, 1989, 231-191.

Total Days: 4
Adjournment Days: 0
In Session Days: 4

101st Congress, 2nd Session

S. 2104—To amend the Civil Rights of 1964, vetoed October 22, 1990. Senate sustained October 24, 1990, 66-34.

Total Days: 2
Adjournment Days: 0
In Session Days: 2

H.J. Res. 660—Making further continuing appropriations for the fiscal year 1991, vetoed October 6, 1990. House sustained October 6, 1990, 260-138.

Total Days: Same Day
Adjournment Days: 0
In Session Days: Same Day

H.R. 20—To restore to federal civilian employees their right to participate in the political process, vetoed June 15, 1990. House overrode June 20, 1990, 327-93. Senate sustained June 21, 1990, 65-35.

Total Days:	6
Adjournment Days:	0
In Session Days:	6

H.R. 770—Family and Medical Leave Act of 1990, vetoed June 29, 1990. House sustained July 25, 1990, 232-195.

Total Days:	26
Adjournment Days:	0
In Session Days:	26

H.R. 2364—To amend the Rail Passenger Service Act, vetoed May 24, 1990. House overrode June 7, 1990, 294-123. Senate sustained June 12, 1990, 64-36.

Total Days:	19
Adjournment Days:	0
In Session Days:	19

H.R. 4328—To provide for the orderly import of textiles, apparel, and footwear, vetoed October 5, 1990. House sustained October 10, 1990, 275-152.

Total Days:	5
Adjournment Days:	0
In Session Days:	5

102nd Congress, 1st Session

S. 1722—Emergency Unemployment Compensation Act of 1991, vetoed October 11, 1991. Senate sustained October 16, 1991, 65-35.

Total Days: 5
Adjournment Days: 0
In Session Days: 5

H.R. 2707—Making appropriations for the Departments of Labor, Health and Human Services, and Education, vetoed November 19, 1991. House sustained November 19, 1991, 276-156.

Total Days: Same Day
Adjournment Days: 0
In Session Days: Same Day

102nd Congress, 2nd Session

H.R. 2212—The United States-China Act of 1992, vetoed March 2, 1992. House overrode March 11, 1992, 357-61. Senate sustained March 18, 1992, 65-38.

Total Days: 16
Adjournment Days: 0
In Session Days: 16

H.R. 4210—The Tax Fairness and Economic Growth Act of 1992, vetoed March 20, 1992. House sustained March 25, 1992, 211-215.

Total Days: 5
Adjournment Days: 0
In Session Days: 5

S. 3—The Congressional Campaign Spending Limit and Election Reform Act of 1992, vetoed May 9, 1992. Senate sustained May 12, 1992, 57-42.

Total Days: 3
Adjournment Days: 0
In Session Days: 3

H.R. 2507—The National Institutes of Health Revitalization Amendments of 1992, vetoed June 23, 1992. House sustained June 24, 1992, 271-156.

Total Days: 1
Adjournment Days: 0
In Session Days: 1

S. 250—The National Voter Registration Act of 1992, vetoed July 2, 1992. Senate sustained September 22, 1992, 62-38.

Total Days: 82
Adjournment Days: 0
In Session Days: 82

S. 5—The Family and Medical Leave Act of 1992, vetoed September 22, 1992. Senate overrode September 24, 1992, 68-31. House sustained September 30, 1992, 258-169.

Total Days: 8
Adjournment Days: 0
In Session Days: 8

S. 323—Title X Pregnancy Counseling Act of 1992, vetoed September 25, 1992. Senate overrode October 1, 1992, 73-26. House sustained October 2, 1992, 266-148.

Total Days: 7
Adjournment Days: 0
In Session Days: 7

H.R. 5318—The United States-China Act of 1992, vetoed September 28, 1992. House overrode September 30, 1992, 345-72. Senate sustained October 1, 1992, 59-40.

Total Days: 3
Adjournment Days: 0
In Session Days: 3

S. 12—The Cable Television Protection and Competition Act of 1982, vetoed October 3, 1992. House overrode October 5, 1992, 308-114. Senate overrode October 5, 1992, 74-25.

Total Days: 2
Adjournment Days: 0
In Session Days: 2

William Clinton

104th Congress, 1st Session

H.R. 1977—Department of Interior appropriations for fiscal year 1996, vetoed December 18, 1995. House sustained January 4, 1996, 239-177.

Total Days: 17
Adjournment Days: 0
In Session Days: 17

H.R. 2076—Appropriations for the Departments of Commerce, Justice, and State, vetoed December 19, 1995. House sustained January 3, 1996, 240-159.

Total Days: 15
Adjournment Days: 0
In Session Days: 15

H.R. 1058—The Securities Litigation Reform Act, vetoed December 19, 1995. House overrode December 20, 1995, 319-100. Senate overrode December 22, 1995, 68-30.

Total Days: 3
Adjournment Days: 0
In Session Days: 3

H.R. 1530—Defense Authorizations for fiscal year 1996, vetoed December 28, 1995. House sustained January 3, 1996, 240-156.

Total Days: 6
Adjournment Days: 0
In Session Days: 6

104th Congress, 2nd Session

H.R. 1561—American Overseas Act of 1996, vetoed April 12, 1996. House sustained April 30, 1996, 234-188.

Total Days:	18
Adjournment Days:	0
In Session Days:	18

H.R. 956—Common Sense Product Liability Legal Reform Act of 1996, vetoed May 2, 1996. House sustained May 9, 1996, 258-163.

Total Days:	7
Adjournment Days:	0
In Session Days:	7

H.R. 1833—Partial Birth Abortion Ban Act, vetoed April 10, 1996. House overrode September 19, 1996, 285-137. Senate sustained September 26, 1996, 57-41.

Total Days:	162
Adjournment Days:	0
In Session Days:	162

105th Congress, 1st Session

H.R. 1122—Partial Birth Abortion, vetoed October 10, 1997. House overrode July 23, 1998, 296-132. Senate sustained September 18, 1998 by 64-36.

Total Days:	313
Adjournment Days:	74
In Session Days:	239

Table 1. Number and Time of Override Attempts

	Number of Days													
Congress/Session	**Same Day**	**1**	**2**	**3**	**4**	**5**	**6**	**7**	**8-14**	**15-30**	**31-50**	**51-100**	**101-150**	**151-200**
$2^{nd}/1^{st}$		1												
$4^{th}/2^{nd}$		1												1
$11^{th}/3^{rd}$			2											
$12^{th}/1^{st}$						1								
$13^{th}/3^{rd}$				1										
$14^{th}/2^{nd}$	1													
$17^{th}/1^{st}$			1											
$21^{st}/1^{st}$	1	1												
$22^{nd}/1^{st}$				1										
$24^{th}/1^{st}$										1				
$27^{th}/1^{st}$		1		1										
$27^{th}/2^{nd}$						1			1					
$28^{th}/1^{st}$	1													
$28^{th}/2^{nd}$									1					
$29^{th}/1^{st}$		1	1											
$33^{rd}/1^{st}$			1			1								
$33^{rd}/2^{nd}$	1													
$34^{th}/1^{st}$			1			1					3			
$35^{th}/2^{nd}$			1											
$36^{th}/1^{st}$		1									1			
$37^{th}/2^{nd}$	1													
$39^{th}/1^{st}$	1	1							1					
$39^{th}/2^{nd}$	2			1					1		1			
$40^{th}/1^{st}$	3													
$40^{th}/2^{nd}$	3		3											
$41^{st}/2^{nd}$														1

Congress/Session	Number of Days													
	Same Day	1	2	3	4	5	6	7	8-14	15-30	31-50	51-100	101-150	151-200
41st/3rd									1					
42nd/2nd										1				
43rd/1st						1								
44th/1st	1	1							1	1		1		
45th/2nd	1													
45th/3rd	1													
46th/1st	3	1	1											
47th/1st		2												
48th/1st		1												
49th/1st					1				1	2	4	2	7	
49th/2nd		1					1		1					
50th/1st												1		
50th/2nd	1								1		1			
51st/1st														1
52nd/1st												1		
52nd/2nd					1									
53rd/2nd							1							
53rd/3rd						1								
54th/1st	1	1			1					2		1	1	
54th/2nd		1								1			1	
55th/2nd	1													
60th/1st		1									1			
62nd/1st	1	1						1		1				
62nd/2nd	2		1											
62nd/3rd	1					1								
63rd/3rd								1						
64th/2nd								1						
65th/2nd	2	1												

Congress/Session	Number of Days												
	Same Day	1	2	3	4	5	6	7	8-14	15-30	31-50	51-100	101-150	151-200
66th/1st		2				1								
66th/2nd	1	2												
66th/3rd	1	1	1			1				1				
67th/2nd		1												
68th/1st					1				1					
70th/1st			3				2	1						
71st/2nd	1	1				1								
71st/3rd	3	1												
72nd/2nd	1					1								
73rd/2nd		1												
74th/1st		1												
75th/1st					1						1			
75th/3rd		1												
76th/3rd	2	1							1			3		
77th/1st						1								
78th/1st	2									1				
78th/2nd	1			1										
79th/2nd	3	1												
80th/1st	1	1		1										
80th/2nd	1	1	1				1	1		1				
81st/1st													1	
81st/2nd		1				1			1	1		1		
82nd/1st		1	2								1			
84th/1st						1								
84th/2nd			1											
85th/2nd									1					
86th/1st		2		1				1			1			
86th/2nd		1		1					1					

	Number of Days													
Congress/Session	**Same Day**	**1**	**2**	**3**	**4**	**5**	**6**	**7**	**8-14**	**15-30**	**31-50**	**51-100**	**101-150**	**151-200**
91st/2nd			2			1		2			1			
92nd/1st		1								1				
92nd/2nd	2	1												
93rd/1st	2			1		2		2	2		1			
93rd/2nd	1	1			1			2		2	1			
94th/1st		3	1	1	1			1		1	2			
94th/2nd		1			1	2	1			5	1			
95th/2nd	1									1				
96th/1st		1			1									
97th/2nd	1				1	1			1	1				
98th/1st							1							
98th/2nd										1				
99th/1st									1					1
99th/2nd							1			1				
100th/1st						1	1							
100th/2nd							2			1				
101st/1st		1			1					1	1	1		
101st/2nd	1		1			1	1			2				
102nd/1st	1					1								
102nd/2nd		1	1	2		1		1	1	1		1		
104th/1st				1			1			2				
104th/2nd								1		1				1
105th/1st														1
Total Number (307)	55	49	25	13	11	24	13	15	19	34	21	13	10	5
Percentage of Total	18%	16%	8%	4%	4%	8%	4%	5%	6%	11%	7%	4%	3%	1%

BIBLIOGRAPHY

1988 proposed amendments to the Constitution of Maryland and the handgun referendum: summary and explanation / prepared by the Department of Legislative Reference.
Published/Created: Annapolis, Md.: The Department, [1988]
Related Authors: Maryland. General Assembly. State Dept. of Legislative Reference.
Description: 9 p.; 22 cm.
Notes: Cover title. At head of title: General Assembly of Maryland.
Subjects: Constitutional amendments--Maryland. Eminent domain--Maryland--Anne Arundel County. Veto--Maryland. Firearms--Law and legislation--Maryland.
LC Classification: KFM1601.A7 M37 1988
Dewey Class No.: 344.752/0533 347.5204533 20

Analyses of the governor's vetoes: appropriation bills, substantive bills / prepared by House Democratic Staff.
Published/Created: [Springfield, Ill.]: The Staff, [1979]
Related Authors: Illinois. House Democratic Staff.
Description: ca. 300 p.; 29 cm.
Notes: Cover title. "October 1979."
Subjects: Bills, Legislative--Illinois. Veto--Illinois.
LC Classification: KFI1215.2 1979
Dewey Class No.: 348.773/01 347.73081 19

Analysis of provisions contained in the Line Item Veto Act (Public Law 104-130) relating to limited tax benefits / prepared by the staff of the Joint Committee on Taxation.

Published/Created: Washington: U.S. G.P.O.: For sale by the U.S. G.P.O., Supt. of Docs., 1997.
Related Authors: United States. Congress. Joint Committee on Taxation.
Description: iv, 68 p.; 24 cm.
ISBN: 0160539749
Notes: At head of title: Joint Committee print. "JCS-1-97." "January 3, 1997." Includes bibliographical references.
Subjects: United States. Line Item Veto Act. Executive impoundment of appropriated funds--United States. Tax expenditures--Law and legislation--United States.
LC Classification: KF4579.I4 A2 1997

Background information on regulatory reform and congressional review of agency rules with a summary of H.R. 1 (as introduced) / prepared by the Subcommittee on Rules of the House of the Committee on Rules, U.S. House of Representatives.
Published/Created: Washington: U.S. G.P.O., 1981.
Related Authors: United States. Congress. House. Committee on Rules. Subcommittee on Rules of the House.
Description: vii, 34 p.; 24 cm.
Notes: At head of title: 97th Congress, 1st session. Subcommittee print. "June 1981." Item 1025-C, 1025-D (microfiche) Includes bibliographical references.
Subjects: Administrative procedure--United States. Legislative oversight--United States. Legislative veto--United States.
LC Classification: KF5411 .A25 1981a
Dewey Class No.: 342.73/066 347.30266 19
Govt. Doc. No.: Y 4.R 86/1:R 26/2

Item veto: state experience and its application to the federal situation / prepared by the Committee on Rules, U.S. House of Representatives, Ninety-ninth Congress, second session.
Published/Created: Washington: U.S. G.P.O.: For sale by the Supt. of Docs., Congressional Sales Office, U.S. G.P.O., 1986.
Related Authors: United States. Congress. House. Committee on Rules.
Description: ix, 291 p.: ill.; 24 cm.
Notes: Cover title. At head of title: Committee print. Distributed to some depository libraries in microfiche. Shipping list no.: 86-993-P. "December 1986." Item 1025-C, 1025-D (microfiche) Bibliography: p.

282-290.
Subjects: Item veto--United States. Item veto--United States--States.
LC Classification: JK586 .I84 1986
Dewey Class No.: 342.73/052 347.30252 19
Govt. Doc. No.: Y 4.R 86/1:V 64/2

Legislative veto of agency rules after INS v. Chadha, twenty-seventh plenary session discussion on December 15, 1983 / Administrative Conference of the United States.
Published/Created: Washington, D.C.: Office of the Chairman, Administrative Conference of the United States: For sale by the Supt. of Docs., U.S. G.P.O., 1984.
Related Authors: Administrative Conference of the United States.
Description: iv, 33 p.; 28 cm.
Subjects: Chadha, Jagdish Rai--Trials, litigation, etc. United States. Immigration and Naturalization Service Trials, litigation, etc. Legislative veto--United States--Congresses. Administrative procedure--United States--Congresses.
LC Classification: KF4944.A75 L44 1984
Dewey Class No.: 342.73/066 347.30266 19

Nightline. [1990-10-22], Bush vetoes civil rights bill / ABC News.
Published/Created: United States: MPI Home Video: ABC-TV, 1990-10-22.
Related Authors: Copyright Collection (Library of Congress) Vanderbilt Television News Archive Collection (Library of Congress)
Related Titles: ABC news nightline. 1990-10-22, Bush vetoes civil rights bill. Bush vetoes civil rights bill.
Description: 1 videocassette of 1 (30 min.): sd., col.; 1/2 in. viewing copy. 1 videocassette of 1 (29 min.): sd., col.; 3/4 in. master.
Summary: George Bush veto of civil rights bill.
Notes: Copyright: ABC News. DCR 1990; PUB 22Oct90; REG 27Oct92; PA591-681. Number 2456. Sources used: label on container, copyright data base and cassette box.
Source of Acquisition: Received: 2-1-93; viewing copy; copyright deposit--RNR; Copyright Collection. Received: 12-10-92; master; purchase; Vanderbilt Television News Archive Collection.
LC Classification: VAC 5232 (viewing copy) VSC 3220 (master)

Nightline. [1992-10-05] / ABC News.
Published/Created: United States: ABC-TV, 1992-10-05.
Related Authors: Vanderbilt Television News Archive Collection (Library of Congress)
Related Titles: ABC news nightline. 1992-10-05.
Description: 1 videocassette of 1 (29 min.): sd., col.; 3/4 in. master.
Summary: Re: the cable television regulation bill passed today over George Bush's veto, and the impact of new technology on the future of television.
Notes: Reference sources used: Television news index and abstracts (Vanderbilt 1992 annual) & container label.
Source of Acquisition: Received: 02-02-95; master; purchase; Vanderbilt Television News Archive Collection.
LC Classification: VSC 8063 (master)

Observations on the late presidential veto: together with a plan for a change of the Constitution relative to this power.
Published/Created: Boston: J. Munroe and company, 1842.
Description: 78 p.; 25 cm.
Subjects: Veto. United States--Politics and government--1841-1845.
LC Classification: JK586 .O2

Pork barrels and principles: the politics of the presidential veto / by Charles J. Cooper ... [et al.]; comment by Ronald W. Reagan; introduction by L. Gordon Crovitz; epilogue by Robert H. Bork.
Published/Created: Washington, D.C.: National Legal Center for the Public Interest, 1988
Related Authors: Cooper, Charles J.
Related Titles: Politics of the presidential veto.
Description: xiii, 62 p.: ill.; 23 cm. ISBN: 093729909X:
Notes: Spine title: The politics of the presidential veto. Includes bibliographical references.
Subjects: Item veto--United States. Executive power--United States.
LC Classification: JK586 .P67 1988
Dewey Class No.: 320.473 20

Presidential vetoes, 1789-1988 / compiled by the Senate Library under the direction of Walter J. Stewart, secretary of the Senate, by Gregory Harness, head reference librarian.
Published/Created: Washington, D.C.: U.S. G.P.O., 1992.

Related Authors: Harness, Gregory. United States. Congress. Senate. Library.
Description: xxvi, 595 p.; 24 cm.
Notes: "February 1992." Shipping list no: 92-178-P. Includes bibliographical references and index.
Subjects: Veto--United States. Bills, Legislative--United States.
Series: S. pub.; 102-12
LC Classification: KF42.2 1992
Dewey Class No.: 320.473/09 20
Govt. Doc. No.: Y 1.3:S.pub.102-12

Presidential vetoes, 1977-1984 / compiled by the Senate Library under the direction of Jo-Anne L. Coe, Secretary of the Senate by Gregory Harness.
Published/Created: Washington, D.C.: U.S. G.P.O.: For sale by the Supt. of Docs, U.S. G.P.O., 1985.
Related Authors: Coe, Jo-Anne L. Harness, Gregory. United States. Congress. Senate. Library.
Description: xiii, 24 p.; 24 cm.
Notes: "May 1985." S/N 052-002-00046-0 Item 998-A-1 Includes bibliographical references and index.
Subjects: Bills, Legislative--United States. Veto--United States.
Series: United States. Congress (99th, 1st session: 1985). Senate. S. pub.; 99-5.
Variant Series: S. pub.; 99-5
LC Classification: KF42.2 1985
Dewey Class No.: 342.73/0262 347.302262 20
Govt. Doc. No.: Y 1.3:S.pub.99-5

Presidential vetoes, 1989-1996 / compiled by the Senate Library under the direction of Gary Sisco, Secretary of the Senate by Gregory C. Harness.
Published/Created: Washington, D.C.: U.S. G.P.O., 1997.
Related Authors: Harness, Gregory. United States. Congress. Senate. Library.
Description: xiii, 35 p.; 24 cm.
Notes: "September 1997." Includes bibliographical references and index.
Subjects: Bills, Legislative--United States. Veto--United States.

Series: S. pub.; 105-22
LC Classification: KF42.2 1997
Dewey Class No.: 016.34873/1 21
Govt. Doc. No.: Y 1.3:S.PUB.105-22

Presidential vetoes, 1989-2000 / compiled by the Senate Library under the direction of Jeri Thomson, by Zoe Davis.
Published/Created: Washington, D.C.: U.S. G.P.O., 2001.
Related Authors: Thomson, Jeri. Davis, Zoe. United States. Congress. Senate. Library.
Related Titles: Presidential vetoes, 1789-1988.
Description: xiv, 42 p.; 24 cm.
Notes: "Supplement to Presidential vetoes, 1789-1988"--Pref. "October 2001." Includes bibliographical references and index.
Subjects: Bills, Legislative--United States. Veto--United States.
Series: S. pub.; 107-10
LC Classification: KF42.2 2001
Dewey Class No.: 016.34873/1 21

The cruel uncle and the vetoed babes in the wood [graphic].
Published/Created: 1866.
Description: 1 print: wood engraving. Summary: Andrew Johnson taking two children "civil rights" and "bureau ..." by their hands in front of forest "veto wood".
Notes: Illus. in: Frank Leslie's illustrated newspaper, v. 22, no. 554 (1866 May 12), p. 128.
Subjects: Johnson, Andrew, 1808-1875. Civil rights--1860-1870. Vetoes--1860-1870.
LC Classification: Illus. in AP2.L52 1866

The Line-item veto: an appraisal (as revised from the January 1984 publication) / Committee on the Budget, U.S. House of Representatives.
Published/Created: Washington: U.S. G.P.O., 1984.
Related Authors: United States. Congress. House. Committee on the Budget.
Description: ii, 18 p.; 24 cm.
Notes: At head of title: Committee print. Distributed to some depository libraries in microfiche. "February 1984." "CP-4A." Item 1035-B-1, 1035-B-2 (microfiche)

Subjects: Item veto--United States. Executive power--United States. United States--Appropriations and expenditures.
LC Classification: KF5067 .L56 1984
Dewey Class No.: 342.73/052 347.30252 19
Govt. Doc. No.: Y 4.B 85/3:V 64/984-2

The line-item veto: an appraisal / Committee on the Budget, U.S. House of Representatives.
Published/Created: Washington: U.S. G.P.O., 1984.
Related Authors: United States. Congress. House. Committee on the Budget.
Description: ii, 16 p.; 24 cm.
Notes: At head of title: Committee print. Distributed to some depository libraries in microfiche. "January 1984." "CP-4." Item 1035-B-1, 1035-B-2 (microfiche)
Subjects: Budget--Law and legislation--United States. Item veto--United States.
LC Classification: KF6221.A55 L56 1984
Dewey Class No.: 343.73/034 347.30334 19
Govt. Doc. No.: Y 4.B 85/3:V 64

INDEX

H

I

J

K

L

M

N

O

P

Q

R

S

T

U

V

W

Y

Contents

Contributors

Pamela Cantor, Ph.D.
Lecturer in Psychology, Department of Psychiatry, Harvard Medical School; Co-Director, Harvard Medical School Suicide Symposium; Lecturer in Psychology, The Cambridge Hospital, Cambridge, Massachusetts

David C. Clark, Ph.D.
Associate Professor of Psychiatry & Psychology, Rush Medical College; Director, Center for Suicide Research and Prevention at Rush-Presbyterian-St. Luke's Medical Center, Chicago, Illinois

Rebecca A. Dulit, M.D.
Instructor in Psychiatry, Cornell University Medical College; Clinical Affiliate, New York Hospital, New York, New York

Jan Fawcett, M.D.
Professor and Chairman of Psychiatry, Rush Medical College; Medical Director, Center for Suicide Research and Prevention at Rush-Presbyterian-St. Luke's Medical Center, Chicago, Illinois

Mark Goldblatt, M.B.B.C.H.
Instructor in Psychiatry, Harvard Medical School; Psychiatrist, Affective Disease Program, McLean Hospital, Belmont, Massachusetts

Frederick K. Goodwin, M.D.
Administrator of the Alcohol, Drug Abuse, and Mental Health Administration, Rockville, Maryland

Thomas G. Gutheil, M.D.
Associate Professor of Psychiatry, Harvard Medical School; Visiting Lecturer, Harvard Law School; Co-Director of the Program in Psychiatry and the Law, Massachusetts Mental Health Center, Boston, Massachusetts

Douglas Jacobs, M.D.
Assistant Clinical Professor of Psychiatry, Harvard Medical School; Supervisor, McLean Hospital; Clinical Director, Professional Psychiatric Associates, Newton, Massachusetts

John T. Maltsberger, M.D.
Lecturer in Psychiatry, Harvard Medical School; Faculty, The Boston Psychoanalytic Society and Institute, Boston; Psychiatrist, Massachusetts General Hospital, Boston, Massachusetts; Senior Consultant, Psychosocial Program, McLean Hospital, Belmont, Massachusetts

Robert Michels, M.D.
Barklie McKee Henry Professor, Department of Psychiatry, Cornell University Medical College; The Stephen and Suzanne Weiss Dean, Cornell University Medical College, New York, New York

Alec Roy, M.B.
Director, Affective Disorders Program, Hillside Hospital, Long Island Jewish Medical Center, Glen Oaks, New York

Bette L. Runck
Science Writer, The Alcohol, Drug Abuse, and Mental Health Administration, Rockville, Maryland

Alan Schatzberg, M.D.
Professor of Psychiatry, Harvard Medical School; Consultant, McLean Hospital; Clinical Director, Massachusetts Mental Health Center, Boston, Massachusetts; Chairman Designate, Department of Psychiatry and Behavioral Sciences, Stanford University, Palo Alto, California

Peggy S. Stephens, M.D.
Director of Chemical Dependency Unit, Jefferson Hospital, Jeffersonville, Indiana

Peter Weiden, M.D.
Director of the Schizophrenia Program, Department of Psychiatry, St. Luke's-Roosevelt Medical Center, New York, New York

Roger D. Weiss, M.D.
Associate Professor of Psychiatry, Harvard Medical School; Clinical Director of the Alcohol and Drug Abuse Program, McLean Hospital, Belmont, Massachusetts

Introduction
to the Clinical Practice Series

Over the years of its existence the series of monographs entitled *Clinical Insights* gradually became focused on providing current, factual, and theoretical material of interest to the clinician working outside of a hospital setting. To reflect this orientation, the name of the Series has been changed to *Clinical Practice.*

The Clinical Practice Series will provide readers with books that give the mental health clinician a practical clinical approach to a variety of psychiatric problems. These books will provide up-to-date literature reviews and emphasize the most recent treatment methods. Thus, the publications in the Series will interest clinicians working both in psychiatry and in the other mental health professions.

Each year a number of books will be published dealing with all aspects of clinical practice, In addition, from time to time when appropriate, the publications may be revised and updated. Thus, the Series will provide quick access to relevant and important areas of psychiatric practice. Some books in the Series will be authored by a person considered to be an expert in that particular area; others will be edited by such an expert who will also draw together other knowledgeable authors to produce a comprehensive overview of that topic.

Some of the books in the Clinical Practice Series will have their foundation in presentations at an annual meeting of the American Psychiatric Association. All will contain the most recently available information on the subjects discussed. Theoretical and scientific data will be applied to clinical situations, and case illustrations will be utilized in order to make the material even more relevant for the practitioner. Thus, the Clinical Practice Series should provide educational reading in a compact format especially written for the mental health clinician–psychiatrist.

Judith H. Gold, M.D., F.R.C.P.(C)
Series Editor
Clinical Practice Series

Clinical Practice Series Titles

Treating Chronically Mentally Ill Women (#1)
Edited by Leona L. Bachrach, Ph.D., and Carol C. Nadelson, M.D.

Divorce as a Developmental Process (#2)
Edited by Judith H. Gold, M.D., F.R.C.P.(C)

Family Violence: Emerging Issues of a National Crisis (#3)
Edited by Leah J. Dickstein, M.D., and Carol C. Nadelson, M.D.

Anxiety and Depressive Disorders in the Medical Patient (#4)
By Leonard R. Derogatis, Ph.D., and Thomas N. Wise, M.D.

Anxiety: New Findings for the Clinician (#5)
Edited by Peter Roy-Byrne, M.D.

The Neuroleptic Malignant Syndrome and Related Conditions (#6)
By Arthur Lazarus, M.D., Stephan C. Mann, M.D., and Stanley N. Caroff, M.D.

Juvenile Homicide (#7)
Edited by Elissa P. Benedek, M.D., and Dewey G. Cornell, Ph.D.

Measuring Mental Illness: Psychometric Assessment for Clinicians (#8)
Edited by Scott Wetzler, Ph.D.

Family Involvement in Treatment of the Frail Elderly (#9)
Edited by Marion Zucker Goldstein, M.D.

Psychiatric Care of Migrants: A Clinical Guide (#10)
By Joseph Westermeyer, M.D., M.P.H., Ph.D.

Office Treatment of Schizophrenia (#11)
Edited by Mary V. Seeman, M.D., F.R.C.P.(C), and Stanley E. Greben, M.D., F.R.C.P.(C)

The Psychosocial Impact of Job Loss (#12)
By Nick Kates, M.B.B.S., F.R.C.P.(C), Barrie S. Greiff, M.D., and Duane Q. Hagen, M.D.

New Perspectives on Narcissism (#13)
Edited by Eric M. Plakun, M.D.

Clinical Management of Gender Identity Disorders in Children and Adults (#14)
Edited by Ray Blanchard, Ph.D., and Betty W. Steiner, M.B., F.R.C.P.(C)

Family Approaches in Treatment of Eating Disorders (#15)
Edited by D. Blake Woodside, M.D., M.Sc., F.R.C.P.(C), and Lorie Shekter-Wolfson, M.S.W., C.S.W.

Adolescent Psychotherapy (#16)
Edited by Marcia Slomowitz, M.D.

Benzodiazepines in Clinical Practice: Risks and Benefits (#17)
Edited by Peter P. Roy-Byrne, M.D., and Deborah S. Cowley, M.D.

Current Treatments of Obsessive-Compulsive Disorder (#18)
Edited by Michele Tortora Pato, M.D., and Joseph Zohar, M.D.

Children and AIDS (#19)
Edited by Margaret L. Stuber, M.D.

Special Problems in Managing Eating Disorders (#20)
Edited by Joel Yager, M.D., Harry E. Gwirtsman, M.D., and Carole K. Edelstein, M.D.

Suicide and Clinical Practice (#21)
Edited by Douglas Jacobs, M.D.

Anxiety Disorders in Children and Adolescents (#22)
By Syed Arshad Husain, M.D., F.R.C.P.(C), F.R.C.Psych., and Javad Kashani, M.D.

Psychopharmacological Treatment Complications in the Elderly (#23)
Edited by Charles A. Shamoian, M.D., Ph.D.

Preface

Suicide, although a rare statistical event, is a clinical phenomenon that impacts all mental health clinicians regardless of professional discipline or composition of clinical practice. This book is intended to enhance the clinical understanding, assessment, and treatment of suicidal phenomena.

It is known that suicide occurs across the entire spectrum of psychiatric illnesses. More than 90% of those who commit suicide suffer from affective disorders, alcoholism, or schizophrenia (Barraclough et al. 1974). Chapter 1, by Dr. Goodwin and Ms. Runck, provides a framework for integrating "core traditions"—the psychosocial, clinical, and biomedical—in psychiatry as they impact on our work with the suicidal patient. The authors make a profound statement about the clinical outcome of suicide: "Mental illness being the necessary condition, our research task becomes identifying the sufficient condition." This statement reflects the reality that most completed suicides consist of persons with high-risk profiles. Fortunately, the reverse statement is not borne out; most high-risk patients do not commit suicide. The authors of this chapter reflect the major thrust of this book: the necessity for continued and individual assessment of patients at high risk for suicide and for the integration of treatment options.

The subsequent two chapters of the book elaborate on the dialectic presented in the introductory chapter: medication issues and the role of psychodynamics in the treatment of the suicidal patient. Chapter 2 concerns medication. The pharmacologic treatment of suicide requires that the psychiatrist be a generalist. The clinician must be familiar with the broad spectrum of psychotropic drugs and must utilize medication that is both diagnostically and symptomatically specific. The issue of prescribing practices must be addressed, acknowledging, as Drs. Goldblatt and Schatzberg state, "medications may be used by the suicidal patient for therapeutic or self-destructive reasons." The recommendation is to pay attention to the therapeutic alliance, which has its application for those conducting pharmacotherapy, as well as psychotherapy.

Understanding the complexity of suicide requires not only diagnostic acumen, but also an appreciation of patient dynamics. Therapists must inquire, explore, and probe to understand fully a patient's suicidality: What does suicide mean? What are the patient's fantasies and wishes? What does death mean? In Chapter 3, Drs. Dulit and Michels emphasize that the appreciation of dynamics, although necessary, is but one component of the management of the suicidal person.

The issue of the complexity of suicide is nowhere more apparent than in the problem of depression. The 6-month prevalence rate for depression is estimated to be 9.6 million people (Regier et al. 1988). Furthermore, 16,000–18,000 of the approximately 30,000 annual suicides in the United States suffer from an affective disorder. Thus the overwhelming majority of people with depression do not suicide in any given year. The challenge for psychiatrists and other mental health professionals is to refine techniques of assessment to determine when, and under what conditions, a person with depression is likely to suicide.

Chapter 4, by Drs. Clark and Fawcett, addresses this issue. They and colleagues of the National Institute of Mental Health Collaborative Study of Depression Clinical Study have conducted prospective studies of suicide among high-risk patients (i.e., those with an affective disorder). The authors' findings from this ongoing study have made an important and novel contribution to the assessment of suicide: the concept of the temporal nature of suicide prediction. They have identified symptom clusters or clinical predictors that are associated with short-term or early suicide (i.e., severe anhedonia, psychic anxiety, and moderate alcohol abuse). The traditional suicide indicators, such as acute suicidal ideation, higher symptom levels of hopelessness, and a history of suicide attempts, were associated with "late" suicide (defined as greater than 1 year from time of assessment).

The clinical application of these studies suggest that many of the short-term risk predictors are modifiable, allowing for timely treatment interventions. Clark and Fawcett's empirically based model can also be applied to other disorders, such as schizophrenia or substance abuse. They emphasize that the suicide risk profile is not only different for early versus late suicide in depressed patients, but is different for alcoholic patients and again different from that for schizophrenic patients. However, it should be stressed that the state of the art of suicide prediction is that the clinician's ability to assess for the imminency of suicide is within a period of 1 year of assessment.

Chapter 5, on schizophrenia, continues with the premise of the necessity for individualized assessment. Drs. Weiden and Roy examine the interaction of traditional suicide risk factors with schizophrenic illness. Suicidal behavior is quite common in schizophrenic patients, with a majority experiencing suicidal ideation at some point during their illness. The authors recommend acknowledging specific suicide risk factors, such as acute psychosis, persistent thought disorder, and despair, and recommend treatment interventions that modify the lethality of the suicidal schizophrenic patient.

In Chapter 6, on substance abuse and suicide, Drs. Weiss and Stephens summarize the prevalence of suicide in substance abusers. They highlight that the relationship between substance abuse and suicide is multifactorial and interrelated. This is particularly true for depression and substance abuse. They identify clinical issues, such as poor medication compliance, impulsiveness, and vulnerability to losses, that increase the likelihood of suicide. The evaluation of the substance abuser must take into account these interrelationships.

In Chapter 7, I focus solely on the suicidal borderline patient. Patients in this diagnostic category challenge clinicians because suicidality is inherent in many of these patients. There is a high incidence of comorbidity, with many patients experiencing an affective disorder and substance abuse, both of which complicate the assessment and clinical outcome. The integration of the biomedical and psychosocial traditions are brought into bold relief in working with these patients. Psychiatrists and other clinicians caring for this patient population must be familiar with dynamics, specific psychopathologic risk factors, and the judicious use of psychotropic medication.

In Chapter 8, on adolescent suicide, Dr. Cantor focuses primarily on the psychological aspects of treating the adolescent. Environmental, educational, and psychological interventions so necessary in the treatment of the suicidal adolescent are presented. Pharmacologic and diagnostic issues, although equally important in the adolescent, are not dealt with in detail.

The book concludes with chapters on liability issues in suicide and the potential adverse reactions that clinicians can experience following a patient's suicide and suggestions to counteract them. In Chapter 9, on liability, Dr. Gutheil examines the medicolegal dimensions of suicide as they impact on the practitioner. There is a practical discussion of suicide litigation and of approaches to liability prevention. Dr. Gutheil emphasizes that despite the primacy of suicide in mental health litigation, clinicians should not respond through "fear, defensive practice, or other adversarializing reactions. Rather, good clinical care augmented by the principles reviewed . . . represent the core of a preventive approach to the unfortunate possibility of liability after suicide."

Finally, in Chapter 10, Dr. Maltsberger addresses the impact of suicide on the clinician. A suicide in one's practice has both professional and personal ramifications. Clinicians may question their own competence or may respond with guilt. Dr. Maltsberger outlines in an exquisite fashion steps to avoid potential adverse reactions, such as the appropriate use of psychological autopsies, consultation, and an acknowledgment that a mourning period should be expected.

Clearly, *Suicide and Clinical Practice* does not embrace every aspect of this challenging and complex subject. The increased attention on rational suicide must be addressed in future work. Are these suicides that are occurring in so-called normal people? Can psychological autopsies in this patient population help us further understand suicidal phenomena? Ed Shneidman, one of the leading figures in the field of suicide, has commented on the role of psychological pain and its relation to suicide, maintaining that it is a person's unwillingness to tolerate the pain that leads to suicide (Shneidman 1991). Is this applicable to rational suicide?

There are endless uncharted waters in the study of suicide. *Suicide and Clinical Practice* provides tools for clinicians to remain afloat in working with patients suffering from suicidal potential. Also, the material in this book allows the clinician to recognize when patients may be approaching a dangerous depth, and what to do about it.

Douglas Jacobs, M.D.

References

Barraclough B, Bunch J, Nelson B, et al: A hundred cases of suicide: clinical aspects. Br J Psychiatry 125:355–373, 1974

Regier DA, Hirschfeld R, Goodwin F: The NIMH Depression Awareness, Recognition, and Treatment Program: structure, aims, and scientific basis. Am J Psychiatry 145:1351–1357, 1988

Shneidman ES: A life in death: notes of a committed suicidologist and epistolary autobiography, in The History of Clinical Psychology in Autobiography. Edited by Walker E. Pacific Brove, CA, Brooks/Cole, 1991, pp 225–292

Acknowledgments

I want to acknowledge the many patients that I have seen over the years, who have struggled with and shared with me their feelings about suicide. These patients have become the meaningful and necessary base of my clinical experience, the essential ingredient in humanizing theoretical models so necessary for relevant and effective psychiatric treatment.

Next, I want to thank each contributor, who so expertly combined theory with clinical practice to produce *Suicide and Clinical Practice,* a book that I hope will enable all health providers to treat better the diverse suicidal patient population.

Several institutions and organizations are responsible for allowing this distinguished group of authors to present their ideas. The industry-sponsored symposia at the annual American Psychiatric Association conventions have been the breeding ground for the chapters that comprise this book. Each symposium was sponsored by the Suicide Education Institute of Boston, The Center for Suicide Research and Prevention at Rush-Presbyterian-St. Luke's Medical Center, and the Hospital Corporation of America (HCA). Special thanks to David Clark and Jan Fawcett at Rush-Presbyterian-St. Luke's and to Jim Don and Jan Pyrce of the HCA Psychiatric Company, without whose participation the programs would never have taken place.

There are several people who also had meaningful input into the production of this book. Marci Klein and Barbara Kopans made editorial revisions on several chapters. Denise Brouillette was instrumental in the conception of the Suicide Education Institute of Boston and worked with me and the faculty on the themes of the individual presentations. Michael Rutstein edited the original oral presentations, which provided a foundation for each contributor. My assistant, Shelley Truett, worked through all phases of correspondence, communication, and production.

I have an ongoing indebtedness to Cambridge Hospital, Department of Psychiatry, for its rich clinical and intellectual atmosphere, and to my two teachers in the field of suicide, John Mack and Les Havens.

Last, I want to acknowledge my family, Mary, Carolyn, and Deborah, who provide me with ongoing support and nurturance.

Douglas Jacobs, M.D.

Chapter 1

Suicide Intervention: Integration of Psychosocial, Clinical, and Biomedical Traditions

Frederick K. Goodwin, M.D.
Bette L. Runck

Suicide is a public health problem of major proportions, one made even more urgent over the last two decades by the appalling upsurge in suicide among the young. Two trends suggest the possibility that we may be facing an escalation of the overall suicide rate. The first trend is that the population is aging. Unless we intervene more effectively than we have in the past, the greater risk of suicide with age can be expected to result in a higher overall suicide rate as the elderly increasingly comprise a larger proportion of the population.*

The second trend that could lead to more suicides is the higher incidence and younger age of onset of major depressive illnesses among

* The relationship between aging and suicide is complex. Whereas the suicide rate among white males continues to rise with age, other groups show more variability across age groups. Further, as Holinger (1987) notes, cohort effects interact with age effects:

> As the population of the older age groups has attained a higher proportion of the total U.S. population, their suicide rates have decreased to the lowest rates ever recorded for those age groups. . . . These data would lead to the prediction that as the proportion of older people increases, their suicide rates would decrease, but probably not to the lower rates seen among the young (due to the fact that suicide rates increase with age). (pp. 192–193)

Related to the aging of the population is the right-to-die issue, a conflict that in some cases may be resolved with "rational" suicides, which until now have not comprised a major portion of actual suicides.

populations born after World War II—the so-called cohort effect (Klerman and Weissman 1989). Although the rising incidence rates appear to have leveled off (Wickramaratne et al. 1989), we can still surmise that at any one time a larger proportion of the population is clinically depressed than in the past. At present, about half of all individuals who commit suicide carry a diagnosis of depression.

Most people who kill themselves are mentally ill at the time, despite the disproportionate amount of attention given to so-called rational suicides. In addition to depression, the most frequently diagnosed disorders are substance abuse (or dependence) and schizophrenia. The presence of both depression and substance abuse appears to be an especially lethal dual diagnosis (Murphy and Wetzel 1990). Identification and effective treatment of these disorders, principally depression, continue to be the most important strategy for preventing suicide. As in the past, that strategy requires refinement because only a minority of patients with any of the high-risk diagnoses actually kill themselves. To burden all diagnosed patients with the extra measures needed to prevent a suicide would be unnecessarily intrusive and expensive. Consequently, identifying those most at risk grows more imperative by the day.

Given the present state of knowledge and clinical practice, how likely is it that the mental health professions can meet these challenges? Judging from the size of the literature on suicide, there is no lack of interest in the subject. We have professional organizations dedicated to the study of self-destruction and symposia at virtually every meeting of our larger organizations. We have even had a White House Conference on adolescent suicide. The epidemiologic data on suicide and suicide attempts are becoming more reliable. Yet, scanning the literature of the last decade, one is struck by the absence of a coherent core of knowledge that represents a widely accepted advance beyond what was known, or at least believed, in the 1960s. With the notable exception of contemporary reports on biological correlates of suicide, little has changed in the research literature. To be sure, shifts of relative emphasis are apparent, clinical recommendations are less purely psychosocial and more concerned with the comprehensive management of the underlying psychiatric disorder, and treatment is more likely to involve pharmacotherapy. Perused as a whole, however, the literature surrenders few pearls.

The malaise evident in the recent discourse on suicide seems to reflect, at least in part, an impasse between different professional traditions in the study of suicide. It hardly needs to be pointed out that biomedical approaches differ substantially from sociological, philosophical, and psychological approaches. The myriad aspects of the study of suicide are reflected in separate sections of books and conferences on the subject. However, merely juxtaposing different frames of reference is not a very useful exercise if their separate languages remain idiosyncratic, their interactions are not even considered, and their relative importance for high-risk individuals remains as imprecise as it is at present. Similarly, calling for a "biopsychosocial approach" serves little purpose unless mechanisms for such interactions are proposed in the form of testable hypotheses.

To revitalize the field of suicide prevention, we are going to have to draw on the best of these separate traditions. The purpose of this chapter is to take a step in the direction of such a rapprochement, with a focus on clinical concerns. We begin by calling attention to the similarities in the interests of all clinicians and speculate on how and why they diverge. After a brief note on the different professional styles and beliefs contributing to the strident discourse that occasionally punctuates the literature on suicide, we discuss how the historical development of the field has tended to focus attention on different populations of self-destructive individuals, a fact that undoubtedly accounts for some (perhaps most) differences in understanding the subject of suicide. Then we suggest a few points of intersection that may serve as grounds for developing new insights. Throughout the discussion, we suggest tentative, testable hypotheses about biological and psychosocial interactions that might have clinical relevance, or we point out strategies by which studies of interactions could be undertaken.

Common Concerns, Disparate Conclusions

Efforts to prevent suicide have traditionally relied on the identification of diagnostic, demographic, and interpersonal risk factors associated largely with suicidal ideation or attempts. This strategy has dominated the vast body of professional literature, both theoretical and clinical, generated during the 20th century, highlighted by the seminal works of Shneidman and Farberow (e.g., *Clues to Suicide*, 1957). Post hoc analyses of risk factors preceding completed suicides have played a less prominent role.

Clinicians, whatever their differences in understanding suicide or approaches to treating suicidal patients, all assess suicidal risk as part of the evaluation of any symptomatic individual who seeks help. The assessment may be preconscious with patients who present little risk, or the clinician may engage in a round-the-clock therapeutic vigil with those in deep despair. Suicide hot lines staffed by nonprofessional volunteers also are geared to assessing risk; however, the lack of professional training and responsibility, deeply troubling to many medical observers (e.g., Himmelhoch 1987), diminishes the quality of such assessments. More importantly, clients who are seen in such settings are only slightly more at risk for actual suicide than the general population and therefore not representative of those at highest risk (see Dew et al. 1987).

Professionals working in more clinical settings disagree over the relative importance of different types of risk and the value of alternative strategies for managing suicidal risk. These differences are a function of the setting in which they work, the type of self-destructive individuals they encounter, the mental set professionals develop during training, and their subsequent clinical or research experience. When professionals share their views, in person or in print, they find themselves talking past each other and sometimes quarreling as they defend the rightness of their own position. These encounters suggest that professional diversity in conceptualizing self-destructive behavior can be profound.

Philosophical-Professional Differences

Although this is not the place to review systematically the factors that contribute to professional differences, we will mention a few of the more obvious. Mental health practitioners begin to develop divergent points of view in professional training: criteria for selecting applicants for a particular course of study vary widely, as do the interests of the individuals who select it, and the curricula, faculty, and clinical supervision to which they are exposed. Given the nature of medical training, for example, the modal psychiatrist probably comes to clinical practice with more commitment to diagnosis and to the regularity of illness processes than the clinical psychologist or social worker. On the other hand, the training of the clinical psychologist and of psychodynamically oriented psychiatrists, especially in an earlier era, makes it more likely that the clinical focus will be on the idiopathic, nonregular characteristics of the patient; on empathic listening; and on the meaning of suicidal ideation or actions for that patient. These differences represent tendencies, not hard and fast universal realities, but they are variations in clinical approach that can lie at the root of disagreements about who is at risk and how to lessen that risk. They can also lead to turf wars, which are further fueled by compensation policies of third-party payers and by the laws prohibiting nonphysicians from prescribing medications. The right to prescribe medications also undoubtedly colors belief systems about the suitability of medication—both among clinicians who have the privilege and among those who do not. (As is plainly obvious in the letters-to-the-editor column of the newspapers of professional organizations, these issues are intensely important to professional self-perceptions.)

As an illustration of one type of the resulting difference between clinical approaches, compare the following descriptions of somatic treatment and psychotherapy for suicidal patients, each of them demonstrating some of the best, most humane advice representative of these approaches:

> In general, somatic therapies for the adult suicidal patient should be aimed at treating symptoms of the underlying, primary condition. . . . Medication should be delivered in the context of a positive physician-patient relationship, one that includes mutual respect and conveys a sense of hopefulness. The clinician should not expect to dissuade patients of their hopelessness; rather the clinician must win the patient's cooperation to undergo, and stick with, treatment. This requires a supportive approach and the building of a working alliance. The clinician's expression of his or her hopefulness that the patient will respond to treatment is an important element in dealing with suicidal patients. (Goldblatt and Schatzberg 1990, p. 430)

> We must be willing to use ourselves to connect with the patient, to feel [his or her] despair. . . . The capacity to understand the plight of our suicidal patients is a central ingredient for successful therapies. . . . The question for therapists becomes both a personal and professional one at the same time. Are we able and willing to accept the despair, are we willing to use more of ourselves in the course of therapy with patients, and can we employ both the psychodynamic and existential perspective in our therapies? . . . The challenge is to be where the patient is—a place where, under ordinary circumstances, we would not choose to go. But in a sense, this is our obligation, our responsibility. (Jacobs 1989, pp. 331, 341)

Quite apart from the fact that the first of these passages describes somatic treatment and the second psychotherapy, the emphases apparent in the choice of language, in the salience of different aspects of the patient's experience, reveal disparate conceptions of the patient's needs in treatment. Reconciling these differences, extracting the best of each approach, may not be an easy undertaking. Because both clearly describe work with patients who present true risk for suicide, however, their similarities may be more important than their dissimilarities.

Tradition and Study Populations

The study of suicide in the United States evolved in separate and, to some extent, isolated intellectual traditions. Shneidman (1970) noted that two major theoretical approaches have dominated suicide studies in the 20th century—the sociological perspective of Durkheim and the psychological concepts of Freud. (Shneidman pointed out, however, that neither is as influential in clinical classification, and thus clinical thinking, as are more commonsensical divisions into committed, attempted, and threatened suicidal behavior.) A third perspective is the biomedical approach, revitalized in the past decade with studies of biochemical correlates of suicide.

The clinical consequences of these primarily research orientations vary enormously. To illustrate, consider the extremes: the disparate perspectives of the community-based suicide prevention movement, on the one hand, and biological psychiatry, on the other. The suicide prevention movement, which emerged in this country in the 1960s, has always been informed primarily by psychological, social, and, to a lesser extent, philosophical and literary studies. Through the many suicide prevention centers that sprang up around the country in the 1960s and 1970s, the people who came to be the subject of concern were most often those who were threatening, contemplating, or attempting suicide. By contrast, clinicians and investigators with a medical focus tend to focus on those who actually committed suicide or whose attempt was sufficiently serious to bring them into an emergency room. This population is largely comprised of people meeting criteria for major psychiatric illness.

A consequence of these different traditions is the confusion of study populations. Despite widespread recognition of this problem, merging dissimilar populations of potentially self-destructive individuals in our research designs remains a primary source of confusion. One all-too-common outcome is that knowledge gathered in such studies loses much of its value because it cannot be compared with other results. In treatment settings, our ability to predict suicidal potential is hampered, and the meaning of an individual's self-destructive behavior is obscured if we base our judgments on overly inclusive or exclusive criteria. Linehan (1986) pointed out that whether one conceives of all suicidal behavior as essentially identical (the one-population model) or as qualitatively different (the multiple-population model) has profound implications for research samples and generalizability of results. It also influences attitudes toward patients:

> The single-population theory defines all subjects with reference to the extreme minority who actually die. The importance of the majority who do not die is contingent on their relationship to the minority who do. It is the risk of suicide that makes suicidal ideation and intentional self-harm important. To the extent that individuals who contemplate suicide and intentionally harm themselves nonfatally differ from suicides, then not only may the behavior be viewed as nonimportant but attitudes toward the individuals can be hostile rather than sympathetic. In contrast a multipopulation perspective views each type of behavior—ideation, self-harm, and suicide—as important in its own right, independent of the relationship of one population to the other. (Linehan 1986, p. 18)

Categorizing self-destructive behavior, especially nonfatal attempts and suicidal ideation, has long been a conceptual problem. Whereas a large percentage of the population may sometime weigh the idea of suicide, community studies have consistently shown that a tiny minority actually attempts it, and the number of completed suicides is still many times smaller. Moscicki and colleagues (1988) reported that 2.9% of the 18,571 respondents in the NIMH (National Institute of Mental Health) Epidemiologic Catchment Area (ECA) Study said that they had attempted suicide during their lifetime; the rate varied from 1.5% at the Piedmont site in North Carolina to 4.3% at the Los Angeles site. The *yearly* rate over all five sites was 0.3% (Moscicki 1989). As with most similar studies, ascertainment of a suicide attempt in this study was problematic. The question was posed as one in a set of criteria to establish whether a diagnosis of major depressive episode could be made. Severity of the attempt was not determined, nor was information given about previous attempts, methods used, or life circumstances surrounding the attempt. Nevertheless, as Moscicki and colleagues demonstrated, the figure is consistent with other community surveys, none of which shows a lifetime rate higher than 5%. Given that the annual suicide rate in the United States is in the range of 12 per 100,000 population (the figure stood at 13.3 in 1977, about the time the ECA study surveys were done) and the comparable yearly figure for attempted suicide in the ECA study was 0.3%, about 23 people attempted suicide for every one who completed it.

Linehan's (1986) analysis led her to a tentative conclusion that one group of suicide attempters—specifically, those with a clear intent to die and significant medical risk—overlaps with the group of individuals who actually commit suicide (see Figure 1–1). But the overlap is probably small, and we must be careful not to confuse these two populations. Despite the need to emphasize research based on individuals who are truly at high risk of suicide, however, we hasten to caution against overlooking what has been learned from studies of suicide attempts and suicidal ideation. Risk factors associated with such behavior, along with risk factors identified in the nonpsychiatrically ill population, may help to predict suicide among those with mental illness. This point will be elaborated on subsequently.

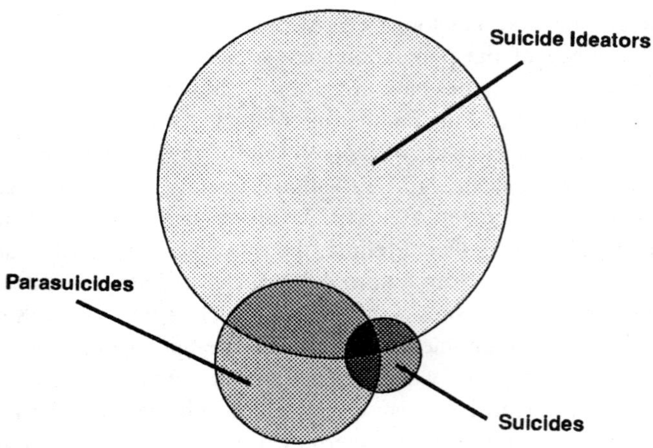

Figure 1–1. Overlapping populations. Reprinted from Linehan (1986) with permission.

Suicide as a Philosophical Issue

Another source of distraction in the literature is the confusion of suicide as a philosophical issue with the clinical risk of suicide. As reviewed by Choron (1972), Western philosophers have considered the possibility of suicide as one of life's most profound paradoxes. Why, when facing overwhelming, unremitting, assuredly endless misery, do the vast majority of human beings choose not to die? Why is suicide such a rare event? In a remarkable article that explores this subject from a medical perspective, Himmelhoch (1988) suggested that evolutionarily determined mechanisms buffer biological organisms from extreme change, a protective barrier that may keep human beings from suicide. "Powerful restraints, neuropsychological, psychological, and social, reside in us all against the completion of self-destruction," he wrote (p. 46).

Thinking about suicide in the abstract is surely commonplace. Many ordinary people, not just poets and philosophers, ponder the subject as part of coming to terms with their own mortality, and patients diagnosed with catastrophic, perhaps terminal, disease may weigh suicide as an alternative to prolonged suffering. Nevertheless, suicide is rare. As noted previously and documented subsequently, it virtually never occurs in the absence of mental illness.

Even though philosophical discussions of the meaning of suicide certainly enrich clinicians' understanding of the thought content of suicidal patients, they probably contribute little to predicting or preventing suicide. Cognitive elements undoubtedly contribute to suicide, and in devising strategies to explore proximate causation, it will probably be most useful to focus on such qualities as the constriction of options described by Shneidman (1986). It is likely that certain cognitive characteristics are among the common factors in suicide, regardless of diagnosis.

Mental Disorder: The Necessary Condition

To zero in on the populations most at risk, we need first to return to the obvious and concern ourselves primarily with patients with symptoms of mental illness. The classic studies of Robins and co-workers (1959) and Barraclough and co-workers (1974) confirmed the long-standing impression that people who kill themselves do so while mentally ill. In the Robins study, 94% of the suicides were in individuals retrospectively diagnosed as psychiatrically ill. Those diagnosed with "manic-depressive depression" or chronic alcoholism and who communicated their suicidal intentions comprised 68% of the total. (As defined, *manic-depressive depression* included individuals with discrete episodes of major depression, with or without manic or hypomanic episodes).

In their study of 100 suicides in England in the late 1960s, Barraclough and Hughes (1987) reported that 93 were judged mentally ill; 70 were diagnosed as depressed, 15 as alcoholic, 3 as schizophrenic, and 27 as having an abnormal personality; 13 were diagnosed as having two or more coexisting disorders. Similar results have been found in studies in several locations, all in Western countries. Stanley and Stanley (1990) recently suggested that the risk of suicide associated with different diagnostic groups documented in such studies should be modified by the rate of various psychiatric illnesses in the population. When the relatively low incidence of schizophrenia is thus considered, for example, the suicide risk associated with it is similar to that for depression. Such analyses could be done prospectively by beginning with a large group of well-diagnosed patients with different illnesses.

In their review of six studies of actual suicides, Black and Winokur (1990) noted that all of the studies found that about 90% of the suicides suffered from a major psychiatric illness at the time of death. These findings were consistent, despite differences in methodology, location, diagnostic criteria, and year of study. As previously mentioned, about half of all the suicides were clinically depressed at the time of the suicide, and about a third were chronic alcoholics. One of the recent studies showed a slightly higher incidence of substance abuse disorders, particularly in subjects under the age of 30. Black and Winokur summarized their findings:

> Taken together, the six studies powerfully demonstrate that major psychiatric illness is, for practical purposes, *necessary* for the suicide. As Murphy (1983) has cogently observed, however, other factors must come into play, for a psychiatric diagnosis itself is not *sufficient* to cause suicide. (p. 136)

It is at this junction—the interplay of the necessary and the sufficient—that psychosocial and biomedical investigators have most to learn from each other.

Intragroup Risk

One attempt to sharpen the focus of clinical attention has been research into the characteristics of suicides within specific diagnostic groups, especially the three most associated with completed suicide: depression, alcoholism, and schizophrenia. As reviewed by Clark and Fawcett (Chapter 4, this volume), the NIMH Collaborative Study of Depression showed that suicide in patients with mood disorders tends to cluster in families, a finding consistent with other findings that suggest a genetic predisposition. For example, evidence from the Danish adoption studies indicates that a tendency to commit suicide may be inherited independently of a depressive diathesis (for reviews, see Kety 1990; Roy 1986). However, in the collaborative study, no association was found between suicide in a patient and completed or attempted suicide in relatives during the first 5 years of follow-up; as Clark and Fawcett noted, the fact that all of these patients had a history of major affective disorder may have erased any further association between patient suicides and family history of suicide. Clinical predictors associated with suicide within the first year of assessment in the collaborative study were anhedonia, severe psychic anxiety, and moderate alcohol abuse. Long-term predictors of suicide (those that occurred after the first year) were severe hopelessness, somatic anxiety, suicidal ideation, and a history of suicide attempts.

Among bipolar patients, suicide rarely occurs during pure mania, but mixed states and the depressions following manias are associated with particularly high risk (Goodwin and Jamison 1990). In general, the period of change between one state and another appears to be a time of great risk for suicide, and thus patients with rapid cycles are particularly vulnerable. In the NIMH collaborative study, when cycling occurred during the intake episode without full remission, the patient was at especially high risk. An early finding that bipolar-II patients—that is, those with major depressions and hypomania—are more prone to suicide than bipolar-I patients (Dunner et al. 1976) was recently confirmed in a study by Rihmer and colleagues (1990). The new study of 100 consecutive suicides in patients with major depression found that 46% had bipolar-II disorder, 1% bipolar-I, and 53% nonbipolar major depression. This study is of particular interest for two reasons. First, it was done in Budapest, Hungary, using diagnostic criteria comparable to other contemporary studies—Research Diagnostic Criteria (Spitzer et al. 1978)—yet because few patients were treated with medications, it approaches a naturalistic study of the type done before the pharmacology era. Second, the results of the study are dramatically suggestive of the potential lethality of bipolar-II illness, since the suicide rate was nearly as high as that for nonbipolar depression despite the lower incidence of bipolar-II disorders. As reviewed by Clark and Fawcett (Chapter 4, this volume), the collaborative study of major depression did not show subgroup differences; since few of the bipolar-II patients were hospitalized during the index episode, however, they may not have been as severely depressed as bipolar-II patients in other studies. In any event, further research should help to clarify whether there is indeed a greater incidence of suicide among bipolar-II patients.

The role of alcoholism in suicide has drawn increasing attention in recent years. The diagnosis of alcoholism is, in itself, predictive of suicide. Suicides frequently occur in the midst of drinking bouts, presumably precipitated by the impaired judgment and poor impulse control associated with alcohol use. Beck and Steer (1989), for example, found that out of 10 clinical and demographic characteristics (i.e., sex, race, marital status, employment status, presence of a depressive diagnosis, presence of a schizophrenia diagnosis, a history of drug abuse, presence of an alcoholism diagnosis, a previous suicide attempt, and age), only a diagnosis of alcoholism predicted the eventual suicide of patients who had previously attempted it. Whether characteristics of alcoholic individuals that are independent of the effects of drinking on judgment, control, and mood contribute to the high risk for suicide is still unclear. In their study, Beck and Steer were unable to determine which of the fatal attempts had been preceded by drinking.

Recent studies of the comorbidity of alcoholism and other psychiatric diagnoses may shed light on this issue. In an important article, Murphy and Wetzel (1990) reviewed the literature on comorbidity, noting that whereas psychopathic or antisocial personality disorders are the diagnoses most often associated with alcoholism, postmortem studies of alcoholics who committed suicide find the highest association with depression:

> Comorbidity plays an important, perhaps crucial, role in the suicide of alcoholics. Complicating depression is the leading factor. Other substance abuse is seen to be not only more frequent now than in the past but to shorten the career from onset of substance abuse to suicide, regardless of which comes first. . . . When the less common contribu-

> tors to suicide are considered, such as antisocial or other personality disorders and Briquet's hysteria, alcoholism or other substance abuse is almost invariably present as well. Thus we may say that *suicide in alcoholism is largely dependent on the supervention of a depressive episode, while in the personality disorders suicide is conditioned on substance abuse* (and possibly depression as well). (p. 390, italics in the original)

Murphy and Wetzel (1990) also recalculated the risk of suicide in alcoholism, suggesting that prevailing estimates of 11–15% are probably wrong and that the more likely lifetime risk is 2–3.4%, a figure that is still much higher than that for the general population.

Alcoholic persons who commit suicide appear to differ from other alcoholics in several respects. The finding that alcoholics who committed suicide had recently suffered the rupture of a close interpersonal relationship has been sufficiently replicated to be considered robust (e.g., Murphy et al. 1979; Rich et al. 1988). In a large prospective study of 1,312 alcoholics, some of whom later committed suicide, Berglund (1984) found that the future suicides had been evaluated as having more depressive and dysphoric symptoms and had been considered more brittle and sensitive than the others. Cognitive impairment and delirium tremens were similar in both groups, suggesting that the vulnerability to alcoholism is related to some factor other than frequent intoxication.

Weiden and Roy's thorough analysis (Chapter 5, this volume) of risk factors in schizophrenia covers risks common to most suicides and also those specific to the illness. Of particular interest here are the relevance of cognitive processes, the thought disorder that persists after florid psychosis has subsided, the counterintuitive finding that illness severity is inversely related to suicide, and the poignant observation that psychosis can protect against suicide.

Identifying the Sufficient Condition

At this stage in our understanding of the factors most predictive of suicide, diagnosis is the first and necessary step to identifying patients at risk. Major depression, unipolar or bipolar, along with alcoholism and schizophrenia, are the diagnoses of most concern. Comorbidity, especially the dual diagnosis of depression and alcoholism, increases the risk still further.

Because a relatively small number of patients who carry any of the high-risk diagnoses actually do commit suicide, the clinician must focus on other individual characteristics that, when combined with the psychiatric disorder, set the stage for the possibility that an underlying suicide risk factor (or factors) may cut across all diagnostic classes. This possibility might be inferred from the observation that suicide rates across diagnoses are roughly the same if differential incidence rates are taken into account (Stanley and Stanley 1990). Because the evaluation of an underlying common suicide factor(s) is an issue facing both the clinician and the researcher, we integrate these two perspectives in the discussion that follows.

We may speculate that it is not the illness itself—that is, the underlying pathopsychological or pathophysiologic processes specific to the illness—that conveys the risk of suicide. Perhaps, instead, the depressive disorder, substance abuse disorder, or psychotic schizophrenic disorder disrupts normal integrative functioning, thus destabilizing the system. This nonspecific disruption of functioning, in turn, "permits" the free expression of an underlying suicidal diathesis.

In searching for a "suicide factor," we must continually remind ourselves of the differences between attempted and completed suicides. As demonstrated in the NIMH collaborative study of depression and other studies, nonlethal attempts appear to be fundamentally different from actual suicides. The task for the clinician is to understand lethal attempts and/or suicide and not to be distracted by nonlethal attempts, which may increase the range of possibilities the clinician must attend to and decrease the signal–noise ratio when determining suicidal risk. Attempted suicide may not be substantially more predictive of actual suicides than other clinical predictors. However, these nonlethal attempts are highly relevant, at least as a comparison group in attempts to tease out characteristics of lethal attempts.

To begin the task of identifying a putative suicide factor, we can draw on the vast psychosocial literature generated over the past four decades, as well as the more recent biomedical findings. Because the psychological literature is well described elsewhere in this volume, we will briefly note a few pertinent findings from studies of the clinical phenomenology of suicide, drawn from both the psychosocial and biomedical traditions.

The clustering of suicide in families suggests either that powerful psychological forces are causing imitative self-destructive behavior or that a vulnerability to suicide is inherited. In all likelihood, both psychological and genetic factors are operating, but for now we shall focus on the genetic. The evidence for a genetic diathesis for recurrent major depression and for early-onset alcoholism is strong, and it is almost as certain that inherited factors play a role in at least some types of schizophrenia as well. As noted earlier, the Danish adoption studies also suggest an inherited vulnerability to suicide itself, independent of diagnosis. Further, personality traits such as impulsiveness that have been associated with low serotonin functioning (see following discussion) themselves involve genetic factors. In one of the largest, most methodologically sophisticated studies of genetic factors in personality ever done, Pedersen and colleagues (1988) compared adult Swedish twins (both monozygotic and dizygotic) reared together and apart on several dimensions of personality. They found that genetic factors accounted for most of the variance in measures of neuroticism, extraversion, impulsivity, and monotony avoidance, whereas shared environment accounted for less than 10% of the variance. The genetic effects appeared to be operating nonadditively in impulsivity and extraversion.

Consistent with these findings are the results of an interesting attempt by Clark and colleagues (1989) to fit data from the NIMH collaborative study to mathematical models predicting the eventual suicide of patients who had previously attempted it. These investigators formulated two models: one that postulated that trait differences would predict who would go on to suicide, the other—the "crescendo hypothesis"—that a first suicide attempt is primarily situational, then each succeeding attempt is more likely because a psychological threshold had been lowered. The model that best fit the data was the trait heterogeneity model, although, as the authors pointed out, methodological limitations must be taken into account: the crescendo process modeled in this study, a reasonable hypothesis, deserves further evaluation. We might add that such a process, if active, is likely to serve as an amplifier of an underlying vulnerability trait.

In searching for an underlying, common risk factor in suicide, how do we evaluate the relative importance of the cluster of personality features (e.g., impulsiveness), behavioral characteristics (e.g., stimulus seeking), cognitive style differences (e.g., rigid, dichotomous thinking), psychophysiologic measures (e.g., augmented response pattern on evoked response), neurobiological factors (e.g., abnormal serotonergic functioning), or experience (e.g., early parental loss) that have been associated with suicide across diagnostic groups? Because many of these features are, in effect, "contaminated" by psychiatric illness, we may learn more about the factors contributing to suicide in our mentally ill patients if we examine what drove that small population who were not ill to commit suicide, as suggested previously (Goodwin 1986). It would be especially important to focus on first-degree relatives of those who have committed suicide in the absence of a psychiatric diagnosis or in the absence of a family history of mental illness. Alternatively, we could conduct psychological and biological autopsies in a sample made up entirely of these so-called normal individuals who committed suicide to examine the variables associated with suicides among the mentally ill.

One use of such strategies would be to evaluate the psychosocial factors contributing to suicide through the back door of biological studies. For example, rather than sorting out the role of impulsivity in the suicide of psychotic patients, it may be easier to examine how personality characteristics associated with suicide correlate with other variables, such as serotonin measures, and then go back to illness populations to evaluate that biological function. The link to abnormal functioning of systems subserved by the neurotransmitter serotonin is the most robust recent finding from biomedical studies of suicide. This indoleamine appears to act as a modulator throughout much of the central nervous system; a wide variety of animal and clinical studies indicates that hypofunction of serotonergic neuronal systems is associated with disinhibition or activation of many types of behaviors. Therefore, most investigators have found low levels of the serotonin metabolite, 5-hydroxyindoleacetic acid (5-HIAA), in the cerebrospinal fluid of suicide victims, and some evidence indicates the association also exists in suicide attempters (for reviews, see Åsberg et al. 1986; Brown and Goodwin 1986; Mann et al. 1989; Ricci and Wellman 1990; Stanley and Stanley 1990).

First reported by Åsberg and colleagues (1976), the suicide-serotonin relationship has been observed in major depression, schizophrenia, adjustment disorders, some personality disorders, and "neurotic" depression. The work has extended beyond metabolite studies, neuroendocrine measures, and postmortem studies of serotonin receptors in the brains of patients who had killed themselves (reviewed by Arora and Meltzer 1989), findings that are consistent with lower-than-normal serotonin functioning. The studies typically show more postsynaptic serotonin receptors than are normal, presumably reflecting a supersensitivity in response to low levels of exposure to serotonin neurotransmitter, and decreased presynaptic autoreceptors, which has been interpreted as the brain's attempt to attenuate the negative feedback that normally constrains neuronal firing. Following the observation of a robust inverse correlation between cerebrospinal fluid 5-HIAA and a life history of aggressive, violent, and impulsive behavior in young males (Brown et al. 1979), Åsberg and her colleagues reported that the link with low serotonin functioning and suicide is stronger in people who commit suicide impulsively, using violent methods. Undoubtedly, the link between the serotonin system and impulsive-aggressive behavior will prove to be complex, probably involving dysregulation of the system as indicated by *either* high or low levels of 5-HIAA or other measures of serotonin function.

The relationship between personality variables associated with a low level of the serotonin metabolite and with aggression and impulsivity—monotony avoidance, stimulus seeking, a tendency to augment stimuli on evoked response—might be conceptualized as a low capacity of the central nervous system for stasis or for constancy; that is, individuals who exhibit these features seem to be constantly looking to change the status quo, the equilibrium of the central nervous system.

The recent report of "intense, violent suicidal preoccupation" in six depressed patients taking fluoxetine (Teicher et al. 1990) is puzzling in light of evidence suggesting a robust relationship between *low* serotonin functioning and the impulsive behavior associated with actual suicide. Fluoxetine, by contrast, is thought to *enhance* serotonin functioning by blocking the presynaptic reuptake of serotonin. In evaluating the meaning of individual case reports, it is important to keep in mind that suicidal behavior is quite common among patients likely to be treated with fluoxetine. A recent analysis (Goodwin, unpublished) indicates that the total number of suicide attempts among patients on fluoxetine reported to the Food and Drug Administration (FDA) represents less than 1% of the attempts that would be expected in that population, as predicted from ECA data on suicide attempts. Even allowing for substantial underreporting to the FDA, it appears that suicide attempts among patients on fluoxetine are low.

In addition to its demonstrated link to impulsivity, serotonin appears to be involved in central pain and punishment mechanisms. A focus on this type of mechanism may help to identify common and differentiating features in attempted and completed suicide. Clinically, survivors of near-lethal attempts often describe their behavior as an act of desperation, a way to escape their pain. People who slash their wrists, a method associated with low lethality, similarly describe their act as a way of calming themselves down; by focusing on identifiable, discreet, physical pain, they relieve or distract themselves from the pervasive, indescribable, unidentifiable psychological pain. The lower 5-HIAA (implying low serotonin functioning) that may be present in people who have attempted suicide could point to a different mechanism than the similar finding of low serotonin activity in those who commit suicide. Those who attempt suicide may have deficiencies in central pain regulation, and by cutting themselves, they release endogenous analgesics, the endorphins. In more lethal attempts and actual suicides, low serotonin functioning might reflect that same dysregulation of central pain mechanisms, plus poor control of violent impulses. In exploring such possible mechanisms, we may ultimately find less of a distinction between lethal and nonlethal suicide attempts, yet the distinction must be drawn to trace these mechanisms.

These speculations are offered as an illustration of how an interactive approach to searching for a suicide factor might proceed. If such an underlying suicide factor exists, it could be a personality trait or a neurobiological abnormality. More likely, it is a proclivity produced by the interaction of genetic, neurologic, and psychological influences, and similar interaction in our research enterprise will have the greatest chance of success.

Summary

Sorting through and reconciling differences in professional approaches to the study of suicide may be key to more effective intervention. Clinically, we must recognize that the individuals most at risk for actual suicide are suffering from major depression, alcoholism, schizophrenia, or more than one of these disorders. Mental illness being the necessary condition, our research task becomes identifying the sufficient condition. One approach to identifying such a "suicide factor" is to study individuals who were not mentally ill when they committed suicide. Another is to examine clinical or personality variables through the back door of biological studies.

References

Arora RC, Meltzer HY: Serotonergic measures in the brains of suicide victims: 5-HT_2 binding sites in the frontal cortex of suicide victims and control subjects. Arch Gen Psychiatry 146:730–736, 1989

Åsberg M, Träskman L, Thorén P: 5-HIAA in the cerebrospinal fluid: a biochemical suicide predictor? Arch Gen Psychiatry 33:1193–1197, 1976

Åsberg M, Nordström P, Träskman-Bendz L: Cerebrospinal fluid studies in suicide: an overview. Ann N Y Acad Sci 487:243–255, 1986

Barraclough B, Hughes J: Suicide: Clinical and Epidemiological Studies. London, Croom Helm, 1987

Barraclough B, Bunch J, Nelson B, et al: A hundred cases of suicide: clinical aspects. Br J Psychiatry 125:355–373, 1974

Beck AT, Steer RA: Clinical predictors of eventual suicide: a 5- to 10-year prospective study of suicide attempters. J Affective Disord 17:203–209, 1989

Berglund M: Suicide in alcoholism: a prospective study of 88 suicides, I: the multidimensional diagnosis at first admission. Arch Gen Psychiatry 41:888–891, 1984

Black DW, Winokur G: Suicide and psychiatric diagnosis, in Suicide Over the Life Cycle: Risk Factors, Assessment, and Treatment of Suicidal Patients. Edited by Blumenthal SJ, Kupfer DJ. Washington, DC, American Psychiatric Press, 1990, pp 135–153

Brown GL, Goodwin FK: Cerebrospinal fluid correlates of suicide attempts and aggression. Ann N Y Acad Sci 487:175–188, 1986

Brown GL, Goodwin FK, Ballenger JC, et al: Aggression in humans: correlates with cerebrospinal fluid amine metabolites. Psychiatry Res 1:131–139, 1979

Choron J: Suicide. New York, Scribner's, 1972

Clark DC, Gibbons RD, Fawcett J, et al: What is the mechanism by which suicide attempts predispose to later suicide attempts? a mathematical model. J Abnorm Psychol 98:42–49, 1989

Dew MA, Bromet EJ, Brent D, et al: A quantitative literature review of the effectiveness of suicide prevention centers. J Consult Clin Psychol 55:239–244, 1987

Dunner DL, Gershon ES, Goodwin FK: Heritable factors in the severity of affective illness. Biol Psychiatry 11:31–42, 1976

Goldblatt MJ, Schatzberg AF: Somatic treatment of the adult suicidal patient, in Suicide Over the Life Cycle: Risk Factors, Assessment, and Treatment of Suicidal Patients. Edited by Blumenthal SJ, Kupfer DJ. Washington, DC, American Psychiatric Press, 1990, pp 425–440

Goodwin FK: Suicide, aggression, and depression. Ann N Y Acad Sci 487:351–355, 1986

Goodwin FK, Jamison KR: Manic-Depressive Illness. New York, Oxford University Press, 1990

Himmelhoch JM: Lest treatment abet suicide. J Clin Psychiatry 48(12, Suppl):44–54, 1987

Himmelhoch JM: What destroys our restraints against suicide? J Clin Psychiatry 49(9, Suppl):46–52, 1988

Holinger PC: Violent Deaths in the United States. New York, Guilford, 1987

Jacobs D: Psychotherapy with suicidal patients: the empathic method, in Suicide: Understanding and Responding. Edited by Jacobs D, Brown HN. Madison, CT, International Universities Press, 1989, pp 329–342

Kety SS: Genetic factors in suicide: family, twin, and adoption studies, in Suicide Over the Life Cycle: Risk Factors, Assessment, and Treatment of Suicidal Patients. Edited by Blumenthal SJ, Kupfer DJ. Washington, DC, American Psychiatric Press, 1990, pp 127–133

Klerman GL, Weissman MM: Increasing rates of depression. JAMA 261:2229–2235, 1989

Linehan MM: Suicidal people: one population or two? Ann N Y Acad Sci 487:16–33, 1986

Mann JJ, Arango V, Marzuk PM, et al: Evidence for the 5-HT hypothesis of suicide: a review of post-mortem studies. Br J Psychiatry 155(Suppl 8):7–14, 1989

Moscicki EK: Epidemiologic surveys as tools for studying suicidal behavior: a review. Suicide Life Threat Behav 19:131–146, 1989

Moscicki EK, O'Carroll P, Rae DS, et al: Suicide attempts in the Epidemiologic Catchment Area study. Yale J Biol Med 61:259–268, 1988

Murphy GE: Problems in studying suicide. Psychiatr Dev 1:339–350, 1983

Murphy GE, Wetzel RD: The lifetime risk of suicide in alcoholism. Arch Gen Psychiatry 47:383–392, 1990

Murphy GE, Armstrong JW, Hermele SL, et al: Suicide and alcoholism: interpersonal loss confirmed as a predictor. Arch Gen Psychiatry 36:65–69, 1979

Pedersen NL, Plomin R, McClearn GE, et al: Neuroticism, extraversion, and related traits in adult twins reared apart and reared together. J Pers Soc Psychol 55:950–957, 1988

Ricci LC, Wellman MM: Monoamines: biochemical markers of suicide? J Clin Psychol 146:106–116, 1990

Rich CL, Fowler RC, Fogarty LA, et al: San Diego suicide study, III: relationships between diagnoses and stressors. Arch Gen Psychiatry 45:589–592, 1988

Rihmer Z, Barsi J, Arató M, et al: Suicide in subtypes of primary major depression. J Affective Disord 18:221–225, 1990

Robins E, Murphy GE, Wilkinson RH, et al: Some clinical considerations in the prevention of suicide based on a study of 134 successful suicides. Am J Public Health 49:888–899, 1959

Roy A: Genetics of suicide. Ann NY Acad Sci 487:97–105, 1986

Shneidman ES: Orientations toward death, in The Psychology of Suicide. Edited by Shneidman ES, Farberow NL, Litman RE. New York, Science House, 1970, pp 3–45

Shneidman ES: Some essentials for suicide and some implications for response, in Suicide. Edited by Roy A. Baltimore, MD, Williams & Wilkins, 1986, pp 1–16

Shneidman ES, Farberow NL (eds): Clues to Suicide. New York, McGraw-Hill, 1957

Spitzer RL, Endicott J, Robins E: Research Diagnostic Criteria: rationale and reliability. Arch Gen Psychiatry 35:773–782, 1978

Stanley M, Stanley B: Postmortem evidence for serotonin's role in suicide. J Clin Psychiatry 51(4, Suppl):22–28, 1990

Teicher MH, Glod C, Cole JO: Emergence of intense suicidal preoccupation during fluoxetine treatment. Am J Psychiatry 147:207–210, 1990

Wickramaratne PJ, Weissman MM, Leaf PJ, et al: Age, period and cohort effects on the risk of major depression: results from five United States communities. J Clin Epidemiol 42:333–343, 1989

Chapter 2

Medication and the Suicidal Patient

Mark Goldblatt, M.B.B.C.H.
Alan Schatzberg, M.D.

Death by suicide may be the final common pathway of expression for patients with a variety of diagnoses. Managing a patient's suicidal ideation and behavior is perhaps the most challenging aspect of psychiatric treatment, reflecting the powerful emotions that are ignited and the inherent dangers of treatment failure. The treatment of the suicidal patient cannot be separated from the treatment of the underlying disorder, whether it be major depression, borderline personality disorder, schizophrenia, alcoholism, and so on. In this chapter, we describe general factors involved in the management of suicidal patients, with particular emphasis on psychopharmacologic treatment of the underlying disorder and the associated supportive psychotherapy.

The factors that precipitate suicidal behavior appear to vary among patients with different diagnoses. For example, depressed patients are more likely to attempt suicide when overcome with hopelessness, especially when compounded by psychosis. Schizophrenic patients tend to commit suicide around poorly understood issues of loss, especially close to the time of discharge from the hospital. Patients with borderline personality disorder are more suicidal when feeling disconnected from key objects in their lives, including their therapists. Alcohol and substance abusers, who often have poor impulse control, may particularly contemplate suicide as a result of confusion or depression induced by the abused substances.

Therefore, each suicidal patient needs to be assessed and understood in the context of his or her diagnosis, as well as any associated risks of acting out these suicidal wishes.

The management of the suicidal patient relies heavily on the relationship that the patient has to a primary therapist or treatment team. The formation and maintenance of this relationship is the cornerstone of any treatment and is crucial for ensuring the safety of patients at risk for suicide. A small percentage of patients may respond to disappointments in this relationship with increased suicidality, but this does not diminish the necessity of this approach nor deny the reality of its shortcomings. In this chapter, we begin by addressing general management issues for suicidal patients with specific psychiatric disorders, and thereafter we propose detailed medication strategies for treating patients and their symptoms within these diagnostic categories.

General Management

Depression

Patients diagnosed with major depression are at great risk for suicide. Studies have shown that approximately 15% of depressed patients will eventually kill themselves (Miles 1977). In this group, hopelessness and pessimism are noticeable features (Beck et al. 1985). Despite reassurances from the therapist that this is a time-limited illness and that it will pass (usually in about 3 weeks or less with appropriate treatment), many depressed patients remain hopeless and distraught. In the darkness of their depression, patients who feel hopeless are often unable to accept and integrate this information. The therapist, however, through his or her own experience of treating depression or observing this treatment during training, can believe that this overwhelming state of gloom will pass. The therapist must convey this sense of hopefulness to the patient, through supportive psychotherapy, to engage the patient in medication trials and delay the acting out of these destructive impulses. Over time, the suicidal period usually passes safely.

Depression can resolve in about 3–4 weeks with adequate levels of medication. Prescriptions for medication require careful consideration. The prescribing physician should take into account the patient's ability to understand directions, the patient's willingness to follow these directions faithfully, and the underlying commitment to engage in this therapeutic trial. As these medications can be lethal in overdose, it is essential to know that both clinician and patient are working together in treating a common problem. If the clinician feels that the patient's reliability is in doubt, then a smaller amount of pills may be prescribed, to last just a few days, and therefore ensure an ongoing dialogue and assessment of the situation. The medicolegal issues concerning prescribing and suicidality are discussed by Gutheil (Chapter 9, this volume).

There are a number of important issues in effecting a hopeful stance. A sense of hopeful optimism in the therapist must be distinguished from a false bravado that devalues the patient's pain and breaks any empathic connection that might be building between patient and therapist. It is unrealistic to try to "talk" depressed patients out of their sadness and desperation. Too often this leads to frustration and anger and ultimately a breakdown in the therapeutic alliance and an increase in the risk of suicidal action.

Depressed patients, who are at greatest risk for suicide, feel isolated and cut off from their supportive network. Finding a way to include the spouse or supportive family members in the treatment is important and challenging. It is important because family members are frequently asked to assist in making painful decisions around hospitalization, involuntary commitment, and safety. It can be a difficult challenge when patients are opposed to their family being involved in the treatment and are ambivalent about admitting to their family the severity of their desperation. However, we have found that this involvement is often critical, both in terms of widening the safety net of relationships and in beginning to repair the breakdowns in communication that so often accompany depression.

Hospitalization is a very helpful and effective tool in the management of the suicidal, depressed patient and should be considered earlier rather than later in the course of the illness. There are several indications for hospitalization. When patient and clinician both agree that the patient's feelings of sadness and death are overwhelming, then hospitalization is obviously appropriate. When a clinician senses that a depressed patient is at risk for acting on suicidal wishes, then the safety of a psychiatric ward is indicated. This decision becomes more ambiguous, and consequently more anxiety provoking, when the patient-therapist alliance is tenuous, usually in the early stages of treatment. When the therapist feels that he or she is not hearing the full story, or that the patient is reluctant to reveal the extent of the problem, then the clinician's ability to make responsible decisions is severely impaired. In many cases, calling in family members can help broaden the clinical picture and clarify the need for safety or hospital level of treatment.

In cases in which there is doubt about hospitalization, it would seem prudent to err on the conservative side, toward hospitalizing the patient.

This provides a number of advantages:

1. The patient is placed in a safe setting and given the message that his or her feelings are important and will be taken seriously by the clinician, even to the extent of ensuring a safe place to recover from this episode.
2. Patients who are actively fantasying about ways to die are relieved by being closely observed in a secure and structured setting. Many self-destructive acts can be averted.
3. An expanded treatment team immediately becomes available to this seriously ill patient. In most hospitals, this would consist of the patient being evaluated by an emergency room psychiatrist, admitting physician, ward nursing staff, mental health worker, social worker, psychologist, behavior therapist, administrator, or inpatient psychiatrist. By enlarging the treatment team, the primary therapist is able to receive other opinions about the severity of the patient's illness and dangerousness. The inpatient stay also makes it possible to observe the patient closely through trained eyes, 24 hours a day.
4. The clinician is provided with valuable information about neurovegetative signs of depression (e.g., sleep disturbance, appetite, weight changes), which are essential for diagnosis.
5. Inpatient wards are also useful for helping patients see that they are not alone in their suffering. Inpatient groups are particularly effective in this regard and can help toward later placement in outpatient groups or in joining self-help educational and support groups.
6. While in the hospital, medication trials can easily and safely be started; if indicated, special diets can be learned and discussed. Although electroconvulsive therapy can be administered as an outpatient procedure, most clinicians feel more comfortable prescribing this highly effective treatment on an inpatient basis.
7. The patient may be seen more intensively, three to five times per week, in supportive therapy, as indicated.

Borderline Personality Disorder

A great deal of the therapy in treating patients with borderline personality disorder lies in the establishment of a working relationship that allows for expression of feelings through verbalization and that contains violent or destructive actions.

The course of treatment of these patients is often punctuated with periods of intense suicidality. At such times, hospitalization can provide a safe, containing environment until more functional defenses are in place. With ongoing psychotherapy, an adequate alliance develops between the patient and the primary therapist or treatment team, resulting in a subsequent decrease in suicidal behaviors. Often merely the knowledge that the patient is able to use the safety of a psychiatric ward is enough to decrease the need for hospitalization of the self-destructive patient.

There is a school of thought that advocates that the therapist should initially set clear limits on the patient's manipulative behavior regarding the need for hospitalization. This can be helpful at some point in therapy; however, when done without explanation or therapeutic alliance, patients can experience this as frustrating and withholding and feel unsafe. In general, we advocate not setting up struggles for suicidal patients who wish to be admitted to a hospital. By giving the patient some degree of responsibility, within the context of the relationship, a more constructive dynamic is established. Patients should be reassured that if their impulses become too intense and uncontrollable, then hospitalization is or will be made available. In our experience, this generally lessens the patient's need to act out and test whether the therapist cares enough about safety to take appropriate action. This type of approach seeks to foster a greater sense of responsibility in the patient and structures the patient-therapist relationship in a healthier fashion.

This sense of responsibility is an outgrowth of the therapy and the therapeutic alliance. It is not always present from the beginning of treatment; but as therapy progresses, it becomes apparent when the patient can use this relationship to discuss his or her self-destructive feelings rather than act them out.

Schizophrenia

Schizophrenic patients are at increased risk for suicide. Several studies have shown that about 10% of schizophrenic patients will eventually kill themselves (Dorpat and Ripley 1960; Miles 1977). Male patients are more likely to act on their suicidal wishes when they are accompanied by depressive symptoms and, in some cases, when the psychosis is marked by command hallucinations. A particularly vulnerable time for this population appears to be around the time of discharge from an inpatient setting (Roy 1982).

Schizophrenic patients who do suicide appear to show an awareness of their loss of function through the illness and loss of a previous capacity to engage in life (Warnes 1968). It seems that these losses are particularly painful soon after admission to, or discharge from, the hospital and may relate to the lack of outpatient treatment facilities and support in the community.

Therefore, we feel that it is crucial for these patients to be connected to a treatment team, usually consisting of a supportive living situation (e.g., a halfway house), a safe way to spend their days (e.g., a supportive day program or work situation), a primary therapist, a psychopharmacologist, and a family therapist (if indicated). The ability to enter the hospital when symptoms increase, particularly when treaters notice an increase in depressive symptoms, is a fundamental necessity for successful treatment. In addition, ongoing antipsychotic medication (decanoate injection if indicated) is a helpful adjunct in ensuring that psychotic decompensations are minimized.

Medication Strategies

Depression

Unipolar and bipolar depressed patients have a relatively high lifetime risk of suicide (Guze and Robins 1970). Although antidepressant response rates are encouraging (Morris and Beck 1974), medications used in the treatment of depression and mood instability can be extremely toxic in overdose. It therefore becomes vitally important in the treatment of these patients that a good mental status examination be performed and that the patient's level of suicidality be assessed.

Most if not all depressed patients will be thinking of death or dying. The quality and intensity of this ideation becomes important to distinguish at which end of the suicide continuum a patient's ideation falls. For example, a patient may have fantasies of "life without pain," with no intent to proceed any further, in contrast to the patient who has a definite suicide plan. Other important aspects to consider are the patient's support system, accessibility to lethal agents, history of previous attempts, and history of compliance with treatment. Perhaps most important of all is the patient-doctor alliance and the degree of trust and communication that this engenders, enabling the clinician to feel safe with a suicidal patient, whether in or out of the hospital.

Suicidal ideation needs to be assessed with every depressed patient, and an ongoing evaluation of dangerousness should be part of the therapeutic work in dispensing medication. Prompt interventions can be lifesaving.

First episodes of major depression are often treated with a tricyclic antidepressant (TCA), such as imipramine if sleeplessness is a problem or desipramine if the patient is slowed down or anergic. The initial dose of 50 mg of imipramine can be raised by 25 mg every 2–3 days, depending on tolerance of side effects. Therapeutic dosage is usually obtained between 150 to 300 mg/day. Patients need to be at this level for at least 3 weeks to ensure an adequate trial. Blood levels may be helpful for evaluating nonresponders and for detecting toxic concentrations that produce severe side effects.

Failure to respond to a trial of a TCA is often related to an inadequate dose, or to an insufficient length of medication trial, or to both these shortcomings. Premature termination of the medication trial due to excessive side effects may be countered by attempting to deal with specific side effects as they arise. If, however, the initial trial of imipramine or desipramine cannot be pursued due to excessive side effects, a trial of a second TCA with a more palatable side-effect profile may be useful. For example, nortriptyline, which is potent in lower dosages, is usually well tolerated. It has a relative lack of orthostatic side effects at lower dosages, and it has a known "therapeutic window." Blood levels of 50–150 ng/ml generally correlate with optimal efficacy, and therefore blood level monitoring is worthwhile. Trimipramine (Surmontil) is another TCA that can be very effective in depressed patients experiencing sleep problems, particularly the elderly. Its sedative qualities, when taken as a nightly dose of 100–300 mg, can prove effective early on in the treatment of depression.

If it becomes impossible to complete a therapeutic trial of a TCA due to excessive side effects, or due to poor compliance, or if there is little or no response to the trial, then switching to a different class of antidepressant is suggested.

Fluoxetine (Prozac), a serotonin reuptake inhibitor, is a relatively new antidepressant that is rapidly becoming a first order treatment option. In light of reports of low cerebrospinal fluid (CSF) levels of 5-hydroxyindoleacetic acid (5-HIAA) in severely depressed patients with suicidal ideation, a serotonin reuptake blocker like fluoxetine may offer particular advantage. Patients are started on 20 mg of fluoxetine per day, and usually remain at this dose for at least 3 weeks. Although some patients require doses of 60–80 mg/day, the vast majority respond to lower dosages (around 20–40 mg/day). Common side effects of nausea, tremor, and nervousness at higher doses argue for the lower dosage, especially in patients experiencing sleep difficulties. In the relatively short period that Prozac has been available, it appears fairly safe in overdosage, although more reports of it being used in suicide attempts are emerging. A report by Teicher and colleagues (1990) suggests that some patients may become more suicidal when treated with fluoxetine; however, this has not been the case in our hands. Other researchers have found fluoxetine to be more effective than mianserin or placebo in treating suicidal feelings in depressed outpatients (Muijen et al. 1988; Teicher et al. 1990), but this has not been repeated in other studies.

Trazodone, another complex antidepressant, is particularly effective in depressed patients who have difficulty sleeping. Patients can be started on 50 mg nightly and increased by 25 mg every 2–3 days according to tolerance of side effects. Although the manufacturer recommends increasing the dose to 600 mg/day, many patients respond at lower levels, usually around 150–300 mg/day. Unfortunately, blood levels here are not particularly helpful. As this is a drug that is usually well tolerated in overdose, it is often used in the treatment of suicidal patients. It does have some worrisome side effects, most notably occasional priapism, and also dizziness when taken on an empty stomach. Priapism is a rare phenomenon but can produce impotence if not treated promptly in the first few hours. We recommend that male patients seek emergency room treatment if they notice any symptoms suggesting priapism. (Transient erections are common and are not a problem with this drug.)

Monoamine oxidase inhibitors (MAOIs) are an effective class of antidepressant drugs that are especially useful for treatment-resistant depressions and for "hysteroid dysphoria." Although there may be hesitation and wariness about treating suicidal patients with MAOIs, we have found this fearfulness is largely misplaced. As with all suicidal patients, a thorough mental status examination will help in monitoring suicidality in a depressed patient who is allied with the treatment team. Contrary to popular fears, most suicidal patients seem to use MAOIs fairly safely. Perhaps the threat of hypertensive crises and its attendant pain and complications are weighted factors that enable suicidal depressed patients to stick to their tyramine-restricted diet. However, we have seen occasional suicidal patients flirt with danger by breaking their diet or by taking unprescribed additional medications.

There are three MAOIs currently available in the United States. Isocarboxazid (Marplan) is started at 20 mg/day and increased by 10 mg every 3–4 days according to the patient's ability to tolerate side effects. Therapeutic effects are usually noted around 30–60 mg/day. Phenelzine (Nardil) is started at 30 mg/day and increased by 15 mg every 3–4 days to a therapeutic dose of 45–90 mg/day. Tranylcypromine (Parnate) is also started at 20 mg/day and increased by 10 mg every 3–4 days to a total of 30–50 mg/day. We often use the guideline of 1 mg/kg/day of phenelzine. Distressing side effects of dizziness and orthostasis can be effectively treated by maintaining adequate hydration (especially in the summer months), by the use of elastic stockings, or by increasing salt intake. Occasionally the addition of Florinef (a mineralocorticoid) at doses of 0.3–0.8 mg has been an effective supplement for this problem. Again, it may take up to 3 or 4 weeks for a therapeutic effect to be realized.

It would appear that this is an effective class of antidepressant in patients with whom the physician has enough of an alliance and who are able both to cooperate and to comprehend the physiologic consequences of monoamine oxidase inhibition and potential hypertensive crises. A 10- to 14-day drug-free period is recommended when changing between an MAOI and a TCA. Although a briefer drug-free period may be sufficient going from a TCA to an MAOI, a 10- to 14-day drug-free period is probably safer.

Wellbutrin (bupropion) is a new unicyclic antidepressant recently released in the United States. Treatment is started at 75 mg/day and increased by 75 mg every 3–4 days to a therapeutic level of 225–450 mg/day. This usually leads to a response in 3–4 weeks. Its favorable side-effect profile makes this a useful additional drug in the treatment of depression, although it is still too soon to report on its safety when taken in overdose.

Lithium carbonate is another useful drug for the treatment of depression. When it is added to a TCA, a substantial proportion of patients show improvement where TCAs alone had been ineffective (de Montigny et al. 1983).

Electroconvulsive therapy remains one of the most effective treatments for depression. Despite negative publicity in the popular press, it continues to be the treatment of choice in severe depression. Its rapid onset and low side-effect profile make it particularly useful in dealing with treatment-resistant depression. Usually at least 12 treatments are needed to ensure an adequate trial. This is usually prescribed during inpatient treatment, but may be an outpatient procedure, especially when considering maintenance treatment.

Psychotic Depression

This category of patients may represent the greatest challenge to the clinician treating suicidal patients. In some studies, delusionally depressed patients have been reported to be much more likely to commit suicide than those who are not delusional (Roose et al. 1983). However, more recent reports seem to indicate that this result may not be consistently found (Coryell et al. 1990). The extent of the psychotic thinking may not be apparent on superficial examination. Often the patient's dangerousness can remain hidden from the physician who has only limited contact with a severely impaired and isolated patient. "Contracts" for safety are notoriously unreliable with these patients, and hospitalization with intense treatment is usually indicated.

Antidepressant and antipsychotic medication in combination treatment, or electroconvulsive therapy, has been shown to be particularly effective for psychotic depressions (Spiker et al. 1981). Low-dose antipsychotic medication (usually less than 300 mg of chlorpromazine, or its equivalent) in combination with antidepressant medication in adequate doses is usually sufficient, although higher doses of both types of medication may be necessary for more refractory conditions. Antipsychotic medications with favorable side effect profiles involving minimal autonomic, sedative, and neuromuscular components are generally well tolerated. These include loxapine (Loxitane) and perphenazine (Trilafon).

Panic Disorder and Attacks

Weissman and colleagues (1989) reported on the increased risk of suicidal ideation and attempts found in patients with panic disorder and panic attacks. Clinically, most panic patients do not appear particularly suicidal, and some investigators have questioned the significance of this finding. One source of variation between investigators may lie in current versus lifetime assessment of suicidal behavior. Many of the adult panic patients who had attempted suicide had done so while they were adolescents. Panic symptoms may not yet have been diagnosed, or later panic may be tied to earlier psychopathology (e.g., suicidal behavior).

Therapeutic interventions for panic patients should begin with a thorough medical evaluation to exclude significant medical illnesses. Thereafter, appropriate psychiatric treatment can be instituted. Behavior therapy and pharmacotherapy are the mainstays of treatment. Imipramine and desipramine in doses lower than those normally prescribed for antidepressant effect (50–150 mg/day) are usually effective. Alprazolam (0.5–1 mg tid) can also be helpful, but patients and clinicians need to be aware of the dependence potential of this and other benzodiazepines.

Mania

Although mania is usually associated with mood elevation and euphoria, several authors have described that manic patients may demonstrate affective lability, irritability, anger, or severe dysphoria characterized by depression and anxiety (Post et al. 1989). Kraepelin first documented such states in 1921 and recognized their relatively poor prognosis. More recent researchers have confirmed this finding and also reported the relatively poor response that these patients have to treatment with lithium carbonate, as compared with "pure" manics (Secunda et al. 1986). Post and colleagues (1987) suggested that this group of patients may show a relatively better therapeutic response to carbamazepine. Occasionally, it may be difficult to distinguish a patient with an agitated depression from another with an irritable and dysphoric mania. The most notable feature in the clinical treatment of the latter patients is their propensity to become worse when treated with antidepressant medication.

The mainstay of treatment for both the dysphoric and nondysphoric manic patient is lithium carbonate. Prior to initiating lithium therapy, the treating physician needs to ensure that the patient's renal and cardiovascular systems are functioning adequately. Usually blood urea nitrogen and creatinine levels are drawn, as well as a chemical profile (including liver function tests) and electrocardiogram. It is also useful to check thyroid function tests prior to initiating therapy so that a baseline level is obtained, should hypothyroidism later develop. Blood should be drawn twice a week while lithium levels are being raised. We recommend starting at 600 mg/day and increasing this every 2–3 days, depending on the blood levels obtained. Adequate blood levels are essential for the management of this illness, and response is generally seen within 10–14 days with blood levels of 0.8–1.2 mEq/L. This usually occurs with dosages between 900 and 1,800 mg/day. Following stabilization of the lithium level, blood levels need be checked only every week and then biweekly or monthly, as the dose stabilizes. Antipsychotic medications can be very helpful in the acute management of this state.

Second-line drugs that are frequently used are carbamazepine (Tegretol) and valproic acid (Depakene). Prior to initiating carbamazepine treatment, blood should be drawn for a complete blood count with differential, and blood levels should be followed initially at weekly intervals to monitor for possible leukopenia. Patients are most at risk for this complication in the first 6 months following initiation of treatment. We recommend starting patients on a relatively low carbamazepine dose of 100 mg at bedtime. If tolerated, an increase to 200 mg at bedtime after 1–2 days may be prescribed, with further increases until a therapeutic level is attained. Antimanic effects are usually observed within 2–3 weeks of treatment at therapeutic levels of approximately 6–8 mg/L.

Before starting patients on valproic acid, baseline laboratory testing of liver function tests, routine chemistry screen, and complete blood count should be obtained. Starting dose is 250 mg/day, and increased after 3 days to 250 mg bid. Blood levels should be followed twice a week while stabilizing dose, and then at less frequent intervals when therapeutic levels are obtained. Common side effects include early acute weight gain, hair loss, and dyspepsia. The dose of valproic acid is increased as tolerated to achieve blood levels of valproic acid between 50 and 100 mg/L. Severe hepatotoxicity is rare, but is a risk in newborns with immature liver (P-450) enzymes systems, particularly those treated with barbiturates.

Borderline Personality Disorder

Of all symptoms of borderline personality disorder, suicidality and self-destructiveness are probably the most distressing to the treating clinician. Although there is controversy as to the effectiveness of medication in the treatment of this disorder, it appears that certain symptoms are more likely than others to respond to pharmacotherapy.

Low-dose phenothiazines have been reported to be effective in the treatment of certain psychotic symptoms. Soloff and colleagues (1986b) reported the improvement noted in a broad range of the psychotic symptoms in borderline patients when treated with haloperidol. Goldberg and colleagues (1986) also showed that thiothixene diminished certain psychotic symptoms in borderline personality disorder. However, depressive symptoms did not appear affected by neuroleptic treatment. In some cases, antidepressant medication may worsen depressive symptoms (Soloff et al. 1986a).

In general, we have found that patients with borderline personality disorder in which psychotic symptoms predominate are noticeably improved on low-dose neuroleptics (i.e., in the range of 100–300 mg of chlorpromazine equivalents). Depressive symptoms may necessitate a trial of antidepressant therapy. However, TCAs have not proven particularly effective. Fluoxetine has been reported to be helpful in a series of patients started on an open-label basis (Nordern 1989). In patients with atypical depressions suggestive of personality disorders, MAOIs have been shown to be effective in decreasing both anxiety and depression.

Cowdry and Gardner (1986) reported on the effective use of carbamazepine (Tegretol) for decreasing self-destructive acts in patients with borderline personality disorder. However, the patients in this study did not report appreciable benefit from this drug. The use of valproic acid in this context is still undocumented.

Alcohol and Substance Abuse

Many authors have reported on the increased rate of suicide attempts and completions in drug and alcohol abusers (Fowler et al. 1986; Kendal 1983). It also appears that alcohol use is significantly found to be connected with suicide. Dorpat and Ripley (1960) found that 89% of alcoholics were drinking at the time of suicide, and that 38% of nonalcoholics were drinking at the time of suicide. Some studies suggest that alcohol abusers are at greatest risk for suicide while drinking and after 20 years of chronic alcoholism (Robins et al. 1959). However, others feel that drug users may be at maximal risk at both an earlier age and after a shorter total period of abuse (Marzuk and Mann 1988).

A difficult aspect of the diagnosis and treatment of these patients relates to the issue of comorbidity with depression. A review by Keeler and co-workers (1979) revealed a prevalence rate of depression ranging from 3% to 98% in alcoholics. Frequently these symptoms are transient and do not require treatment, as abstinence alone leads to a resolution of depressive symptoms. However, in certain cases, it appears that alcoholism may be masking an underlying depressive disorder that the patient is trying to "self-medicate" with alcohol. It is still unclear exactly how long patients should be observed drug free before the diagnosis of depression can be made. However, many authorities argue that at least 3 weeks should elapse, drug free, before making a diagnosis of major depression. Once such a diagnosis is made, treatment with antidepressants appears reasonable.

It is difficult to assess and treat suicidal substance abusers (Wolk-Wasserman 1987). They seem to do best with long-term care through supportive and stable treatment, with attention paid to any underlying illness and maintenance of abstinence.

Much of the treatment of these patients is psychoeducational, focusing on the need for abstinence and on techniques for managing the addictive behaviors, while treating any underlying psychiatric disorder. Self-help groups such as Alcoholics Anonymous are usually very effective in helping to maintain sobriety. Clinicians working with this population should be aware of the availability of Alcoholics Anonymous and its usefulness. Individual, family, or group psychotherapy with dual-diagnosis patients should initially be supportive, present-oriented, and practical (Weiss and Mirin 1989).

Pharmacotherapy is most useful when aimed at the patient's underlying or coexisting psychiatric illness. Antidepressants can be useful in the treatment of a coexisting depression; lithium carbonate is effective in treating comorbid bipolar disease. Benzodiazepines should generally be avoided in this population because of their abuse potential. Disulfiram (Antabuse) can be used effectively in certain alcoholic patients to help maintain abstinence. It is usually started during hospitalization at a dosage of 250 mg/day. However, the use of disulfiram must be carefully evaluated, especially in potentially suicidal patients who may intentionally mix it with alcohol. In addition, disulfiram can increase TCA blood levels.

Schizophrenia

Patients diagnosed with schizophrenia carry an increased risk of suicide. Approximately 10% of schizophrenic patients die by suicide, and approximately 3,800 schizophrenic patients commit suicide each year in the United States (Miles 1977). Tsuang (1978) found that suicide is a significant factor in the long-term outcome of both schizophrenia and primary affective disorders. That study noted a trend for the suicides to cluster near the beginning of the follow-up period, suggesting that early in the course of the illness the relative risk of suicide is increased.

Although the causes of suicide in schizophrenia are still unclear, it appears that there are several risk factors that are associated with lethality. Roy and colleagues (1983) pointed to the incidence of depression in chronic schizophrenic patients, in particular those whose schizophrenic illness is controlled by neuroleptics. They noted that chronic schizophrenic patients who developed a depressive episode had more negative symptoms (e.g., lack of volition, slowness, flat affect, social withdrawal) than those schizophrenic patients who did not develop depression. In addition, this depressed group had more hospital admissions than the other group. Others have noted that depression is most prevalent during acute exacerbations of schizophrenia, and less prevalent in the stable or maintenance phase (Knights and Hirsh 1981).

Other authors have noted that schizophrenic patients often fail to communicate their suicidal intent directly, and that they generally used highly lethal suicide methods (Breier and Astrachan 1984). This population appears to be at most risk shortly after discharge from an inpatient facility (Roy 1982). This may in part be due to the awareness these patients have of their debilitating illness, and speaks to the increased need for the massive outpatient support necessary when these patients are discharged from the hospital.

Standard pharmacologic treatment has been available for the treatment of schizophrenia for approximately the past 30 years (Baldassarini 1977). Current therapy focuses on treating the psychotic aspects of the illness with low-dose neuroleptics (up to 300-mg equivalents of chlorpromazine). The choice of antipsychotic agent is usually based on the side-effect profile of the particular drug in the patient's past experience, any family history of effectiveness, and the physician's degree of comfort with a particular agent. Haloperidol and fluphenazine are particularly useful as they are available in decanoate preparations and can be administered biweekly in long-acting injectable form, thus increasing compliance.

Although thioridazine is approved by the Food and Drug Administration in the treatment of anxious depression, we have found it to be of no greater benefit than other antipsychotic agents in the treatment of schizophrenia, even in schizophrenic patients with depressed symptoms.

Clozapine, a new antipsychotic, is an exciting addition to the pharmacologic treatment of schizophrenia. It has recently been released for use in the United States and is innovative because it appears to lack the extrapyramidal side effects of other neuroleptics. In addition, it appears not to cause tardive dyskinesia and in some cases may even improve tardive dyskinesia symptoms. It does, however, have potentially harmful side effects; therefore, complete blood counts need to be monitored weekly for leukopenia, a potentially fatal blood disorder. Clozapine-induced leukopenia is reportedly rare; however, when diagnosed, clozapine must be discontinued immediately, and treatment for the blood disorder should be aggressively pursued.

Although it has been claimed that treatment with neuroleptics is a cause of depressive symptoms in schizophrenic patients, many researchers have failed to validate this finding (Roy et al. 1983). For a long time, controversy has raged over the use of antidepressants in the treatment of schizophrenia. Although there is some evidence to suggest that schizophrenic patients in remission from their psychosis who demonstrate depressive symptomatology may benefit from combined neuroleptic-antidepressant treatment (Siris et al. 1978), this is not universally true. Other authors have noted that antidepressants should not be routinely prescribed in an attempt to reduce depressive symptomatology in actively psychotic schizophrenic patients, as there was no apparent benefit to adding the antidepressants to an adequate antipsychotic regimen. The data suggest that antidepressants may attenuate postpsychotic depressive syndromes (Kramer et al. 1989). Often it is difficult to distinguish depression in schizophrenia from negative symptoms and motoric or cognitive effects of anticholinergic or neuroleptic agents. The issue of using antidepressants in this population is not clear-cut, and physicians should additionally consider whether anticholinergic side effects may be accounting for apparent anergia or withdrawal.

Summary

The treatment of suicidal patients is a complex and demanding aspect of psychiatric work. Special consideration needs to be paid to diagnostic issues and to the development of the therapeutic alliance. Medication can play an important role in treatment, especially when judiciously applied within the context of a comprehensive treatment program. Antidepressants are extremely effective for depressed patients with suicidal ideation and need to be prescribed in adequate doses and for adequate periods of time before being abandoned as ineffective. Psychotic (delusional) depression is most likely to respond to a course of electroconvulsive therapy or a combination of TCA and antipsychotic medication. Patients with panic disorder show an increased risk of suicide and are responsive to treatment with imipramine or desipramine. Dysphoric manic patients present a confusing picture but appear to respond to thymoleptic medication. The reports on the efficacy of medication for borderline personality disorder is mixed, but careful and considered drug trials may be helpful. Alcohol and substance abusers may benefit from treatment with antidepressants or lithium carbonate for comorbid or underlying affective disorders, but these trials can occur only after sobriety is achieved. Antipsychotic medication is essential for the ongoing treatment of schizophrenia and may be combined with antidepressants under certain circumstances. In all cases, medications may be used by the suicidal patient for therapeutic or self-destructive reasons, and therefore needs to be monitored very carefully.

References

Baldassarini RJ: Chemotherapy in Psychiatry, 2nd Edition. Cambridge, MA, Harvard University Press, 1977, p 2

Beck AT, Steer RA, Kovacs M, et al: Hopelessness and eventual suicide: a 10-year prospective study of patients hospitalized with suicidal ideation. Am J Psychiatry 142:5:559–563, 1985

Breier A, Astrachan BM: Characterization of schizophrenic patients who commit suicide. Am J Psychiatry 141:206–209, 1984

Coryell W, Kleller M, Lavori P, et al: Affective syndromes, psychotic features and prognosis, I: depression. Arch Gen Psychiatry 47:651–657, 1990

Cowdry RW, Gardner DC: Pharmacotherapy of borderline personality disorder. Arch Gen Psychiatry 45:111–119, 1986

de Montigny C, Cournoyer G, Morissette R, et al: Lithium carbonate addition in tricyclic antidepressant-resistant unipolar depression. Arch Gen Psychiatry 40:1327–1334, 1983

Dorpat TL, Ripley H: A study of suicide in the Seattle area. Compr Psychiatry 1:349–359, 1960

Fowler RC, Rich CL, Young D: San Diego suicide study, II: substance abuse in young cases. Arch Gen Psychiatry 43:962–965, 1986

Goldberg SC, Schulz SC, Schulz PM, et al: Borderline and schizotypal personality disorders treated with low-dose thiothixene vs placebo. Arch Gen Psychiatry 43:680–686, 1986

Guze SB, Robins E: Suicide and primary affective disorders. Br J Psychiatry 117:437–438, 1970

Keeler MH, Taylor I, Miller WC: Are all recently detoxified alcoholics depressed? Am J Psychiatry 136:585–588, 1979

Kendal RE: Alcohol and suicide. Substance and Alcohol Actions Misuse 4:121–127, 1983

Knights A, Hirsh S: "Revealed" depression and drug treatment for schizophrenia. Arch Gen Psychiatry 38:806–811, 1981

Kraepelin E: Manic-Depressive Insanity and Paranoia. Edited by Robertson GM. Edinburgh, Scotland, E&S Livingstone, 1921

Kramer MS, Vogel WH, DiJohnson C: Antidepressants in "depressed" schizophrenic inpatients: a controlled trial. Arch Gen Psychiatry 46:922–928, 1989

Marzuk PM, Mann JJ: Suicide and substance abuse. Psychiatric Annals 18:639–644, 1988

Miles CP: Conditions predisposing to suicide: a review. J Nerv Ment Dis 164:231–246, 1977

Morris JB, Beck AT: The efficacy of antidepressant drugs: a review of research 1958–1972. Arch Gen Psychiatry 30:667–674, 1974

Muijen M, Roy D, Silverstone T, et al: A comparative clinical trial of fluoxetine, mianserin and placebo in depressed outpatients. Acta Psychiatr Scand 78:384–390, 1988

Nordern MJ: Fluoxetine in borderline personality disorder. Prog Neuro-psychopharmacol Biol Psychiatry 13:885–893, 1989

Post RM, Uhde WT, Roy-Byrne PP, et al: Correlates of antimanic response to carbamazepine. Psychiatry Res 21:71–83, 1987

Post RM, Rubinow DR, Uhde TW, et al: Dysphoric mania: clinical and biological correlates. Arch Gen Psychiatry 46:353–358, 1989

Robins E, Murphy GE, Wilkinson RH, et al: Some clinical considerations in the prevention of suicide based on a study of 154 successful suicides. Am J Public Health 49:888–899, 1959

Roose SP, Glassman AH, Walsh TB, et al: Depression, delusions and suicide. Am J Psychiatry 140:9:1159–1162, 1983

Roy A: Suicide in chronic schizophrenia. Br J Psychiatry 141:171–177, 1982

Roy A, Thompson R, Kennedy S: Depression in chronic schizophrenia. Br J Psychiatry 142:465–470, 1983

Secunda SK, Katz MM, Swann AC, et al: Mixed mania: diagnosis and treatment, in Mania: New Research and Treatment. Edited by Swann AC. Washington, DC, American Psychiatric Press, 1986, pp 79–94

Siris SG, van Kammen DP, Docherty JP: Use of antidepressant drugs in schizophrenia. Arch Gen Psychiatry 35:1368–1377, 1978

Soloff PH, George A, Nathan RS, et al: Paradoxical effects of amitriptyline on borderline patients. Am J Psychiatry 143:1603–1605, 1986a

Soloff PH, George A, Nathan RS, et al: Progress in pharmacotherapy of borderline disorders: a double-blind study of amitriptyline, haloperidol and placebo. Arch Gen Psychiatry 43:691–700, 1986b

Spiker DG, Hanin I, Cofsky JE, et al: Pharmacological treatment of delusional depressives. Psychopharmacol Bull 17:201–202, 1981

Teicher MH, Glod C, Cole JO: Emergence of intense suicidal preoccupation during fluoxetine treatment. Am J Psychiatry 147:207–210, 1990

Tsuang MT: Suicide in schizophrenics, manics, depressives, and surgical controls. Arch Gen Psychiatry 35:153–155, 1978

Warnes H: Suicide in schizophrenia. Diseases of the Nervous System (Suppl) 29(5):35–40, 1968

Weiss RD, Mirin SM: The dual diagnosis alcoholic: evaluation and treatment. Psychiatric Annals 19:262–265, 1989

Weissman MM, Klerman GL, Markowitz JS, et al: Suicidal ideation and suicide attempts in panic disorder and attacks. N Engl J Med 321:1210–1214, 1989

Wolk-Wasserman D: Contacts of suicidal alcohol and drug abuse patients and their significant others with public care institutions before the suicide attempt. Acta Psychiatr Scand 76:394–405, 1987

Chapter 3

Psychodynamics and Suicide

Rebecca A. Dulit, M.D.
Robert Michels, M.D.

A psychodynamic approach to suicide requires an understanding of the common fantasies, wishes, fears, and conflicts found in suicidal patients as well as the psychodynamics of the suicidal act itself. This understanding both contributes to the clinical management of suicidal patients and elucidates the special challenges and countertransference problems experienced by their therapists.

The concept of psychodynamics refers to the mental content and themes associated with a particular phenomenon. Of course, an understanding of the psychodynamics of suicidality is only one critical component of a comprehensive assessment of a suicidal patient. Furthermore, one must be cautious in drawing conclusions about the relationship between psychodynamics and etiology. Psychodynamic themes sometimes seem to have an important causal role in suicidal behavior, but often the patient's psychopathology is more closely related to the etiology of suicidality and particularly the prediction of risk.

Psychodynamics of Suicidal Motivation

Suicidality exists on a spectrum from no suicidal intent through nonspecific passive suicidal ideation to active suicidal intent. A variety of mental states and fantasies may be associated with suicidality and warrant exploration during assessment and treatment. The most striking affects are despair and hopelessness. Clinical studies indicate that these affects are highly correlated with risk for suicide (Beck 1975; Dyer and

This work was partially supported by a Reader's Digest Fellowship (R.A.D.).

Kreitman 1984; Minkoff 1973; Wetzel 1976). The experience of despair is characterized by intolerable emotional pain and abandonment of the self (Maltsberger 1986). Suicidal despair is often associated with a subjective sense of aloneness in which the person feels devoid of all external and self-regulatory support structures and without hope that the aloneness will ever be relieved. The subjective experience of worthlessness is also related to suicidal despair if patients believe they deserve their state of aloneness.

The fantasy of reunion with a lost object through death probably accounts for most anniversary suicides and for many that occur during bereavement (Furst and Ostow 1979; Hendin 1951). When a loved object with whom an individual has identified dies, suicide may unconsciously represent a means of rejoining the lost object. The fantasy of identification with a lost object occurs in suicidal individuals whose object relations are characterized by a wish to abolish distance from the loved object and whose self-esteem is contingent on their relationship with the lost object (Hendin 1956).

The fantasy of spiritual rebirth (Klopfer 1961) is closely related to the fantasy of identification with the lost object. Patients who see themselves as incomplete or less than total in the absence of an important lost object may view suicide as a means of regaining totality. This illustrates a common paradox in suicidal fantasies; they are often characterized by a desire to remain alive or to start over rather than to die.

The wish to be reunited with an all-giving mother of early infancy appears in the fantasies of some suicidal individuals (Furst and Ostow 1979; Klopfer 1961; Maltsberger 1986). The person's magical desire for an ideal state of passivity and helplessness here assumes the form of wishing to return to the mother's body. In death, the human body returns to the earth (a common maternal symbol) and mixes with it as in early infancy, when there was no subjective sense of separateness. By fusing with the earth, the person unconsciously hopes to experience again the peace of the early anaclitic relationship.

For persons suffering from intolerable emotional or physical pain, suicide may be experienced as a release or an escape from suffering (Furst and Ostow 1979; Grinker 1967; Kilpatrick 1948). Suicide appears to be an adaptive solution to an unbearable situation. This psychodynamic theme may be most commonly experienced by elderly depressed or physically ill individuals who become preoccupied with all that they have lost (Hendin 1956). Withdrawal of emotional investment in the painful real world may then precipitate escape by suicide.

In certain suicidal persons, intrapsychic conflicts may induce a defensive splitting of the subjective self-image into a "good self" that wants to live and a "bad self" that is experienced as an alien killer (Furst and Ostow 1979; Maltsberger 1986; Menninger 1933). The bad self remains within the ego and becomes the target of the punitive superego with which the good self is identified (Kernberg 1970). Splitting of the self-representation may be so intense as to lead to depersonalization, and the suicidality that ensues represents an attempt to eliminate the bad self (Kilpatrick 1948).

Some psychoanalytic thinkers have emphasized the role of aggression in suicide, which may involve a death wish against another that is turned against the self (Freud 1914; Hendin 1956; Menninger 1933; Sifneos and McCourt 1962). The suicidal act represents unconscious hostility directed toward an introjected ambivalently viewed love object and is essentially an ultimate act of revenge. Freud (1914) first set forth this formulation and theorized that in depression an individual identifies with an object that is both hated and loved. Through suicide, the person destroys both the self and the internalized object. Additionally, there may be guilt about hatred of the object, and through suicide the self is punished for this hatred (Hendin 1951; Menninger 1933).

Finally, certain theorists have emphasized the importance of social context in the understanding of suicidal motivation. Durkheim (1897) first postulated that suicide can be conceptualized as a pathologic reaction to society's control over the individual. He emphasized the role of social disintegration, social isolation, and status loss in suicide. Horney (1950) expanded on this sociological model by adding that suicide is related to infantile dependency needs and deep-rooted feelings of inadequacy resulting from a sense of having failed to meet societal standards.

Thus there are several common psychodynamic themes that emerge in the study of suicidal individuals. These themes are not mutually exclusive, and several may be found in the same patient. Of course these observations are based almost exclusively on data from anecdotal clinical case material. Essentially no systematic empirical research has examined the psychodynamics of suicidal ideation. Furthermore, each of these psychodynamic themes may also be found in a great many patients who never entertain thoughts of suicide or who do have suicidal ideation but never actually attempt or commit suicide. The question of the psychodynamics of the transition from suicidal ideation to suicidal action is obviously extraordinarily difficult to study from a psychodynamic perspective as most of the raw data lie with the deceased. However, some inferences can be made from suicidal patients who recover and from suicide notes and final communications.

The Psychodynamics of the Suicidal Act

Suicide is generally assessed in terms of the severity of the suicidal intent and the lethality of the actual suicide act. Furst and Ostow (1979) postulated that no suicidal act is ever completely free of conflict and suggested that the severity of intent is determined by two competing factors: 1) the intensity of suicidal motivation, and 2) the degree to which this motivation is counterbalanced by a conflicting desire to live. These competing factors must be explored in the assessment and treatment of suicidal patients.

The selection of the mode of suicide—the method, setting, and style—can have important symbolic meaning. Freud (1920) discussed the possible sexual meaning of several common methods; jumping from a height represented giving birth, and taking poison suggested fantasies of oral impregnation. Sifneos and McCourt (1962) suggested that, in some cases, the selection of the method of suicide is associated with the person whom the suicidal individual wants to punish; thus one might select a "weapon" that belongs to the other person. They cited the example of a woman who used her lover's prescription to get pills for an overdose and then took the overdose in his bedroom. A particularly common version of this dynamic is the patient who expresses hostile transference feelings by making a suicide attempt with pills prescribed by the doctor or who times the attempt in relation to the treatment process, either interfering with a session or responding to an interruption.

Furst and Ostow (1979) suggested that suicidal persons may choose a method of dying that represents either an extreme variant or the opposite of the fantasied crime for which they are punishing themselves. For example, a male homosexual may shoot or stab himself, representing his wish to be attacked by another man's penis. A person with guilt over an Oedipal triumph represented by the symbolic fantasy of flying high may choose to jump to suicide, while one who overdoses may have suffered disappointment in a dependent relationship. People who find erotic excitement in the sense of smell may inhale poisonous gas; those who find excitement in the sensation of heavy breathing or breathlessness may choose hanging.

Finally, we would emphasize that suicide is an act that requires the capacity to organize behavior actively and effectively. It is partly for this reason that depressed patients are most likely to commit suicide during the early phases of recovery rather than when they are most severely depressed. As a result, depressed suicidal patients who have recently been started on pharmacotherapy may be at higher risk for suicide than untreated and more severely depressed patients because the antidepressant-induced activation or hypomania can mix with residual depression, resulting in a depressed person with a proneness to action and a capacity to organize his or her behavior effectively (Brent et al. 1988).

An individual's threshold for suicidality is also important for the clinician to assess. For some individuals, alcohol and other substances may be disinhibiting and decrease the threshold for impulsive action (Marzuk and Mann 1988). Substance abuse is a risk factor for suicide in part because suicidal patients may become more action oriented under the influence of certain substances. Interestingly, alcohol and other substances may also be used by patients to modulate emotional suffering and protect or guard against suicidality. The paradox of self-destructive behavior (substance abuse) defending against suicide (Himmelhoch 1988) complicates the assessment of suicide risk in a substance abuser.

In summary, the mode of suicide probably has symbolic meaning to the suicidal individual. Exploration of this meaning is one important component of the assessment and treatment of suicidal patients. Information about the psychodynamics of the act of suicide may aid the clinician in evaluating the seriousness of suicide risk. Certainly, the psychodynamic meaning of the suicidal act should be addressed over time in the ongoing psychotherapy of a suicidal patient, with the goal of providing alternate strategies serving the same psychodynamic functions so that the suicidal behavior no longer offers a solution to the patient's problems.

Psychodynamics of the Management of Suicidality

Managing a suicidal patient is one of the most challenging and stressful tasks for a psychiatrist. The ever-present possibility of death evokes intense emotions in the therapist. The ability of a therapist to treat a suicidal patient depends in large part on the degree to which the therapist has been able to face and come to terms with his or her own unconscious fantasies and conflicts about death (Klopfer 1961) and helplessness in being able to control it.

Working with a suicidal patient challenges the psychiatrist's personal narcissism and sense of professional grandiosity. Halperin (1979) suggested that therapists of suicidal patients experience an intense awareness of their own personal and professional limitations. Fromm-Reichmann (Green 1961) warned clinicians to attend to their own attitudes about their emotional stake in their patient's survival. Rosenbaum (1967) argued that some patients will inevitably commit suicide regardless of the quality of the treatment they receive, and psychiatrists must accept this reality to avoid compromising personal integrity and professional skill. We would agree that the experience of working with a suicidal patient generally has a profound effect on the professional (and sometimes the personal) identity of the psychiatrist.

One of the most basic and important tasks of the clinician managing any patient at risk is to inquire about suicidality. Inexperienced clinicians often fear that asking a patient about suicidal ideation will actually put ideas of suicide in the patient's head and increase the danger of suicidality (Grollman 1988). In fact, not asking about suicidality is most likely to lead a patient to believe that the physician is anxious about the issue and therefore may increase the patient's emotional distress and risk for suicide. In one interview study of nonpsychiatrist physicians who had treated patients who suicided, a striking finding was the frequent failure of physicians to inquire about suicidality. Only one physician in six was aware that a patient had had suicidal ideation, and the reason for this lack of information was generally the failure to inquire (Murphy 1988).

Another reason psychiatrists may hesitate to inquire about suicidality is to avoid the responsibility that comes with the knowledge of such information. It is often difficult for psychiatrists to recognize the subtle but significant difference between being responsible for treating a suicidal patient and being responsible for a patient's suicide. In fact, psychiatrists have extremely limited power in predicting, treating, and preventing suicide. Fromm-Reichmann (Green 1961) urged the psychiatrist to remind the suicidal patient that no other person, not even the psychiatrist, can carry the total burden of responsibility for the self-induced death of a patient. The psychiatrist can, however, actively convey concern and desire to explore and help the patient with suicidal feelings.

In addition to serving a clinical function, inquiring about suicidal ideation serves an important psychotherapeutic function: to communicate to the patient that the assessment and treatment of suicidality is part of routine clinical practice. In fact, the psychiatrist must convey to the patient that contemplating suicide is neither shameful nor reprehensible (Green 1961). Asking about suicidality in a professional manner may itself be therapeutic to the suicidal patient, who is often relieved to be able to finally talk about this "taboo" subject and to begin an exploration of his or her feelings (Grollman 1988). The impact of the doctor-patient relationship itself is often an important factor in the ongoing psychotherapy of a chronically suicidal patient.

One problem that sometimes arises during the assessment and treatment of an acutely suicidal patient is the patient's request for complete confidentiality. A patient who asks the doctor to keep information about suicidality hidden from others may be unconsciously testing the physician's priorities. The clinical, ethical, and legal priorities are clear: there is no basis for confidentiality when that confidentiality conflicts with the preservation of life or health. The discussion of this "rule" with a suicidal patient may itself be reassuring and therapeutic.

Countertransference Pitfalls in the Treatment of Suicidality

Countertransference occurs in all encounters with patients and, as used in this chapter, refers to both the conscious and unconscious mental responses the therapist has to the patient. This broad sense of the term needs to be differentiated from the narrower definition of countertransference as the therapist's neurotic reactions to the patient. Countertransference is often intense and sometimes problematic in the treatment of suicidal patients.

Suicidal patients arouse countertransference hate in the clinicians who treat them. Maltsberger (1986) described the two components of this hate as malice and aversion and noted that the aversive component is paradoxically more dangerous to the patient since it may result in abandonment. The malicious, sadistic component, on the other hand, results in the preservation of the patient-therapist relationship as a sadomasochistic struggle; suicidal patients generally have a higher tolerance for sadomasochistic interactions than for abandonment.

Therapists will mobilize a variety of defensive maneuvers against countertransference hate, some of which may lead to disturbed and potentially dangerous therapist-patient interactions (Maltsberger and Buie 1974). Countertransference hatred may be repressed, and therapists may find themselves detached and unable to pay attention, which may be experienced by patients as a lack of interest or concern. Countertransference hatred may be turned against the self, and therapists may become overly preoccupied with their own feelings of inadequacy and helplessness rather than focusing on these emotions in their patients. Some therapists may utilize reaction formation and feel an overwhelming urgency to protect suicidal patients, leading to excessive use of restrictions and hospitalization. Countertransference hatred is sometimes projected onto patients; some therapists may then have difficulty distinguishing between their realistic concerns and their exaggerated concerns for their patients' safety. Finally, to validate countertransference hate, the therapist may distort or deny reality by seeing the patient as completely hopeless. In this case, the therapist would be without empathic understanding and in danger of inappropriately giving up on treatment of the patient.

Therapists who treat suicidal patients must learn to utilize countertransference constructively to avoid creating pathologic clinical interactions in which the patient is attacked or rejected. First, the therapist must recognize and acknowledge emotional responses to the patient and remain alert to impulses to deviate from empathic attunement and an appropriate professional role. Second, the therapist must put countertransference into perspective by identifying its source. Third, the therapist must decide whether and when to acknowledge countertransference feelings to the patient. Sharing the therapist's feelings may be useless and even dangerous with an actively suicidal patient, but it may be helpful for a therapist to discuss countertransference responses in the ongoing psychotherapy of an episodically suicidal patient to help the patient recognize the responses his or her behavior may lead to in others.

Finally, we would emphasize the special role of consultation and supervision in the treatment of suicidal patients, especially when an apparent impasse has been reached. Not only may a consultation provide a fresh perspective on the treatment, but countertransference issues are often paralleled in the consultation process and should be explored. The risk of a suicidal patient feeling abandoned in response to a therapist's request for a consultation must be considered, but often a consultation will illuminate the nature of an impasse and allow the therapy to continue.

In summary, the countertransference that suicidal patients evoke in psychiatrists can be a major obstacle to successful treatment. The management of countertransference through conscious awareness, inhibition of antitherapeutic acting out, and on occasion appropriate discussion can be important tools in the treatment of suicidal patients.

Summary

A psychodynamic approach to the understanding of suicide is one component of the management of the suicidal patient. It must be emphasized, however, that addressing dynamic suicidal themes alone is unlikely to "cure" suicidality. To treat suicidality successfully, the psychiatrist must diagnose and treat the underlying psychopathology. At times, this may require a combination of therapeutic modalities, including psychotherapy, pharmacotherapy, and environmental manipulation (e.g., hospitalization). There is no single type of psychiatric treatment that is most effective for all suicidal patients. The appropriate treatment will depend on a number of factors, including both the psychopathology and the psychodynamics of the particular patient, the nature of the suicide risk, and the nature of the relationship between patient and psychiatrist. The therapist-patient relationship can have an enormous impact on a suicidal patient, and this relationship must be considered in the management of suicidality.

References

Beck AT, Kovacs M, Weissman A: Hopelessness and suicidal behavior: an overview. JAMA 234:1146–1149, 1975

Brent DA, Kupfer DJ, Bromet EJ, et al: The assessment and treatment of patients at risk for suicide, in Psychiatry Update: American Psychiatric Association Annual Review, Vol 7. Edited by Frances AJ, Hales RE. Washington, DC, American Psychiatric Press, 1988, pp 353–385

Durkheim E: Suicide (1897). New York, Free Press, 1951

Dyer JAT, Kreitman N: Hopelessness, depression and suicidal intent in parasuicide. Br J Psychiatry 144:127–133, 1984

Freud S: Mourning and melancholia (1914), in The Standard Edition of the Complete Psychological Works of Sigmund Freud, Vol 14. Translated and edited by Strachey J. London, Hogarth Press, 1957, pp 239–258

Freud S: A case of homosexuality in a woman (1920), in The Standard Edition of the Complete Psychological Works of Sigmund Freud, Vol 18. Translated and edited by Strachey J. London, Hogarth Press, 1955, pp 147–172

Furst SS, Ostow M: The psychodynamics of suicide, in Suicide: Theory and Clinical Aspects. Edited by Hankoff LD, Einsidler B. Littleton, MA, PSG Publishing, 1979, pp 165–178

Green MR: Suicide: the Sullivanian point of view, in The Cry for Help. Edited by Farberow NL, Shneidman ES. New York, McGraw-Hill, 1961, pp 220–235

Grinker RR: The psychodynamics of suicide and attempted suicide, in Symposium on Suicide. Edited by Yochelson L. Washington, DC, George Washington University, 1967, pp 60–70

Grollman EA: Suicide. Boston, MA, Beacon Press, 1988

Halperin DA: Psychodynamic strategies with outpatients, in Suicide: Theory and Clinical Aspects. Edited by Hankoff LD, Einsidler B. Littleton, MA, PSG Publishing, 1979, pp 363–372

Hendin H: Psychodynamic motivation factors in suicide. Psychiatr Q 25:672–678, 1951

Hendin H: Suicide. Psychiatr Q 30:267–282, 1956

Himmelhoch J: What destroys our restraints against suicide? J Clin Psychiatry 49:46–52, 1988

Horney K: Neurosis and Self-Growth. New York, WW Norton, 1950

Kernberg O: A psychoanalytic classification of character pathology. J Am Psychoanal Assoc 18:800–822, 1970

Kilpatrick E: A psychoanalytic understanding of suicide. Am J Psychoanal 8:13–23, 1948

Klopfer B: Suicide: the Jungian point of view, in The Cry for Help. Edited by Farberow NL, Shneidman ES. New York, McGraw-Hill, 1961, pp 193–203

Maltsberger JT: Suicide Risk: The Formulation of Clinical Judgement. New York, New York University Press, 1986

Maltsberger JT, Buie DH: Countertransference hate in the treatment of suicidal patients. Arch Gen Psychiatry 30:625–633, 1974

Marzuk PM, Mann JJ: Suicide and substance abuse. Psychiatric Annals 18:639–645, 1988

Menninger KA: Psychoanalytic aspects of suicide. Int J Psychoanal 14:376–390, 1933

Minkoff K: Hopelessness, depression, and attempted suicide. Am J Psychiatry 130:455–459, 1973

Murphy GE: Prevention of suicide, in Psychiatry Update: American Psychiatric Association Annual Review, Vol 7. Edited by Frances AJ, Hales RE. Washington, DC, American Psychiatric Press, 1988, pp 403–421

Rosenbaum M: Recognition of the suicidal individual, in Symposium on Suicide. Edited by Yochelson L. Washington, DC, George Washington University, 1967, pp 73–82

Sifneos PE, McCourt WF: Wishes for life and death of some patients who attempted suicide. Mental Hygiene 46:543–552, 1962

Wetzel RD: Hopelessness, depression, and suicidal intent. Arch Gen Psychiatry 33:1069–1073, 1976

Chapter 4

An Empirically Based Model of Suicide Risk Assessment for Patients With Affective Disorder

David C. Clark, Ph.D.
Jan Fawcett, M.D.

Our empirical studies of suicide risk prediction among patients with major affective disorders rest on a number of assumptions about the phenomenology of suicidal behavior that have been supported by previous studies. Briefly stated, these assumptions are: 1) those who make nonfatal suicide attempts and those who die by suicide are drawn from qualitatively different clinical populations, for the most part; 2) suicide risk predictors vary as a function of the major psychiatric disorder(s) implicated; and 3) clinical characteristics associated with risk of *imminent* suicide (i.e., death within 6–12 months) and those associated with risk of later suicide differ in important ways. The evidence for the first assumption will be summarized briefly. Evidence for the second assumption emerges from follow-up mortality studies and record-linkage studies of patients by specific and reliably defined diagnostic categories; these studies will be highlighted. Evidence for the third assumption emerges from our own studies of suicide risk prediction among patients with major affective disorders. Thus the evidence for the latter two assumptions will be summarized in due turn.

Assumption 1: The Differences Between Nonfatal Attempters and Suicide Completers

Our first assumption is that suicide completers and suicide attempters are more different than alike. There is some overlap between the two groups (i.e., some nonfatal attempters eventually die by suicide), but that overlap is small. Psychological autopsy studies of community-based populations (i.e., systematic studies of a large number of suicides occurring in a specific geographic area over a specified period of time) show that only 18–38% of those who die by suicide had ever attempted suicide on a prior occasion (Barraclough et al. 1974; Dorpat and Ripley 1960; Rich et al. 1986; Robins 1981). Turning this observation around, long-term follow-up studies of persons who have made nonfatal suicide attempts show that only 7–10% eventually die by suicide (Cullberg et al. 1988; Ettlinger 1964; Motto 1965; Weiss and Scott 1974). Since 1.5% of the United States population eventually dies by suicide (National Center for Health Statistics 1989), the 7–10% risk associated with a history of nonfatal suicide attempts is clearly five or six times greater than that for the general population. Thus a history of nonfatal attempts does constitute one definition of a group at elevated risk for completed suicide, but 90–93% of all attempters never go on to die by suicide in their lifetime.

We do not want to be misunderstood as minimizing the plight of the attempter or the danger of completed suicide among those with a history of nonfatal attempts. Instead, we want to emphasize the fact that there are many demographic and clinical differences between completers and nonfatal attempters. Men die by suicide three to four times more often than women, but women make nonfatal attempts three to four times more often than men (Murphy 1986). Prevalence rates of major psychiatric disorder are much higher among suicide completers, and prevalence rates of personality disorder are much higher among nonfatal attempters (Murphy 1986). Living conditions, social circumstances, and acute life upset appear to play a much greater role in the shaping of nonfatal attempts than of death by suicide (Murphy 1986; Robins 1986). The appropriate conclusion to draw is one of caution about generalizing from one group to the other.

Most of our clinical knowledge about suicidal behavior is based on studies of "ideators" and attempters because these patients are accessible to study and because of historically prevalent assumptions that attempters (especially attempters who employed medically serious methods of self-harm) resemble suicide completers in most important ways. It is much more difficult to characterize persons who have died than those who have survived and are available to be interviewed. But increasing evidence shows that profiles of persons who make nonlethal attempts are not very good profiles of persons who die by suicide (Linehan 1986;

Murphy 1986). It is fair to conclude that prior studies provide some basis for characterizing persons likely to make nonfatal suicide attempts, persons likely to make serious nonfatal attempts, and persons likely to repeat nonfatal attempt behavior, but that knowledge about those who kill themselves is much less adequate.

One might argue that clinical reports of individual psychiatric inpatients and outpatients in treatment who later die by suicide provide a relatively more complete description of the modal suicide completer (e.g., Black et al. 1985a, 1985b; Martin et al. 1985a, 1985b; Tsuang 1978; Winokur and Tsuang 1975). Treatment records and the firsthand experiences of therapists with these patients often yield rich and detailed records of their character and the complexity of their life story. Once again, however, psychological autopsy studies of community-based populations show that only 35–50% of all persons dying by suicide ever had contact with a mental health professional in their lifetimes, even once (Barraclough et al. 1974; Beskow 1979; Dorpat and Ripley 1960; Hagnell and Rorsman 1979). Thus the data demonstrate that persons in treatment are not representative of all or most cases of death by suicide. The bottom line is that as clinicians we must be aware that existing clinical knowledge and experience conspire to make us more familiar with nonfatal attempters and with the minority of suicide victims who access mental health services. As a result, one must call into question the accuracy or legitimacy of much that is assumed about suicide completers from the data available to us. At the very least, we must be tremendously humble about the usefulness of available knowledge when it comes to detecting or assessing risk of death by suicide.

Epidemiology of Completed Suicide

A review of United States vital statistics trends as they relate to completed suicide shows that three times as many men as woman die by suicide. The rates are significantly higher for whites than for nonwhites. The only ethnic or subcultural groups that are associated with elevated suicide rates are certain specific native American Indian and Eskimo tribes. When one stands back and looks at the proportions of deaths by suicide in the United States each year, one finds that 72% are white males and 20% are white females (National Center for Health Statistics 1989).

The age trends have been confused, we think, by the incomplete media coverage of youth suicide trends. The suicide rate for the United

States general population has increased to a small degree over the last 30 or 40 years. This statistic masks the fact that youth rates have increased threefold since 1955, and that rates for the elderly (those over 60 years old) have decreased just as dramatically over four decades. Despite the dramatic extent of these changes by age group, it continues to remain true that those under age 25 years have a lower suicide rate and those over age 60 have a higher suicide rate than those between the ages of 25 and 60. Thus the youth suicide rate went from a very low value to being almost as high as the general adult rate during the period between 1955 and 1977, and the elderly suicide rate went from an extremely high value to being almost as low as the general adult rate between the 1940 and 1980. Since 1980, the youth rates have been relatively level, but the elderly rates have been on the increase. One way of interpreting the changes in youth rates observed between 1950 and 1980 is to say that our youth moved from resembling preadolescent children to resembling adults with respect to their suicidal behavior (Holinger 1987).

There is a controversy about whether married marital status is related to risk of suicide. Veevers (1973) was the first to hypothesize, then demonstrate the variable "marital status" functions as a proxy for another variable, "responsibility for children under age 18 years," which is not generally reported in vital statistics data. According to this theory, the presence of children under age 18 years in a home imputes some parental responsibilities, and these responsibilities (not marital status) are associated with lower risk of death by suicide. The few replication studies reported support Veevers' hypothesis (Fawcett et al. 1987; Lindesay 1989; Smith et al. 1988).

Community-Based Psychological Autopsy Studies

The most reliable source of clinical data about deaths by suicide have come to us from community-based psychological autopsy studies. The first were reported by Robins and colleagues (1959a, 1959b) in St. Louis and Dorpat and Ripley (1960) in Seattle. Since those first studies, there have been five other community-based studies that included large samples and involved entailed interviews with knowledgeable informants: Barraclough and colleagues (1974) in England; Beskow (1979) in Sweden; Hagnell and Rorsman (1978, 1979; Hagnell et al. 1982) in Sweden; Chynoweth and colleagues (1980) in Australia; and Rich and colleagues (1986, 1989; Fowler et al. 1986) in San Diego.

The essential design of community-based psychological autopsy studies involves identifying the geographic boundaries of the catchment area (usually one or more counties), identifying a time period, and then working with the local coroner or medical examiner to identify 100 or more consecutive deaths by suicide occurring in that geographic area within that time frame for investigation. The hallmark of the psychological autopsy method is the identification of several knowledgeable informants for every case of suicide, so that structured interviews may be administered and reconciled to yield psychological and psychiatric data about the suicide victim's functioning in the weeks or months preceding death. The results of informant interviews are generally integrated with all available official records (e.g., school records, health records, arrest records, death investigation records) to try to understand precisely what happened.

Five findings have been replicated across most of the reported psychological autopsy studies, and thus are a good point of departure for clinical investigations. The first two important observations have already been cited. First, about 60% of all persons who die by suicide never made a prior suicide attempt in their lifetime. Second, 50–60% of all persons who die by suicide never had any contact with a mental health professional in their lifetime, not even once.

The third observation is that for two-thirds of all persons who die by suicide, there is evidence of direct communication of suicidal intent to several close family members or friends in the weeks prior to the suicide. Casual friends, co-workers, and health professionals are much less likely to hear the communication. It is common, however, to find two or three family members or friends who heard direct communications of suicidal intent, although they did not always recognize the gravity of the communication at the time (Robins et al. 1959b).

The fourth observation we want to note is a high rate of physician contact in the months before death. The psychological autopsy studies that have examined this phenomenon tend to agree that 50% of those who die by suicide saw a physician in the 6 months before death, and 80% saw a physician in the month before death. Yet it is also true that half or more of all persons who die by suicide had never seen a mental health professional in their lives. This suggests that people struggling with lethal suicidal impulses realize that something is profoundly wrong with themselves, and either conceptualize the crisis in somatic terms or expect that their physician will be able to recognize and address the underlying problem. It is very common for persons struggling with severe episodes of major depressive disorder, for example, to focus on the vegetative symptoms of their illness (e.g., anorexia, weight loss, insomnia, fatigue, loss of libido), to believe the symptoms represent a physical illness, and to seek physical remedies for their distress. Thus most persons who will imminently die by suicide often present their symptoms to a primary care physician, a general practice physician, a gynecologist, or other specialists who are not always prepared to screen for and detect acute psychiatric illness, much less suicide risk.

The fifth and final observation to be gleaned from community-based psychological autopsy studies is that 93–95% of all cases of suicide qualify for one or more DSM-III-R (American Psychiatric Association 1987) Axis I psychiatric diagnoses on the basis of evidence provided by family members, friends, and colleagues. An episode of psychiatric illness is almost invariably present in the weeks or months before the suicide. The diagnoses most often implicated are affective disorders, alcoholism, and schizophrenia.

Between 40% and 50% of suicide victims can be reliably diagnosed as evidencing major depressive disorder in the weeks or months before they died. The second most common diagnosis encountered is alcoholism, especially chronic alcoholism, which appears in roughly 20% of the cases explored. Chronic schizophrenia appears in about 10% of the cases studied. These findings can be considered from another perspective by examining the results of follow-up mortality studies.

When one identifies a large sample of patients with major affective disorder and follows them for 20 or more years, 15% are found eventually to die by suicide (Murphy 1986), as opposed to the general population base rate of 1.5%. In patients with chronic schizophrenia, 10% ultimately die by suicide in their lifetime (Bleuler 1978). It is commonly repeated that 15% of all persons with alcoholism eventually die by suicide (Miles 1977), but Murphy and Wetzel (1990) recently clarified that the true figure is closer to 3.4% in the case of persons ever hospitalized for treatment of alcoholism.

Thus the community-based psychological autopsy studies help define what are clearly high-risk groups for suicide. Although most patients with major affective disorder, alcoholism, or schizophrenia never die by suicide, their very diagnosis identifies them as a group of persons at elevated risk for death by suicide. This information can be combined with other kinds of risk estimates to help fashion an empirically based set of risk assessment guidelines. For example, persons hospitalized on an inpatient psychiatric unit experience a 7–12% risk of eventually dying by suicide (Miles 1977). Persons with a functional psychosis (i.e., any delusions or hallucinations) experience a 10–12% risk for dying by suicide (Miles 1977). As previously mentioned, persons who have ever made a nonfatal suicide attempt are exposed to a 7–10% risk for dying by suicide. One might reasonably expect that patients qualifying for one or more of these empirical risk factors might be at cumulatively higher risk for suicide (e.g., hospitalized depressed patients, depressed patients with a history of suicide attempts, or schizophrenic patients experiencing a depressive episode).

Assumption 2: Suicide Risk Profiles Vary as a Function of Clinical Diagnosis

Murphy (1972, 1983, 1984), Motto and colleagues (1985), and Pokorny (1983), among others, have wisely pointed out that one has to be very modest about what one can expect from suicide risk prediction models. They demonstrated that in the case of a behavior as infrequent in the general population as is death by suicide, it is inevitable that a large number of false positives will be generated under the best of circumstances. They suggested that the best one can do is to identify *groups* of persons at elevated risk without being able to pinpoint the precise persons who are likely to die. They also reminded us that there will always be persons not identified as at-risk with the screening instruments and criteria we employ who will nonetheless go on to die.

One way to bring optimal precision (i.e., sensitivity and specificity) to the task of suicide risk prediction is to tailor risk prediction formulas to identify suicide completers narrowly defined and not the wider band of completers and nonfatal attempters considered together. We have already suggested that risk assessment formulas meant to identify persons likely to make nonfatal attempts, medically serious nonfatal attempts, or repeated nonfatal attempts differ qualitatively from those characterizing suicide completers.

A second way to bring optimal precision to the task of suicide risk prediction is to tailor risk assessment formulas to the principal psychiatric diagnosis implicated. We prefer to think that the final behavioral outcome of suicide is the product of a complex multivariate equation, and that one necessary variable in that equation is a DSM-III-R Axis I psychiatric disorder. The remainder of the equation resulting in suicide may take different forms, depending on whether the critical diagnostic variable is major depression, alcoholism, schizophrenia, or some other disorder. Thus clinicians should be prepared to think that the suicide risk profile for depressed patients is pronouncedly different than that for alcoholic patients, and again different from that for schizophrenic patients. Although there is likely to be some overlap among these diagnostic profiles, they may be substantively more different than alike, in which case it would be premature or erroneous to screen all patients using a single concatenated risk profile that failed to be useful in any situation in its ambition to serve all situations.

Investigators have reported studies that shed light on clinical features associated with greater risk for death by suicide among those with alcoholism (Berglund 1984; Motto 1980; Murphy and Wetzel 1990; Murphy et al. 1979) and those with schizophrenia (Allebeck et al. 1987; Breier and Astrachan 1984; Drake and Cotton 1986; Drake et al. 1984; Roy 1982). We will now describe a prospective follow-up mortality study of patients under treatment for major affective disorder and summarize findings that clarify clinical features associated and not associated with death by suicide in this sample.

NIMH Collaborative Depression Clinical Study

Beginning in 1974, after many years of planning, five university medical center-affiliated hospitals in the United States (Massachusetts General in Boston, Massachusetts; New York State Psychiatric Institute in New York, New York; Renard Hospital in St. Louis, Missouri; University of Iowa Hospital in Iowa City, Iowa; and Rush-Presbyterian-St. Luke's Medical Center in Chicago, Illinois) banded together to recruit a series of 954 patients entering treatment for affective disorder (Katz and Klerman 1979). The sample was made up of routine admissions to the hospitals (80%) and several outpatient services; these were cases coming through all five hospitals for routine care, not recruited for treatment in the context of a research study. They were under the care of a variety of attending and private psychiatrists not selected by the study. Their clinical care was not supervised in any way by the study; all treatment administered was simply documented over time.

All patients admitted to the study had to have a diagnosis of major affective disorder as ascertained by a structured clinical interview (the Schedule for Affective Disorders and Schizophrenia) (SADS) (Endicott and Spitzer 1978) and Research Diagnostic Criteria (Spitzer et al. 1978). The diagnoses of inclusion were depression (79.2%), manic disorder (13.2%), and schizoaffective disorder (6.9%). The diagnostic interviewers were all experienced clinicians trained for reliability under the direction of Endicott and Spitzer.

On admission to treatment and the study, patients were systematically interviewed using a variety of measures of clinical state, personality traits, acute life stress, social supports available, and work-social functioning. In addition, complete family histories for psychopathology were elicited and all available first-degree adult relatives were interviewed face-to-face.

After 4 years of follow-up interviews at 6-month intervals, there were 25 patient deaths by suicide. We can look back and ask the question that clinicians must pose all the time: namely, in a sample of depressed patients, most of whom have affective disorder severe enough to warrant hospitalization, most of whom have suicidal ideation, and half of whom have made prior suicide attempts, which are the ones that die by suicide? The clinical problem is one of "searching for a needle in a haystack," insomuch as all the patients began the study at relatively high risk for suicide. Which among the high-risk group died by suicide?

Attempt to Validate Motto's Risk Estimator for Suicide

As a beginning point, we were eager to test Motto's published Risk Estimator Scale for Suicide (Motto et al. 1985), which is certainly the best-developed suicide prediction scale available, due to the prospective nature of the study and the psychometric rigor of scale development. The Risk Estimator Scale is the result of following a sample of 2,753 patients hospitalized for a depressive or suicidal state for 2 years, noting which ones died by suicide, and partitioning the sample to identify 15 signs and symptoms that identify a subgroup at relatively high suicide risk. Motto collaborated with us to pick the items from our database corresponding closest to the key 15 items of the Risk Estimator Scale. Then we applied his scale algorithm to test whether it could identify the 14 patients who died by suicide within 2 years in our sample. Patients identified as high risk were no more likely to die by suicide than those identified as low risk (Clark et al. 1987).

It is possible that the quality or intensity of clinical care available to the patients at university medical centers during and after hospitalization (particularly follow-up care) accounted for some of the differences observed between our sample and Motto's. The samples might also have been different because there was not the same degree of diagnostic reliability demonstrated in Motto's sample, nor was the extent of comorbidity (i.e., complicating nonaffective disorders) documented in his sample. Other factors that might contribute to the discrepant results include the fact that the rating items we employed were not identical to Motto's, and the racial makeups of the two samples were different.

Family History as a Predictor of Suicide Risk Among Those With Mood Disorders

Suicides appear to cluster in some biological families (Egeland and Sussex 1985; Farberow and Simon 1969; Tsuang 1983), but there are a number of mechanisms that might explain this phenomenon in addition to that of genetics (Wender et al. 1986). For example, Pitts and Winokur (1964) showed that 68% of 37 psychiatric inpatients with a family history of suicide had an affective disorder. Roy (1983) showed that of 243 psychiatric inpatients with a family history of suicide, 56% had a current primary depressive disorder, and 84% had a history of major depressive disorder. These findings suggest the possibility that family members of a suicide victim are at greater risk for suicide because a genetic predisposition for specific psychiatric disorders (e.g., mood disorders) runs in the family, and the latter predisposition is what raises the risk for suicide.

This position is supported by our group's analyses of the collaborative depression study data (Scheftner et al. 1988). Among 954 affectively disordered psychiatric patients and their 5,042 relatives aged 18 years and over, no association was observed between completed or attempted suicide in relatives and completed suicide by patients during a 5-year follow-up. The lack of any association between familial and patient suicide may be attributable to the fact that all the patients shared a history of major affective disorder. That is, once a background of affective disorder is common to all subjects, any unique relationship between familial and patient suicide disappears.

Clinical Predictors of Suicide

What were the clinical features associated with death by suicide at the 4-year follow-up, when 25 patients in our sample had died by suicide? We will briefly summarize the most useful clinical findings (Fawcett 1988; Fawcett et al. 1987, 1990). Severe levels of hopelessness, as reported in retrospective and prospective studies by Beck and colleagues (1974), was one of the good predictors. This was true despite the fact that we used a different measure of hopelessness than Beck and colleagues did. The SADS hopelessness item is a single clinical rating scored on a scale of 1 to 6. Anhedonia (i.e., loss of interest or pleasure compared with one's normal interest and pleasure levels) was another good predictor. Although the great majority of patients evidenced hopelessness and significant loss of pleasure interest, those who died by suicide scored extremely high compared with the rest of the patients in the sample in both cases.

Depressive turmoil, which in the SADS is defined as "rapid shifts from one dysphoric state to another without the persistence of one affect," was also associated with a greater likelihood of the patient's death by suicide. In the case of depressive turmoil, no one dysphoric affect (i.e., not sadness, anxiety, depression, or agitation) predominates, but instead the characteristic pattern is one of change among all these states.

Patients who cycled between depressed and manic or hypomanic states during the intake episode (without full remission in between) were at greater risk for suicide, but patients classified as bipolar I or bipolar II by history (i.e., with a lifetime history of both depression and mania or hypomania) were not at greater risk. Thus it appeared that it was the lability of an affective state (i.e., cycling) and not the history of manic or hypomanic disorder that increased risk.

Other variables related to subsequent death by suicide included depressed appearance (an observational rating), fewer adolescent friendships by history, and more social withdrawal.

Probably most surprising to the clinician was the list of variables *not* associated with subsequent suicide in this very large stratified sample. Neither bipolar nor schizoaffective patients were at higher risk compared to other patients with affective disorder. Affective disorder subtypes (e.g., psychotic, endogenous, incapacitated, agitated, primary) were of no predictive value for suicide. The 11% of depressed patients who had delusions or hallucinations were not at higher risk. Severity of suicidal ideation as rated by experienced clinicians at the index evaluation, a history of recent suicidal attempts, and a lifetime history of suicide attempts were not associated with greater likelihood of death by suicide. Nor was duration of the index episode, number of prior episodes of affective disorder, clinician-rated life stress levels, or subject-rated life stress levels.

At the 1-year follow-up point, there were 14 deaths by suicide in the sample, which is a little bit less than the expectation of 2–4% estimated by most clinical studies (Murphy 1986). At the 1-year follow-up point, we conducted a discriminant function analysis to establish (retrospectively) what combination of clinical variables collected at intake might efficiently identify those who died by suicide within 1 year. The discriminant function that resulted correctly identified 13 of the 14 suicides, but yielded a high false-positive rate (as all suicide prediction formulas must) of 41%.

According to the function, patients more likely to die by suicide yielded higher scores on measures of hopelessness, severity of hallucinations, alcohol abuse, panic attacks, anhedonia, and somatic anxiety; and lower scores on measures of hypochondriasis, fatigue, phobic symptoms, antisocial behavior, subjective stress, and reactivity. At the 5-year follow-up point, when a total of 28 suicides had occurred, we tested whether this profile developed at the 1-year follow-up point would "predict" the suicides occurring during years 3, 4, and 5 of follow-up. It did not.

There are three conclusions one can draw from the fact that the discriminant function could not predict subsequent suicides. The first conclusion is that the low base rate of suicide makes it statistically unpredictable on an individual basis, particularly when the database is limited to a cross-sectional assessment. The second is that discriminant function formulas rarely generalize. The third possibility is that the function identifying patients who die within 1 year of initial assessment might be qualitatively different than the profile for those who died by suicide later on. This third possibility led us to compare the intake symptom levels of patients who died by suicide in the first year of follow-up ("early suicides"), those who died during the next 4 years of follow-up ("late suicides"), and all patients still alive after 5 years of follow-up ("nonsuicides").

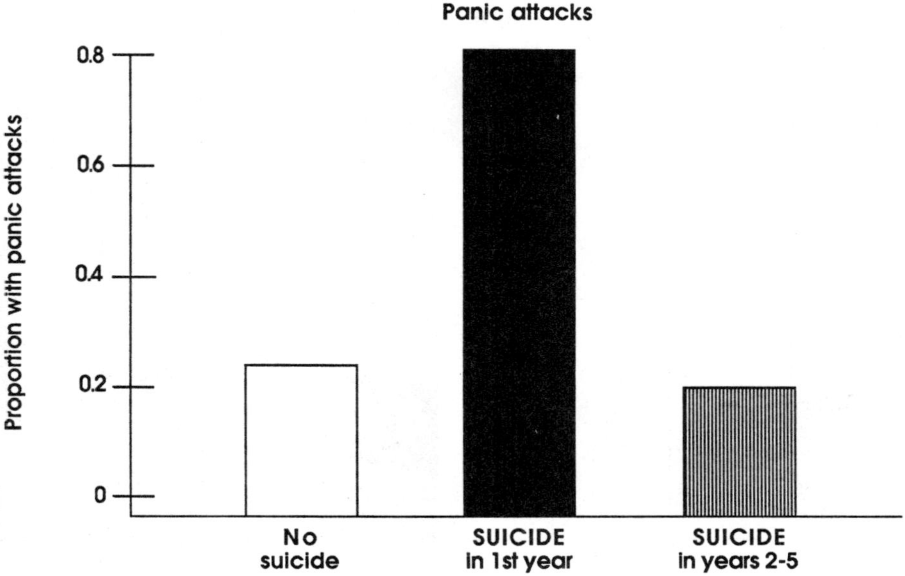

Figure 4–1. Association between panic attacks and death by suicide.

Assumption 3: Predictors of Imminent Suicide Differ From Those of Later Suicide

These comparisons yielded a very interesting story. Higher symptom levels of psychic anxiety, panic attacks, anhedonia, and alcohol abuse were associated with early suicide, whereas higher symptom levels of hopelessness, suicidal ideation, and a history of suicide attempts were associated with late suicide. For example, Figure 4–1 illustrates that panic attacks in the context of a major affective episode was an early predictor. Figure 4–2 illustrates that recent history of suicide attempts was a late predictor. Figure 4–3 illustrates that "hopelessness" was best interpreted as a late predictor.

The implication of our findings is that imminent suicide risk has a different quality than chronic or long-term suicide risk. Studies that relate a baseline clinical evaluation to death by suicide over an extended follow-up period of years or decades combine subsamples of early and late suicides, inadvertently obfuscating distinct early and late prediction profiles. The priorities of the clinician correspond to the time frame of

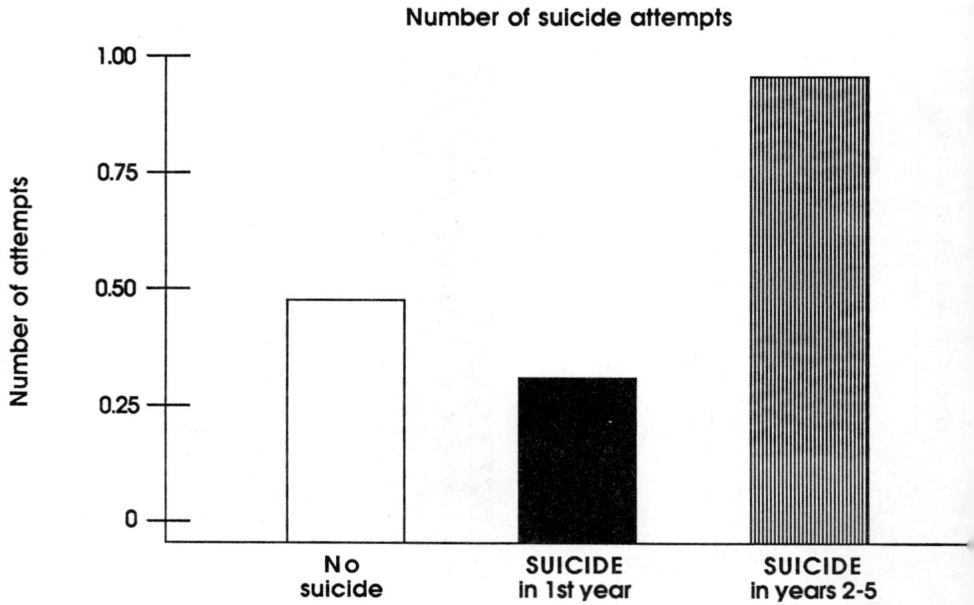

Figure 4–2. Association between history of suicide attempts and death by suicide.

the early suicides. The clinician assessing an individual patient for suicide risk is most interested in appraising the risk of suicidal behavior for the immediate days or weeks that follow, and only secondarily interested in what might happen months or years later. Pokorny (1983) was perhaps the first researcher to draw attention to the clinician's time frame with regard to suicidal crisis, defined in minutes, hours, or days, in the context of voicing pessimism about the possibility of doing prospective research on "short-range" prediction of suicide, since it would be unethical to withhold taking appropriate emergency steps to ensure a patient's safety.

On the basis of these findings, clinical decision making and research about suicide may benefit from conceptualizing clinical assessment in terms of the difference between acute and long-term risk factors, on the one hand, and modifiable or nonmodifiable risk factors, on the other. The anxiety-related symptoms associated with short-term risk, for example, may be modifiable through clinical and therapeutic efforts, thus potentially decreasing the likelihood of suicide.

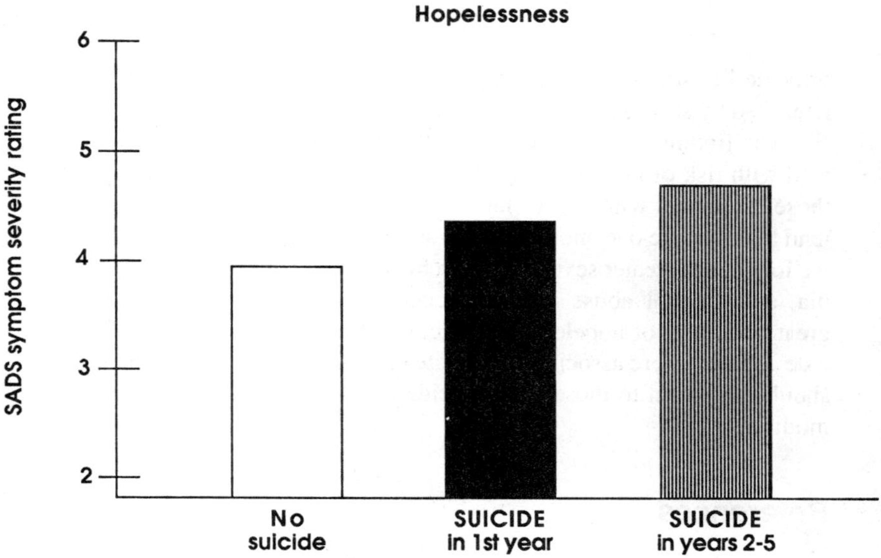

Figure 4–3. Association between hopelessness and death by suicide.

Summary

A number of investigations have yielded findings suggesting that suicide risk predictors vary as a function of the major psychiatric disorder(s) implicated. The clinical features to consider when assessing a depressed patient for suicide risk, for example, may be different than those to consider when assessing an alcoholic or schizophrenic patient. The findings summarized here contribute to a better understanding of those clinical features associated with suicide risk among patients with moderate to severe major affective disorder. The great majority of these patients manifested suicidal ideation at initial assessment, and 49% evidenced a history of suicide attempts. In these and other respects, most of the sample were at risk for suicide according to conventional clinical standards.

In this diagnostically homogeneous sample, few of the clinical features associated with suicide risk in the clinical literature (e.g., not bipolar course, schizoaffective presentation, psychotic or endogenous subtypes, severity of suicidal ideation, history of suicidal attempts, duration of the index episode, number of prior episodes of affective disorder, or acute life stress levels) helped to identify the subset of patients who later died by suicide.

The findings led us to conclude that clinical characteristics associated with risk of *imminent* suicide (i.e., death within 6–12 months) and those associated with risk of later suicide differ in important ways and tend to obfuscate one another if they are not considered separately. Thus we found that greater severity of psychic anxiety, panic attacks, anhedonia, and alcohol abuse were associated with early suicide, whereas greater severity of hopelessness, suicidal ideation, and a history of suicide attempts were associated with late suicide. The clinician's attention should be drawn to those early suicide risk factors that are potentially modifiable.

References

Allebeck P, Varla A, Kristjansson E, et al: Risk factors for suicide among patients with schizophrenia. Acta Psychiatr Scand 76:414–419, 1987

American Psychiatric Association: Diagnostic and Statistical Manual of Mental Disorders, 3rd Edition, Revised. Washington, DC, American Psychiatric Association, 1987

Barraclough B, Bunch J, Nelson B, et al: A hundred cases of suicide: clinical aspects. Br J Psychiatry 125:355–373, 1974

Berglund M: Suicide in alcoholism: a prospective study of 88 suicides, I: the multidimensional diagnosis at first admission. Arch Gen Psychiatry 41:888–891, 1984

Beck AT, Weissman A, Leste A, et al: The measurement of pessimism: The hopelessness scale. J Consult Clin Psychol 42:861–865, 1974

Beskow J: Suicide and mental disorder in Swedish men. Acta Psychiatr Scand Suppl 277:1–138, 1979

Black DW, Warrack G, Winokur G: Excess mortality among psychiatric patients: the Iowa record-linkage study. JAMA 253:58–61, 1985a

Black DW, Warrack G, Winokur G: The Iowa record-linkage study, I: suicides and accidental deaths among psychiatric patients. Arch Gen Psychiatry 42:71–75, 1985b

Bleuler M: The Schizophrenic Disorders. New Haven, CT, Yale University Press, 1978

Breier A, Astrachan BM: Characterization of schizophrenic patients who commit suicide. Am J Psychiatry 141:206–209, 1984

Chynoweth R, Tonge JI, Armstrong J: Suicide in Brisbane: a retrospective psychosocial study. Aust N Z J Psychiatry 14:37–45, 1980

Clark DC, Young MA, Scheftner WA, et al: A field test of Motto's risk estimator for suicide. Am J Psychiatry 144:923–926, 1987

Cullberg J, Wasserman D, Stefansson C-G: Who commits suicide after a suicide attempt? an 8 to 10 year follow up in a suburban catchment area. Acta Psychiatr Scand 77:598–603, 1988

Dorpat TL, Ripley HS: A study of suicide in the Seattle area. Compr Psychiatry 1:349–359, 1960

Drake RE, Cotton PG: Depression, hopelessness and suicide in chronic schizophrenia. Br J Psychiatry 148:554–559, 1986

Drake RE, Gates C, Cotton PG, et al: Suicide among schizophrenics: who is at risk? J Nerv Ment Dis 172:613–617, 1984

Egeland JA, Sussex JN: Suicide and family loading for affective disorders. JAMA 254:915–918, 1985

Endicott J, Spitzer RL: A diagnostic interview: the Schedule for Affective Disorders and Schizophrenia. Arch Gen Psychiatry 35:837–844, 1978

Ettlinger RW: Suicides in a group of patients who had previously attempted suicide. Acta Psychiatr Scand 40:363–378, 1964

Farberow NL, Simon MD: Suicides in Los Angeles and Vienna: an intercultural study of two cities. Public Health Rep 84:389–402, 1969

Fawcett J: Predictors of early suicide: Identification and appropriate intervention. J Clin Psychiatry 49 (suppl):7–8, 1988

Fawcett J, Scheftner WA, Clark DC, et al: Clinical predictors of suicide in patients with major affective disorders: a controlled prospective study. Am J Psychiatry 144:35–40, 1987

Fawcett J, Scheftner WA, Fogg L, et al: Time-related predictors of suicide in major affective disorder. Am J Psychiatry 147:1189–1194, 1990

Fowler RC, Rich CL, Young D: San Diego suicide study, II: substance abuse in young cases. Arch Gen Psychiatry 43:962–965, 1986

Hagnell O, Rorsman B: Suicide and endogenous depression with somatic symptoms in the Lundby study. Neuropsychobiology 4:180–187, 1978

Hagnell O, Rorsman B: Suicide in the Lundby study: a comparative investigation of clinical aspects. Neuropsychobiology 5:61–73, 1979

Hagnell O, Lanke J, Rorsman B: Suicide and depression in the male part of the Lundby study. Neuropsychobiology 8:182–187, 1982

Holinger PC: Violent Deaths in the United States. New York, Guilford Press, 1987

Katz MM, Klerman GL: Introduction: overview of the clinical studies program. Am J Psychiatry 136:49–51, 1979

Lindesay J: Age, sex and suicide rates within birth cohorts in England and Wales. Soc Psychiatry Psychiatr Epidemiol 24:249–252, 1989

Linehan MM: Suicidal people: one population or two? Ann N Y Acad Sci 487:16–33, 1986

Martin RL, Cloninger CR, Guze SB, et al: Mortality in a follow-up of 500 psychiatric outpatients, I: total mortality. Arch Gen Psychiatry 42:47–54, 1985a

Martin RL, Cloninger CR, Guze SB, et al: Mortality in a follow-up of 500 psychiatric outpatients, II: case-specific mortality. Arch Gen Psychiatry 42:58–66, 1985b

Miles CP: Conditions predisposing to suicide: a review. J Nerv Ment Dis 164:231–246, 1977

Motto J: Suicide attempts: a longitudinal view. Arch Gen Psychiatry 13:516–520, 1965

Motto JA: Suicide risk factors in alcohol abuse. Suicide Life Threat Behav 10:230–238, 1980

Motto JA, Heilbron DC, Juster RP: Development of a clinical instrument to estimate suicide risk. Am J Psychiatry 142:680–686, 1985

Murphy GE: Clinical identification of suicide risk. Arch Gen Psychiatry 27:356–359, 1972

Murphy GE: On suicide prediction and prevention. Arch Gen Psychiatry 40:343–344, 1983

Murphy GE: The prediction of suicide: why is it so difficult? Am J Psychother 38:341–349, 1984

Murphy GE: Suicide and attempted suicide, in The Medical Basis of Psychiatry. Edited by Winokur G, Clayton P. Philadelphia, PA, WB Saunders, 1986, pp 562–579

Murphy GE, Wetzel RD: The lifetime risk of suicide in alcoholism. Arch Gen Psychiatry 47:383–392, 1990

Murphy GE, Armstrong JW, Hermele SL, et al: Suicide and alcoholism: interpersonal loss confirmed as a predictor. Arch Gen Psychiatry 36:65–69, 1979

National Center for Health Statistics: Advance report of final mortality statistics, 1987 (NCHS Monthly Vital Statistics Rep 38, No 5). Washington, DC, National Center for Health Statistics, 1989

Pitts F, Winokur G: Affective disorder, III: diagnostic correlates and incidence of suicide. J Nerv Ment Dis 139:176–181, 1964

Pokorny AD: Prediction of suicide in psychiatric patients: report of a prospective study. Arch Gen Psychiatry 40:249–257, 1983

Rich CL, Young D, Fowler RC: San Diego suicide study, I: young vs old subjects. Arch Gen Psychiatry 43:577–582, 1986

Rich CL, Fowler RC, Young D: Substance abuse and suicide: the San Diego study. Ann Clin Psychiatry 1:79–85, 1989

Robins E: The Final Months: A Study of the Lives of 134 Persons who Committed Suicide. New York, Oxford University Press, 1981

Robins E: Completed suicide, in Suicide. Edited by Roy A. Baltimore, MD, Williams & Wilkins, 1986, pp 123–133

Robins E, Gassner S, Kayes J, et al: The communication of suicidal intent: a study of 134 consecutive cases of successful (completed) suicide. Am J Psychiatry 115:724–733, 1959a

Robins E, Murphy GE, Wilkinson RH, et al: Some clinical considerations in the prevention of suicide based on a study of 134 successful suicides. Am J Public Health 49:888–899, 1959b

Roy A: Suicide in chronic schizophrenia. Br J Psychiatry 141:171–177, 1982

Roy A: Family history of suicide. Arch Gen Psychiatry 40:971–974, 1983

Scheftner WA, Young MA, Endicott J, et al: Family history and five-year suicide risk. Br J Psychiatry 153:805–809, 1988

Smith JC, Mercy JA, Conn JM: Marital status and the risk of suicide. Am J Public Health 78:78–80, 1988

Spitzer RL, Endicott J, Robins E: Research Diagnostic Criteria: rationale and reliability. Arch Gen Psychiatry 35:773–782, 1978

Tsuang MT: Suicide in schizophrenics, manics, depressives, and surgical controls: a comparison with general population suicide mortality. Arch Gen Psychiatry 35:153–155, 1978

Tsuang MT: Risk of suicide in the relatives of schizophrenics, manics, depressives, and controls. Arch Gen Psychiatry 44:396–400, 1983

Veevers JE: Parenthood and suicide: an examination of a neglected variable. Soc Sci Med 7:135–144, 1973

Weiss JMA, Scott KF: Suicide attempters ten years later. Compr Psychiatry 15:165–171, 1974

Wender PH, Kety SS, Rosenthal D, et al: Psychiatric disorders in the biological and adoptive families of adopted individuals with affective disorders. Arch Gen Psychiatry 43:923–929, 1986

Winokur G, Tsuang M: The Iowa 500: suicide in mania, depression and schizophrenia. Am J Psychiatry 132:650–651, 1975

Chapter 5

General Versus Specific Risk Factors for Suicide in Schizophrenia

Peter Weiden, M.D.
Alec Roy, M.B.

This chapter focuses on suicidal behavior in schizophrenia: why it occurs and how to manage it. Schizophrenia is a cruel illness, and it is not surprising that schizophrenic persons kill themselves. However, it is surprising how little we know about suicide in schizophrenia. To understand this phenomenon, we will also have to consider issues apart from the schizophrenic diagnosis. Nondiagnostic predictors of suicide include demographics, social and cultural factors, personal and family history of suicide, psychodynamic issues, comorbidity with other high-risk diagnoses, biological vulnerability, and treatment issues. Because these are risk factors for all psychiatric patients, we will first focus on how these "general" risk factors interact with the schizophrenic illness. However, schizophrenic patients also kill themselves for reasons not often seen in other diagnostic groups. Put another way, some risk factors for suicide in schizophrenia are different (or behave differently) than risk factors for other illnesses. In the second section of this chapter, we will cover risk factors "specific" to schizophrenia. Although such a distinction between general versus specific risk factors is somewhat artificial, it can be helpful for the evaluation and management of the suicidal schizophrenic patient.

The authors would like to thank Carolyn O'Carroll for her assistance in the preparation of this manuscript. This paper was supported by National Institute of Mental Health Grant MH 43635.

General Risk Factors

Demographics

A diagnosis of schizophrenia carries with it a dramatically increased risk of suicide. At least 10% of schizophrenic patients will die by suicide (Miles 1977). Many other schizophrenic patients attempt suicide sometime during their illness (Planansky and Johnston 1973). With such high rates, identifying schizophrenic suicides means attempting to find very-high-risk patients within a baseline high-risk population. With that in mind, schizophrenic patients who commit suicide tend to be young and predominantly male. Table 5–1 summarizes all demographic studies of completed schizophrenic suicides since 1980; the mean age of death was 32, and 72.2% were male. The male predominance is found in other psychiatric disorders; however, the sex distribution of suicide attempts is not as weighted toward females as in other diagnoses. Female schizophrenic patients do not attempt suicide more frequently than do male schizophrenic patients (Wilkinson and Bacon 1984). The early age of suicide in schizophrenia is not typical of all diagnoses. For example, patients with affective illness or alcoholism tend to be older at the time of suicide and have a longer lag time from onset of illness to the completed suicide.

Table 5–1. Age and sex ratio in studies reported since 1980 of chronic schizophrenic suicide victims

Reference	Suicides (*N*)	Mean age (years)	Male (%)
Cheung 1981	12	31.0	83.3
Roy 1982	30	27.9	80
Hogan & Awad 1983	67	35.5	80.6
Breier & Astrachan 1984	20	30.3	90
Drake and Cotton 1986	15	31.7	60
Wilkinson & Bacon 1984	17	42	47
Nyman & Jonsonn 1986	10	30.4	90
Allebeck and Wistedt 1986	33	35.9	54
TOTAL	204	33	73.1

Suicidal Ideation and Attempts

A completed suicide is, by definition, unchangeable. Since clinical practice focuses on the living patient, it is important to consider the natural history of nonlethal suicidal behavior. Ideation and attempts certainly are very common for this patient population. Suicide completion (1.0%), attempts (33–56%), and ideation (60–80%) are all very common in schizophrenia (Drake et al. 1985). The high baseline rate of suicidal ideation is well illustrated in one study (Landmark et al. 1987), where only 27% of hospitalized schizophrenic patients did show suicidal ideation. A history of a prior attempt was present in 40–60% of schizophrenic suicide attempters (Planansky and Johnston 1973; Wilkinson and Bacon 1984). Therefore, the imminently suicidal patient is hard to identify based on presence or absence of ideation or the past history of an attempt. At least two studies comparing schizophrenic suicides versus schizophrenic controls did not show significant differences in number of previous attempts. One control group was matched for age and sex (Roy 1982); the other control group consisted of unsuccessful attempters (Drake et al. 1985).

A past history of suicide attempt is relevant when considered in the context of the phase and course of the patient's illness. Schizophrenic patients who repeat their suicidal behavior often have an episodic illness with many exacerbations and remissions (Planansky and Johnston 1973). Patients may not be suicidal between episodes, but revert back to a suicidal status at the time of relapse. The time lag between repeated attempts is longer for schizophrenic patients than for those with other diagnoses (Breier and Astrachan 1984). Unfortunately, the long lag time between attempts does not diminish the risk of suicide over a lifetime. Compared with those with other psychiatric diagnoses who had made an attempt, schizophrenic patients have an eightfold greater likelihood of a future "successful" completion (Hawton and Fagg 1988).

Social and Cultural Factors

In general, persons who suicide do so in social settings of loneliness and isolation (e.g., being unmarried, being unemployed, or living alone). For example, early epidemiologic studies of suicide found that, compared with chance, suicides were much more likely to be living alone. Schizophrenia is no exception. In a comparison of schizophrenic suicide completers versus attempters, the completers tended to live alone, and the attempters lived with others (Drake and Cotton 1986). However, other studies seem to contradict this notion (Breier and Astrachan 1984; Roy 1982), but these negative studies base their sample from outpatient treatment settings treating patients who are likely to have social supports. For example, only 27% of the Breier and Astrachan study sample lived alone. In Roy's study, unemployment rather than living alone did appear to be a significant risk factor for suicide. Schizophrenic persons in the community are more likely to be socially isolated compared with those with other major mental illnesses. Deterioration associated with schizophrenia ("downward drift") increases the chances that the schizophrenic patient will remain isolated over long periods of time. For example, homeless schizophrenic persons are more likely to remain homeless than other homeless individuals (Koegel et al. 1988). Also, schizophrenic persons who live alone or lack social supports are more likely to become noncompliant with medication (Weiden et al. 1986), and noncompliance is another risk factor for suicide (Cohen et al. 1964).

Comorbidity With Depression

Depression is very common for all subtypes of schizophrenic disorders, with a lifetime risk estimated at 60% (Roy 1986). Comorbidity of schizophrenia and secondary depression greatly increases the risk of suicide. Chronic schizophrenic patients who suicided were more likely than matched schizophrenic controls to have an associated depressive episode and were more likely to receive tricyclic antidepressants or electroconvulsive therapy for depression (Roy 1986). The eventual suicides had shown higher rates of suicidal impulses and depressive symptoms during their last hospitalization (Table 5–2).

How does the depression in schizophrenia compare with depression seen in other psychiatric diagnoses? Drake and Cotton (1986) examined the nature of the depressive symptoms in schizophrenic patients who committed suicide. They blindly reviewed 15 schizophrenic suicide victims and 89 schizophrenic controls. The suicides were much more likely to manifest *persistent* depressed mood than the controls. Surprisingly, the severity of depression as measured by vegetative symptoms was not higher for the suicides. Rather, the schizophrenic suicides were more *psychologically* distressed. Depressed *but not hopeless* schizophrenic patients were not at greater risk for suicide, and the suicides were no

Table 5–2. Studies reporting rates of depression during last period of contact among schizophrenic suicide victims

Reference	Suicide (*N*)	Depressed *N*	Depressed %
Levy & Southcombe 1953	29	10	34.5
Cohen et al. 1964	40	28	70
Warnes 1968	16	12	75
Yarden 1974	20	13	65
Virkkunen 1976	82	57	69.5
Cheung 1981	12	12	100
Roy 1982	30	16	53.3
Drake and Cotton 1986	15	12	80
TOTAL	244	160	65.6

more likely than controls to fulfill DSM-III (American Psychiatric Association 1980) criteria for a comorbid major depressive episode. Hopelessness rather than severity of depression seems to cut across all psychiatric diagnoses as a key symptom predictor for suicide (Beck et al. 1990).

Comorbidity With Substance Abuse

Schizophrenic patients often have a secondary substance abuse diagnosis. Comorbidity rates of schizophrenia and substance abuse (the so-called dual-diagnosis patient) range from 40% to 80% (Schneier and Siris 1987). Dual-diagnosis schizophrenic patients paradoxically seem to prefer psychotomimetic drugs rather than sedating drugs (e.g., marijuana and cocaine, not the sedative-hypnotics). It is easy to understand why dual-diagnosis patients may have a higher suicide risk than schizophrenic patients who do not abuse drugs. First, substance abuse by itself is an independent risk factor for suicide. Second, dual-diagnosis patients have more hospitalizations and are more impaired than schizophrenic patients who do not abuse drugs (Drake and Wallach 1989). Third, there may be a vicious cycle interaction between the abused drug, the schizophrenic illness, and suicidality. Consistent with this notion are several case series that have noted high rates of suicidality in substance-induced schizophrenic psychosis (Bowers 1977). In these case studies, the patients' suicidal behavior seemed to parallel the substance-induced psychosis. Although this observation may simply reflect a reporting bias for dramatic cases, it is also possible that a substance-induced psychosis is more likely to induce suicidal behavior than a usual relapse. Dopamine-agonist agents given to normal subjects will decrease insight; acute cocaine administration caused paranoid symptoms (as determined by nurse raters) that were not reflected in the subject's self-report of the experience (Sherer et al. 1988). Thus, should this finding generalize to schizophrenic patients, acute drug intoxication could selectively disrupt insight.

Treatment Issues

Many individuals who suicide have made contact with a mental health treatment within the week before death. For example, Roy's (1982) study showed that of 75 outpatient suicides, 12 (16%) made contact with hospital psychiatric emergency services immediately before their suicides (none were admitted). Of these 12 patients, 7 were already receiving outpatient treatment. Of the 12 patients who made their first contact through the emergency service, 5 suicided before the next outpatient visit. At least with the benefit of hindsight, it often is possible to prevent suicide with hospitalization.

Hospitalization seems to protect the patient (at least temporarily) from suicide. Inpatient suicide is uncommon. In Roy's (1982) study, only 17% of the suicides were inpatients. Even "inpatient" suicides do not usually occur on the ward. Rather, the suicide usually occurs on the hospital grounds, on a pass, or after eloping. Most of the time, suicides occur shortly after hospitalization. The postdischarge phase is the highest risk period for all psychiatric diagnoses (reviewed in Roy 1986) (Table 5–3). For example, more than 80% of 75 outpatient suicides had recently changed status from inpatient to outpatient care (10% suicided within 4 days, 29% within 2 weeks, and 65% by 3 months) (Roy 1982). This pattern is seen in schizophrenia; 30% of all schizophrenic suicides occurred during this phase. Therefore, a suicide soon after discharge may be indirectly associated with the hospitalization experience or the psychological trauma of returning to outpatient life.

Biological Factors

Interest in neurochemical vulnerability to suicide was reawakened in 1976, when Åsberg and colleagues reported a bimodal distribution of

Table 5–3. Comparison of schizophrenic patients who did and did not commit suicide: significant findings

	Suicides[a] (*N* = 15) (%)	Nonsuicides (*N* = 89) (%)
College education	73	29
Explicit suicide threat	67	28
Lives alone	60	27
Depressed mood	80	48
Inadequacy	80	36
Hopelessness	60	27
Suicidal ideation	73	38
Awareness of pathology	47	11
Fears of mental disintegration	33	1
High self-expectations	47	12

[a] All significant findings to the $P < .01$ level are taken from the original analysis.
Source. From Drake et al. 1984, with permission from *The Journal of Nervous and Mental Disease.*

levels of the serotonin metabolite 5-hydroxyindoleacetic acid (5-HIAA) in the lumbar cerebrospinal fluid (CSF) of 68 depressed patients. More "low" than "high" CSF 5-HIAA patients had attempted or completed suicide. Reduced central serotonin metabolism is hypothesized to be associated with suicidal behavior (reviewed in Roy et al. 1989; see also Goodwin and Runck, Chapter 1, this volume).

The results of the CSF 5-HIAA studies in suicidal versus nonsuicidal schizophrenic patients have been mixed; two studies have reported significant decreases of CSF 5-HIAA (Ninan et al. 1984), and two studies have reported no decrease in 5-HIAA levels (Roy et al. 1985). Therefore, the evidence for serotonergic abnormalities as an explanation for suicide in schizophrenia is less robust than other diagnoses. What this means is unclear. Perhaps a serotonergic abnormality is obscured by alterations in dopaminergic systems. Alternatively, it would not be surprising if dopamine systems were involved in the biology of suicide in schizophrenia. Dopamine is implicated both in mediating normal pleasure responses and in the pathogenesis of psychosis (Moore and Bloom 1978).

Specific Risk Factors

Symptoms of Schizophrenia

Acute psychosis. Does psychosis lead to suicide? This issue is more complicated than would first appear. Consider, for example, the timeworn observation that the presence of command auditory hallucinations is a predictor of suicide in schizophrenia. However, at least four studies have not found command hallucinations to be a risk factor for suicide in schizophrenia (Breier and Astrachan 1984; Roy 1982). Does this mean that acute psychosis is not a risk factor for suicide? Being psychotic could cause deaths in ways that are not emphasized in the current literature. A major source of methodological bias in metanalyses of suicide in schizophrenia involves secondary treatment effects; clinicians are more likely to hospitalize schizophrenic persons for their psychotic symptoms than for their depressive or suicidal symptoms (Mezzich et al. 1984; Segal et al. 1988). Symptoms of impulsivity and thought disorder seem to be heavily weighed in decisions to admit or commit. In contrast, depression and distress actually predict *outpatient* disposition from an emergency room (Mezzich et al. 1984) or a decision to commit (Segal et al. 1988). Therefore, we hypothesize that 1) acutely psychotic schizophrenic persons (compared with nonpsychotic and depressed schizophrenic persons) are more likely to be admitted and protected from killing themselves, and 2) clinicians in emergency room settings view symptoms of disorganization, impulsivity, and psychosis as more dangerous than depression or distress. The net effect of these treatment decisions during emergency situations may make our current efforts at suicide prevention in schizophrenia relatively more effective for psychotic symptoms than for depressive symptoms. As a result, longitudinal studies of schizophrenic suicides may understate the intrinsic (i.e., untreated) risk of patients' psychotic symptoms.

Accidental death versus intentional suicide. Psychosis may cause death through the unfortunate—and inadvertent—consequences of dangerous behavior. Accidental deaths during a psychosis are not necessarily considered or reported as suicides, yet are very common in schizophrenia. For example, Allebeck and Wistedt (1986) found that excess mortality in schizophrenia was particularly high for what they called "unnatural deaths." Of these deaths, injuries caused 68 deaths; the standardized mortality rate would predict only 8.1 deaths. Of the 68 "injuries," the authors found 47 suicides, but 14 of these 47 were actually considered "undetermined." Similarly, Buda and colleagues (1988) found the relative risk of "accidental" death (compared to the general population) in a long-term follow-up of nonschizoaffective schizophrenic patients was 3.5 (versus 1.6 for suicide). Of the 124 deaths (37% overall mortality), 15 deaths were "unnatural" and only 6 were suicides. Kendler (1986) evaluated mortality in a cohort of 590 schizophrenic twins and found 38 "trauma" deaths (versus 17.15 expected) and 21 suicide deaths (versus 3.59 expected). We are left with the strong impression that a schizophrenic person has at least as great a chance of dying from a so-called accident as a suicide. We suspect that many of these "accidental" deaths are really from behaviors that are secondary to acute psychosis. The fact that the patient does not perceive his or her behavior to be dangerous or suicidal does not bring the accidental or undetermined death back to life. Therefore, we feel that it is reasonable to broaden our discussion of suicide in schizophrenia to include inadvertent deaths resulting from delusional or disordered thinking. We leave it to the reader to decide whether to call this kind of death a suicide.

> Mr. A was a 30-year-old schizophrenic auto mechanic who had been ill for 10 years. His early history of multiple relapses were caused by neuroleptic noncompliance. After repeated hospitalizations he finally had been able to remain stable as an outpatient. This change seemed due to family work and personal involvement on the part of his outpatient physician. After 3 relatively stable years he developed tardive dyskinesia, and his neuroleptic medication was lowered. He relapsed 1 month later. A day before his death, he reported to his physician that he was a messenger from God but denied suicidal ideation. The following day, a few minutes before his death, he was watching television with his mother and had casually mentioned to her his delusion of being able to fly. He died after jumping from the roof of his building.

Persistent thought disorder. Schizophrenic symptoms may persist long after the florid psychosis is over. In particular, a thought disorder may interfere with the patient's ability to think through ambiguous, complex, or conflicting ideas. Judgment may be affected. Persistent thought disorder is a very common chronic symptom. In a series of follow-up studies, Harrow and colleagues (1983) found a significant thought disorder in 75% of recently discharged schizophrenic patients. This system was persistent (despite the resolution of other psychotic symptoms) for approximately one-third of the sample. Patients who had persistent thought disorder had a much worse long-term outcome, as measured by rehospitalizations and psychosocial functioning. A thought disorder may also make it difficult for patients to understand and accept treatment. This symptom distinguished a group of involuntary patients who subsequently agreed to take medication from involuntary patients who steadfastly refused medication (Marder et al. 1984). Since the control group was also committed to the hospital, this finding is not an artifact of general uncooperativeness. Therefore, a thought disorder may be a relatively refractory psychotic symptom that, when present, may interfere with a patient's judgment about suicidal impulses or following treatment recommendations.

Cognitive and perceptual deficits. Some schizophrenic patients have striking deficits in the ability to learn from past experiences, especially in new situations (Goldberg et al. 1987). The biological basis of this finding has been demonstrated with neuropsychological deficits (Wisconsin Card Sorting Test [Heaton 1985]), which correlate with decreased frontal lobe blood flow (Weinberger 1987). The clinical implication of inability to learn is that the patient may expose himself unwittingly to stressful situations, or may unknowingly behave in a dangerous manner. The following case illustrates this point.

> Mr. B, a schizophrenic 24-year-old, had rheumatic heart disease requiring an aortic valve replacement and anticoagulation. He was admitted to a medical unit for retroperitoneal bleeding after an overdose of warfarin (Coumadin). During the initial interview, the patient denied that the overdose was a suicide attempt. According to him, the overdose happened because his prescription of Coumadin had run out and when he refilled the prescription he believed that he had to "take the entire week's worth to catch up." The patient's family confirmed this version of the history.

Perceptual deficits can also lead to dangerous self-neglect states. Patients who do not perceive adequately may not be able to preserve an ability to regulate, avoid, or minimize exposure to noxious situations. Self-neglect may not really be suicide, but the end result is identical. Bleuler (1911) described this phenomenon: "The sense of self-preservation is often reduced to zero. The patients do not bother about whether they starve or not, whether they be on a snowbank or in a red hot oven" (p. 40).

Psychological Issues

Distress from deterioration. Schizophrenic patients who have multiple psychotic episodes along with a deteriorating course of illness may be at particular risk for intentional suicide (Roy 1982). Drake and Cotton (1986) suggested that hopelessness and distress over loss of functioning is a major cause of suicide in schizophrenia. Their psychological autopsies of schizophrenic suicide victims found that these patients had high premorbid achievement, high self-expectations of performance, and extensive awareness about their illness (Cotton et al. 1985; Drake et al. 1984). For example, 73% of the suicide victims in the Drake study were college educated compared with 29% of the controls (Table 5–3). The authors concluded that

> Given the schizophrenic suicides' inability to achieve major life goals, they felt inadequate, feared further deterioration of their mental abilities, and decided to end their lives rather than continue living with chronic mental illness. . . . Perhaps these patients should be considered to suffer from despair rather than depression.

Insight seems necessary for these motivations. Therefore, moderate (versus severe) levels of deterioration may paradoxically be associated with a greater suicide risk. Severe deterioration may cause loss of insight or loss of capacity to experience distress.

Narcissistic injury. Distress from deterioration may not completely explain the patient's determination to "succeed." Why is the despair experienced by someone suffering from schizophrenia so often lethal? Before we accept the notion that suicide in schizophrenia is justifiable and realistic, please consider the hardships posed by other chronic and progressively deteriorating diseases of young adulthood (e.g., end-stage renal disease, cystic fibrosis, or severe sickle cell anemia). While these chronic medical illnesses are also associated with suicide, the suicide rates found in these conditions are not nearly as high as in schizophrenia. To explain this discrepancy, we speculate that it is the experience of *cognitive* deterioration that is particularly associated with self-destruction. Kohut (1972) postulated that a brain injury is likely to invoke a response of severe narcissistic injury and narcissistic rage. He considered the "catastrophic reaction" in brain-injured patients to be a response to recognition of cognitive loss. Psychologic precipitants of a catastrophic reaction in schizophrenia might include the sudden feelings of shame, humiliation, stigma, and anger at being controlled by other people (e.g., needing disability payments, having to take medication). Unfortunately, for many schizophrenic patients, chances are good that these intrapsychic struggles are exacerbated by the patient's real life predicaments.

Treatment Issues

Neuroleptic-mediated insight. The observation that psychosis can be psychologically protective goes back to Roman times: "There is a pleasure, sure, in being mad which none but madmen know" (Horace, 20 B.C.). This finding was replicated almost two thousand years later by Van Putten and colleagues (1976), who reported that persistent medication refusers are chronically grandiose. Neuroleptic treatment can improve insight and change psychotic grandiosity to realistic demoralization. Another possible reason for neuroleptics to increase suicide rates is that "successful" treatment results in faster discharges into the community. The unprepared patient is then exposed to stresses of outpatient life. The following case illustrates a "successful" neuroleptic treatment of a life-threatening psychosis. The suicide that followed was caused, in part, by neuroleptic-mediated insight.

> Ms. C was a 27-year-old woman admitted to the hospital for a first episode of schizophrenia. Her symptoms developed over 2 years and culminated with an admission for cachexia secondary to paranoia about her food being poisoned. The admission occurred after her internist diagnosed an electrolyte imbalance and malnutrition. She initially had no insight into the psychiatric nature of her illness. Nonetheless, she had an excellent response to neuroleptic treatment, regained her weight, and (reluctantly) admitted to being psychiatrically ill. She was discharged after 6 weeks and was seen weekly after discharge as an outpatient. At her third outpatient visit, she did not appear psychotic and denied suicidal ideation. After that day, however, she suicided by overdose after being rejected by her boyfriend. After her suicide, her

mother informed the staff of the patient's secret concern about whether or not the illness would ruin her marriage chances.

Neuroleptic-mediated distress. Neuroleptic-induced suicidal behavior can be directly mediated through neuroleptic-induced depression (Van Putten and May 1978), akathisia (Drake and Ehrlich 1985), and other behavioral toxicities (e.g., dysphoria) (Weiden and Bruun 1987). Of all of the side effects, akathisia is most clearly associated with suicidal behavior. This side effect is very common during acute neuroleptic treatment. Estimates range from 40% to 90%. Akathisia may occur within hours of a single neuroleptic dose. Normal volunteers who take single doses of neuroleptics report developing severe and unrelenting distress from akathisia (Anderson et al. 1981). Akathisia occurs in nonpsychiatric medical patients (Weiden 1985). Suicide from akathisia may occur in apparently normal individuals.

The following suicide note was left by Mrs. D, a 42-year-old married mother of four who shot herself shortly after receiving prochlorperazine (Compazine) for treatment of nausea. "I love you all, but I just cannot bear this mental anxiety anymore. I am a fighter, but I just could not fight this time. My mind won out. I can't even explain what happened. . . . " A careful review of her case failed to reveal any prior history of psychiatric illness, suicidal ideation, or other risk factors. Distress from akathisia (combined with lack of awareness of this side effect) seemed to cause the suicide.

Medication discontinuation. Discontinuation of neuroleptics in stable schizophrenic outpatients carries with it a very high risk of relapse (Cheung 1981). With the relapse comes risk of suicide, either directly from psychosis or indirectly from the posthospitalization depression. The most common reason that clinicians abruptly discontinue neuroleptics is the diagnosis of tardive dyskinesia. In a previously stable patient, the ensuing relapse and suicide can be considered an indirect complication of tardive dyskinesia.

Ms. E was a 59-year-old magazine editor. She had taken thioridazine (Mellaril) for many years after suffering a psychotic episode during her 20s. Over the years, she remained socially isolated, but never was psychotic or suicidal. She developed abnormal mouth movements consistent with tardive dyskinesia. A neurologic consultant recommended discontinuation of the thioridazine, which she did. Within 3 months, she became psychotic, lost her job, and suicided by placing a plastic bag over her head.

Deinstitutionalization. Deinstitutionalization has increased rehospitalization rates for schizophrenia more than for any other diagnosis. A schizophrenic patient living in the 1990s can expect many more hospitalizations (and discharges) than a schizophrenic patient living in the 1950s. Every readmission means there is a corresponding high-risk postdischarge phase. Therefore, "revolving door" rehospitalizations have the unfortunate effect of multiplying the high-risk periods for suicide.

Suicide Management

Understanding the risk factors behind suicide in schizophrenia is already a large step toward effective treatment. In this section, we will focus on assessment and management issues.

Risk Factor Assessment

Mental status examination. The mental status evaluation of a suicidal schizophrenic patient differs somewhat from the suicide evaluation of patients with other diagnoses. Schizophrenic symptoms complicate the evaluation. In particular, symptoms of denial of illness, cognitive disorganization, loss of drive, and social unrelatedness can confound the examination. Denial may be more extensive than the usual psychological defensiveness seen in other suicidal patients. Schizophrenic patients do not complain of pain during acute surgical conditions (Marchaud et al. 1959) or side effects (Weiden et al. 1989). Similarly, denial of illness may make the patient unable (not unwilling) to report suicidal ideation. Even if suicidal ideation is elicited, problems with social relatedness can create a false impression that the suicidal ideation is not serious. Therefore, the clinician should be cautious about using lack of affect about the suicide as a guide to the short-term risk of completion.

Mr. F was a single 42-year-old suffering from paranoid schizophrenia. He was evaluated for suicidality after his discharge from the hospital. He had joined a right-to-die society (Hemlock Society), which had prompted the suicide evaluation. He described his decision to join the Hemlock Society in a bland and unrelated manner. He stated "it is an intellectual interest of mine," and denied any imminent suicide plan.

He indifferently mentioned that he would suicide in the distant future should he not improve. He suicided by overdose later that week.

Other important schizophrenic symptoms include the presence of a subtle thought disorder, which can be easy to miss. One clinical method to evaluate how a thought disorder might affect judgment during periods of suicidal feelings is to review the patient's own plan—step by step—to avoid suicide during those times. Logical inconsistencies in such a plan should alert the clinician that the suicidal ideation might be more dangerous than would otherwise appear. The content of the suicide ideation should be carefully examined. Whereas the presence or absence of suicidal ideation does not seem to be a strong predictor of suicide, *explicit ideation* is a particular cause of concern. A history of explicit suicide threats was twice as common in the suicide completers versus controls (Drake and Cotton 1986). Similarly, it has been our clinical experience that there really is no such thing as a "suicide gesture" in schizophrenia. What is usually a low-lethality attempt (e.g., superficial wrist slashing) for someone with a personality disorder diagnosis should be considered to be a serious attempt in a schizophrenic patient. In contrast, one aspect of the mental status that should be minimized for schizophrenic patients versus patients with other diagnoses is the psychodynamic evaluation. Explicit use of psychodynamic formulations can be counterproductive for this patient population. Admittedly, psychodynamic conflicts can promote suicidal behavior for schizophrenic patients, but the problem facing the examiner is that psychodynamics are often obscured for overtly psychotic patients. For example, impulsive suicidal acts arising from a delusion make an understanding of the patient's unconscious motivations difficult, if not impossible.

Suicide history and phase of illness. Schizophrenic patients go through different phases of illness (Docherty et al. 1978). Many schizophrenic patients are suicidal during one phase of illness but not during another. For example, the demoralized schizophrenic patient is typically most suicidal during periods of relative remission. In contrast, the impulsive, thought-disordered patient is often most suicidal during the height of the psychotic relapse. Therefore, the suicide evaluation needs to establish a link between the patient's current phase of illness and history of suicidality. In particular, an understanding of the relationship between the patient's past suicidality and stage of the illness at the time of the past attempts is very helpful. Moreover, changes in states of illness can be used as a guide for when a suicide evaluation needs to be done. Neuroleptic responsiveness and relative remission should not convince the physician that a suicide attempt or completion cannot happen in the near future. Schizophrenic patients change states rapidly; remission may change to relapse within hours. Therefore, a suicide evaluation should be scheduled promptly if there is a change back to the state of illness where the patient was most suicidal.

Prodromal states. In this section, we deal with the stable and nonsuicidal schizophrenic patient. After "knocking on wood," the clinician should consider the possibility that future suicide attempts will occur during periods of decompensation. The patient's history should be reviewed; often important information about past suicidality is "buried" in voluminous charts. A good history, although necessary, is often missing. Rapid clinical interventions during early stages of relapse (prodromal periods) can be a life-saving preventative measure. In one study of recovering schizophrenic patients, 47 (70%; 93% of their families) reported the presence of a prodromal period immediately before relapse (Herz and Melville 1980). Typically, the prodromal period consisted of *nonpsychotic* symptoms (e.g., anxiety, depression) lasting days to weeks prior to the full-blown psychotic relapse. Recognition of prodromal episodes becomes a crucial clinical task in outpatient suicide prevention because, if recognized, prompt and aggressive use of neuroleptics (either restarting or increasing the dose) can sometimes stop the patient's progression to a full relapse. Important prodromal symptoms to evaluate include 1) the presence or worsening of thought disorder, 2) the disappearance of insight and/or distress over symptoms, 3) the time course of symptom progression (especially suicidal behavior), 4) the pattern of the past history of suicidal behavior, 5) the time course of neuroleptic responsiveness, and 6) the patient's past ability to cooperate with outpatient treatment during prior prodromal episodes. When the patient becomes prodromal, a medication approach is indicated and should take priority over psychological interventions.

> Mr. A was a stable schizophrenic patient in a combined weekly medication-supportive therapy treatment. His course and suicide are described in an earlier vignette. Several weeks before his suicide, he began discussing memories of early childhood sexual abuse by an

uncle and did so under appropriate circumstances and was not psychotic. After his relapse and suicide in retrospect, the report of sexual abuse had been a prodromal symptom during past episodes.

Depressive symptoms. Depression in schizophrenia can arise from different etiologies. Depression can represent a prodromal symptom, be a part of the acute psychosis, be a side effect from neuroleptics, or represent an independent secondary syndrome (postpsychotic depression). For the depressed and suicidal schizophrenic patient, it is very important to consider the differential diagnosis because the various treatments are so different. Since neuroleptic-induced akinesia can present as a cause of depression and is readily treatable, typically the first step is to rule out akinesia (Van Putten and May 1978). The association between akinesia and suicide is anecdotal. One study reported higher rates of suicide in a schizophrenia outpatient clinic where, because of policy changes, patients were converted from oral to intramuscular fluphenazine (Alarcon and Carney 1969). Another report noted that patients with severe side effects from depot neuroleptics had preoccupations with death and suicide (66% versus 4% of controls) (Blum 1980). However, most studies do not find neuroleptic treatment to be a common cause of postpsychotic depression. Therefore, akinesia cannot explain the high suicide rates in recently discharged schizophrenic outpatients. Nonetheless, anecdotal reports and clinical experience suggest that akinesia may promote suicidal behavior for a few vulnerable individuals, and aggressive treatment to rule out akinesia is usually indicated.

Since many prodromal episodes begin with affective symptoms (Docherty et al. 1978; Herz and Melville 1980), the clinician should be fairly certain that the depressive symptoms are psychotic before instituting somatic treatment for depression. This distinction is not always so easy to make, because the difference between a prodrome and postpsychotic depression can be subtle. Sullivan (1962) observed that

> While the true depressive is preoccupied with thoughts of the enormity of the disaster of punishment and hopelessness, the incipient schizophrenic . . . becomes more and more wrapped up in fantastic explanation and efforts at remedy. . . . While the pure depression may end in suicide of a practical sort, the schizophrenic depression leads to fantastic methods of self destruction often preceded by fear of being killed. (p. 151)

Neuroleptic noncompliance. The suicidal schizophrenic patient's compliance with neuroleptic therapy warrants detailed evaluation. Neuroleptic noncompliance can be "two strikes" for these patients. First, as mentioned, neuroleptic noncompliance increases vulnerability to relapse. Warnes (1968) reported that suicidal schizophrenic persons were on lower doses of neuroleptics; Virkkunen (1976) observed that prior to their suicide, many patients had become less cooperative to treatment. The second and often less obvious issue about noncompliance is that the noncompliant patient often suffers a personal loss. On refusing medication, the patient may lose a valued and trusted support system as a secondary consequence. (Often the patient is required to leave a day program or therapy.) In a follow-up study of schizophrenic persons who were drop-outs from outpatient psychotherapy, Katz and colleagues (1984) observed that "most strikingly, 5 patients (out of the 48 dropouts) were deceased at the time of follow-up. Four had committed suicide and one had been murdered." The major determinants of medication noncompliance include complexity of treatment regimen, severity of treatment side effects, and the doctor-patient relationship variables, especially patient dissatisfaction (Blackwell 1976). In contrast, physician belief in medication is associated with neuroleptic compliance (Irwin et al. 1971). Two issues that stand out in this illness are 1) the schizophrenic patient's tendency toward lack of insight and denial of illness, and 2) distress from neuroleptic side effects, especially akinesia and akathisia (Van Putten 1978).

Management

Psychoeducation. The patient and family should be informed of the high suicide risk in schizophrenia. For first-episode psychosis, this discussion should come only after the schizophrenic diagnosis has been established and accepted. The discussion should occur after the patient is stable. Maintaining an attitude of hopefulness is helpful in suicide prevention, especially among demoralized patients and families. "The schizophrenic appreciates all too definitely the attitude of the physician regarding the life situation of the patient" (Sullivan 1962, p. 246). Without expressing false cheerfulness, it is important to be optimistic. Optimism and realism can be combined by noting that the patient's suicide risk should decrease with time, so that if the patient can get through the high-risk time period (usually about 5 years after the diagnosis of schizophrenia is made), the lifetime risk will be much lower.

Psychoeducation can be helpful even for "battle scarred" families of chronically suicidal patients. One of the rare benefits of being a chronic patient is that specific prodromal patterns of suicidal behavior often can be established. Early identification of these patterns can then be used as a management guide for future episodes. For patients who have recently recovered from suicidal episodes, it is helpful to review the patient's individual pattern of suicidal behavior and discuss preventative measures. The clinician should communicate that the suicidal behavior will return, perhaps many years later. The goal of anticipation and advanced planning is to decrease the risk of potentially lethal "glitches" that might arise during a suicide crisis. Rehearsing what to do for future crises hopefully will allow for a smoother course of action when the crisis occurs.

A side benefit of advanced planning is to provide the patient and family with a sense of some control over the situation. If the pattern of suicidal behavior is known, there can be "nuts and bolts" planning. For example, window guards could be installed for a city-dwelling patient who, when relapsing, is known to have a delusion about being able to fly. If such specifics are not known, psychoeducation about suicide in schizophrenia can review general issues of vulnerability to stress. It could be helpful to review which stressors might be worth the risk of relapse to the patient and which ones are not. For example, a patient who gets suicidal on relapsing may decide that "getting high" on marijuana is not worth relapsing, but that the stress of dating is a chance worth taking.

Psychological management. According to Sullivan (1962):

> Even should the physician see clearly the (psychodynamic) mechanism of the symptom, he may not consider it advisable to put his views as definitely before the patient. The age of the patient, the educational level, the degree of contact with and confidence in the physician, the ability to assimilate unfamiliar ideas, must all be carefully weighed. Frequently the physician will find it most judicious to avoid complicating the patient's mental state with explanations that will be ill digested. (p. 313)

An acutely psychotic person can misunderstand a dynamic interpretation. Misunderstandings can be dangerous.

> A student therapist attempted to explore an acutely psychotic patient's "feelings of anger towards his family." He advised the patient that he had harbored hidden rage against his domineering brother and suggested that he "get his anger out." The patient did just that, by smashing and breaking his hand against the office wall!

Psychodynamic understanding *without interpretation* can be helpful. This seems especially true for those fortunate stabilized patients who, through the benefit of financial resources and ability to form a bond, have an ongoing long-term relationship with a therapist. These schizophrenic patients have preserved their ability to communicate feelings and to relate to others. The therapist, in turn, is able to offer a long-term commitment (e.g., years) to psychological treatment. By knowing the patient well, it can be easier for the therapist to distinguish between ongoing psychodynamic issues and symptoms of impending relapse. Even where the patient is less familiar (e.g., the inpatient unit or emergency room), modified forms of psychological management can be useful. The use of commonsense psychological principles can help guide the clinician in establishing a relationship with the patient and/or help establish effective communication with the patient despite their psychosis.

Formal psychotherapy is not the same as sound psychological management. May (1968) found formal analytically oriented psychotherapy to be ineffective for the inpatient treatment of schizophrenia, but emphasized the clinical importance of good psychological management. This point seems to have been forgotten. Skilled psychological management can take place without formal psychotherapy.

> A supervisor was asked by a resident to do a suicide evaluation on a recently admitted inpatient. The reason for the patient's suicidality was not known. At the start of the interview, the patient (who was about the same age as the examiner) commented "you are too young to be the supervisor . . . you must be very successful." This comment helped focus the interview on the patient's sense of shame about his unemployment, which seemed to be contributing to his suicidality. This was *not* interpreted. However, the understanding of the self-esteem problem helped guide appropriate clinical interventions designed to decrease his suicide risk.

Psychopharmacologic management. Relapse prevention is probably the single most important preventative measure for decreasing suicide in schizophrenia. Increasing compliance is one way to decrease relapse rates. During inpatient treatment, before discharge, the pattern of outpatient compliance should be evaluated. For example, it would make little sense to use lithium as an adjunct for a homeless patient who is unable to receive outpatient follow-up monitoring. If repeated noncompliance contributes to a pattern of suicidality, one could consider switching medications from oral to long-acting intramuscular medication. Often this treatment is best done in the hospital. Neuroleptic dosage reductions that are initiated by the clinician should be done cautiously. Fortunately, there can be more control when the doctor lowers the neuroleptic compared with patient-initiated noncompliance. Especially when the neuroleptic dose is lowered because of tardive dyskinesia, it is important not to convey a sense of urgency. The dosage should be lowered *slowly* (e.g., 10–20% a month). A slow and cautious dosage lowering may help avoid a precipitous relapse and anxiety from a withdrawal dyskinesia. Finding the best neuroleptic (optimizing benefit and minimizing side effects) and optimum dose for each patient is very important. For those patients with treatment-refractory psychotic symptoms, adjunctive antipsychotic therapies and ultimately clozapine may be indicated. After all of this, should the patient remain medication nonresponsive and at high risk for self-destruction, long-term protective care may be indicated.

A thorough side-effect history and physical examination should be done on suicidal schizophrenic patients. Extrapyramidal side effects from neuroleptics often go unrecognized; for example, akathisia was missed in 70% of inpatients (Weiden et al. 1987). The clinician should look for 1) distressing extrapyramidal side effects that may be causing or exacerbating suicidality (especially akathisia and akinesia, 2) distress from side effects as a cause of noncompliance or a cause of eroding family support for medication treatment, 3) the possible contribution of extrapyramidal side effects as a reason for using illicit drugs (e.g., marijuana is very anticholinergic), and 4) anxiety (the patient's or clinician's) over tardive dyskinesia, which then may result in too rapid a dosage lowering. The clinician should keep in mind that extrapyramidal side effects may present purely behaviorally or subjectively with no physical findings. Depression as a prodrome or during an acute psychotic episode should be treated with neuroleptics. For patients who are "stabilized" but persistently depressed, Siris and colleagues (1987) have found adjunctive imipramine to be effective for schizophrenic patients with postpsychotic depression. Distress from negative symptoms should be approached in a manner as reviewed by Carpenter and colleagues (1985).

Decision to hospitalize. Hospitalization is a two-edged sword. Hospitalization is life-saving when it protects the patient from self-destruction during an acute psychosis. On the other hand, a hospitalization could increase the future suicide risk during the postdischarge period. The reasons to hospitalize for the suicidal patient are usually obvious. However, it is less obvious to assess the risks of hospitalization *before hospitalization.* Factors that tend to increase long-term suicide risk include the stigma from hospitalization and reexposing the patient to the postdischarge phase. To discover only after admission that hospitalization is riskier in the long run is not helpful. This trade-off can be evaluated along with the evaluation of the history of the time course of the patient's suicidality. Not all prodromal or acutely psychotic patients need admission. Relative indications for outpatient management of the relapsing schizophrenic patient include 1) the patient's motivation and insight to stay in treatment and to request hospitalization, should it become necessary, 2) the availability of the outpatient treatment system to respond to emergencies, 3) the estimated dangerousness of the relapse, and 4) the time course of symptom resolution. Even if outpatient management is safe in the short run, a strong case can be made for hospitalizing relapsed patients who, by history, take a long time to respond to neuroleptics. Outpatients who remain acutely ill over months place a severe burden on their caretakers and often come to hospitalization anyway. In the meantime, these patients can act in dangerous and unpredictable ways. The next case is a relapsing patient who probably was going to have to be hospitalized sooner or later. The attempt at outpatient management created an unnecessary risk for accidental death.

> Mr. G is a "negative-symptom" schizophrenic 40-year-old living with his mother. He was stable for long periods of time, but when he became psychotic, he would require 3–6 months of high-dose neuroleptic treatment before he would improve. He relapsed in the setting of psychosocial stress. He remained under close supervision by his mother and was not hospitalized. He denied suicidal ideation, but his mental status showed severe thought disorganization. Two weeks later, however, he was hospitalized after he drank a bottle of dishwashing soap believing it was soda. This and other behaviors seemed to be quite dangerous and could have resulted in an accidental death. In retrospect, our attempt to

manage him as an outpatient was not realistic given Mr. G's known length of recovery time.

Summary

Until better treatments are found, suicide will remain a major complication for patients with schizophrenia. In the meantime, a careful, focused, and commonsense approach to this problem can make a difference. In particular, the clinician should pay attention to inherent risk factors, match patient's current phase of the illness with the past suicide history, and know how the schizophrenic symptoms alter the mental status evaluation. We know all too well that, despite our best efforts, many schizophrenic patients go on to kill themselves. Of the surviving patients, we will never know who we have saved by learning more about suicide in schizophrenia.

References

Alarcon R, Carney MWP: Severe depressive mood changes following slow-release intramuscular fluphenazine injection. Br Med J 3:569–677, 1969

Allebeck P, Wistedt B: Mortality in schizophrenia. Arch Gen Psychiatry 43:650–653, 1986

American Psychiatric Association: Diagnostic and Statistical Manual of Mental Disorders, 3rd Edition. Washington, DC, American Psychiatric Association, 1980

Anderson B, Reker D, Cooper T: Prolonged adverse effects of haloperidol in normal subjects. N Engl J Med 305:643–644, 1981

Beck AT, Brown G, Berchick RI, et al: Relationship between hopelessness and ultimate suicide: a replication with psychiatric outpatients. Am J Psychiatry 147:190–195, 1990

Blackwell B: Treatment adherence. Br J Psychiatry 129:513–531, 1976

Bleuler E: Dementia Praecox, or the Group of Schizophrenias (1911). New York, International Universities Press, 1961

Blum A: Patients at risk of developing severe side effects from depot fluphenazine treatment. Am J Psychiatry 137:254–255, 1980

Bowers MB: Psychosis precipitated by psychotomimetic drugs. Arch Gen Psychiatry 34:832–835, 1977

Breier A, Astrachan BM: Characterization of schizophrenic patients who commit suicide. Am J Psychiatry 141:206–209, 1984

Buda M, Tsuang MJ, Fleming JA: Causes of death in DSM-III schizophrenics and other psychotics (atypical group). Arch Gen Psychiatry 45:283–285, 1988

Carpenter WT, Heinrichs DW, Alphs ID: Treatment of negative symptoms. Schizophr Bull 11:440–452, 1985

Cheung HK: Schizophrenics fully remitted on neuroleptics for 3–5 years: to stop or continue drugs? Br J Psychiatry 138:490–494, 1981

Cohen S, Leonard CV, Farberow AC, et al: Tranquilizers and suicide in schizophrenic patients. Arch Gen Psychiatry 11:312–321, 1964

Cotton PG, Drake RE, Gates G: Critical treatment issues in suicide among schizophrenics. Hosp Community Psychiatry 36:534–536, 1985

Docherty JP, Van Kammen DP, Siris SC, et al: Stages of onset of schizophrenic psychosis. Am J Psychiatry 135:420–426, 1978

Drake R, Cotton PG: Depression, hopelessness and suicide in chronic schizophrenia. Br J Psychiatry 148:554–559, 1986

Drake R, Ehrlich J: Suicide attempts associated with akathisia. Am J Psychiatry 142:499–501, 1985

Drake RE, Wallach MA: Substance abuse among the chronic mentally ill. Hosp Community Psychiatry 40:1041–1046, 1989

Drake R, Gates C, Cotton PC, et al: Suicide among schizophrenics: who is at risk? J Nerv Ment Dis 172:613–617, 1984

Drake R, Gates C, Whitaker A, et al: Suicide among schizophrenics: a review. Compr Psychiatry 26:90–100, 1985

Goldberg TE, Weinberger DR, Berman KF, et al: Further evidence for dementia of the prefrontal type in schizophrenia: a controlled study of teaching the Wisconsin Card Sorting Test. Arch Cen Psychiatry 44:1008–1014, 1987

Harrow M, Silverstein M, Marengo J: Disordered thinking. Arch Gen Psychiatry 40:769–777, 1983

Hawton K, Fagg J: Suicide, and other causes of death, following attempted suicide. Br J Psychiatry 152:359–366, 1988

Heaton R: Wisconsin Card Sorting Test. Odessa, TX, Psychological Assessment Resources, 1985

Herz MI, Melville C: Relapse in schizophrenia. Am J Psychiatry 137:801–805, 1980

Hogan TP, Awad AG: Pharmacotherapy and suicide risk in schizophrenia. Can J Psychiatry 28:277–281, 1983

Irwin DS, Weitxell WD, Morgan DW: Phenothiazine intake and staff attitude. Am J Psychiatry 127:1631–1636, 1971

Katz HM, Frank AF, Gunderson JG, et al: Psychotherapy of schizophrenia: what happens to treatment dropouts? J Nerv Ment Dis 172:326–331, 1984

Kendler KS: A twin study of mortality in schizophrenia and neurosis. Arch Gen Psychiatry 43:643–649, 1986

Koegel P, Bumam A, Farr RK: The prevalence of specific psychiatric disorders among homeless individuals in the inner city of Los Angeles. Arch Gen Psychiatry 45:1085–1092, 1988

Kohut H: Thoughts on narcissism and narcissistic rage. Psychoanal Study Child 27:360–400, 1972

Landmark J, Cernovsky ZZ, Merskey H: Correlates of suicide attempts and ideation in schizophrenia. Br J Psychiatry 151:18–20, 1987

Levy S, Southcombe RH: Suicide in a state hospital for the mentally ill. J Nerv Ment Dis 117:504–514, 1953

Marchaud WE, Sarota B, Marble HC, et al: Occurrence of painless acute surgical disorders in psychotic patients. N Engl J Med 260:580–585, 1959

Marder SR, Swann E, Winslade WJ, et al: A study of medication refusal by involuntary psychiatric patients. Hosp Community Psychiatry 37:724–726, 1984

May PRA: Treatment of Schizophrenia. New York, Science House, 1968

Mezzich JE, Evanczok KJ, Mathias RJ, et al: Symptoms and hospitalizations decisions. Am J Psychiatry 141:764–769, 1984

Miles C: Conditions predisposing to suicide. J Nerv Ment Dis 164:231–246, 1977

Moore RY, Bloom FE: Central catecholamine neuron systems: anatomy and physiology of the dopamine systems. Annu Rev Neurosci 1:129–169, 1978

Ninan P, Van Kammen D, Scheinin M, et al: CSF 5-hydroxyindoleacetic acid levels in suicidal schizophrenic patients. Am J Psychiatry 141:566–569, 1984

Nyman A, Jonsson H: Patterns of self-destructive behavior in schizophrenia. Acta Psychiatr Scand 73(3):252–262, 1986

Planansky K, Johnston R: Clinical setting and motivation in suicide attempts in schizophrenics. Acta Psychiatr Scand 49:680–690, 1973

Roy A: Suicide in chronic schizophrenia. Br J Psychiatry 141:171–177, 1982

Roy A: Depression, attempted suicide, and suicide in patients with chronic schizophrenia. Psychiatr Clin North Am 9:196–206, 1986

Roy A, Ninan P, Mazonson A, et al: CSF monoamine metabolites in chronic schizophrenic patients who attempt suicide. Psychol Med 15:335–340, 1985

Roy A, DeJong J, Linnoila M: Cerebrospinal fluid monoamine metabolites and suicidal hehavior in depressed patients. Arch Gen Psychiatry 46:609–612, 1989

Schneier FR, Siris SG: A review of psychoactive substance use and abuse in schizophrenia: patterns of drug choice. J Nerv Ment Dis 175:641–642, 1987

Segal SP, Watson MA, Goldfinger SM, et al: Civil commitment in the psychiatric emergency room, I: the assessment of dangerousness by emergency room clinicians. II: mental disorder indicators and three dangerousness criteria. III: disposition as a function of mental disorder and dangerousness indicators. Arch Gen Psychiatry 45:748–752, 753–758, 759–763, 1988

Sherer MA, Kumor KM, Cone EJ, et al: Suspiciousness induced by four-hour intravenous infusions of cocaine. Arch Gen Psychiatry 45:673–677, 1988

Siris S, Morgan V, Fagerstrom R, et al: Adjunctive imipramine in the treatment of postpsychotic depression. Arch Gen Psychiatry 44:533–539, 1987

Sullivan HS: Schizophrenia as a Human Process. New York, WW Norton, 1962

Van Putten T, May PRA: "Akinetic depression" in schizophrenia. Arch Gen Psychiatry 35:1101–1107, 1978

Van Putten T, Crumpton E, Yale C: Drug refusal in schizophrenia and the wish to be crazy. Arch Gen Psychiatry 33:1443–1446, 1976

Virkkunen M: Attitude to psychiatric treatment before suicide in schizophrenia and paranoid psychosis. Br J Psychiatry 128:47–49, 1976

Warnes H: Suicide in schizophrenics. Diseases of the Nervous System (Suppl) 29(5):35–40, 1968

Weiden PJ: Akathisia from prochlorperazine. JAMA 253:635 1985

Weiden PJ, Bruun R: Worsening of Tourette's Disorder due to neuroleptic-induced akathisia. Am J Psychiatry 144:4, 1987

Weiden PJ, Mann JJ, Haas G, et al: Clinical nonrecognition of neuroleptic-induced movement disorders: a cautionary study. Am J Psychiatry 144:1148–1153, 1987

Weiden PJ, Mann JJ, Dixon L, et al: Is neuroleptic dysphoria a healthy response? Compr Psychiatry 30:546–552, 1989

Weiden PJ, Mann JJ, Shaw E: Causes of neuroleptic noncompliance. Psychiatric Annals 16:571–575, 1986

Weinberger DR: Implications of normal brain development for the pathogenesis of schizophrenia. Arch Gen Psychiatry 44:660–669, 1987

Wilkinson G, Bacon N: A clinical and epidemiological survey of parasuicide and suicide in Edinburgh schizophrenics. Psychol Med 14:899–912, 1984

Yarden PE: Observations on suicide in chronic schizophrenics. Compr Psychiatry 15:325–333, 1974

Chapter 6

Substance Abuse and Suicide

Roger D. Weiss, M.D.
Peggy S. Stephens, M.D.

Alcoholism and drug abuse are the most common psychiatric disorders in the general population (Regier et al. 1984) and are among the leading causes of death in the United States (Vaillant 1983). One of the reasons for this high mortality rate is the elevated incidence of suicide among substance abusers (Frances et al. 1987; Murphy 1988). Investigating the relationship between alcoholism, drug abuse, and suicide is difficult; methodological problems include disagreements over how to define terms such as *substance abuse* and *suicide*. However, it is clear that clinicians are frequently called on to treat patients with suicidal behavior and alcohol or drug abuse. In this chapter, we will therefore review 1) the relationship between substance abuse and suicidal behavior, 2) recognition and assessment of suicidality in the alcohol- or drug-dependent patient, and 3) treatment of the suicidal substance abuser.

Prevalence of Suicide in Substance Abusers

Although studies of patients who are substance abusers have revealed an elevated risk of suicide, estimates of the prevalence rate of suicide among this population are highly variable. Although some authors have cited a suicide rate among substance abusers of up to 15% (Marzuk and Mann 1988; Schuckit 1989), others have estimated a lifetime risk of suicide among alcoholics of only 2–3% (Murphy and Wetzel 1990). The latter estimate nevertheless represents a significantly higher prevalence rate than that found in the general population; the overall risk of completed suicide in the United States is less than 1%. Approximately 15–25% of all suicides are committed by alcoholic patients (Jaffe and Ciraulo 1986; Murphy and Wetzel 1990), and alcohol has been associated with up to 50% of all suicides (Frances et al. 1987; Marzuk and Mann 1988).

Suicide in alcoholics is more common among men and among people who have been drinking heavily for a long time; the mean duration of alcoholic drinking in one study was 20 years (Robins et al. 1959). Although suicide in alcoholics has traditionally been most prevalent in the fifth and sixth decades (Murphy 1986), adolescents and young adults may also be at particular risk for both suicide and substance abuse. Indeed, suicide has been reported to be the second leading cause of death in the 15- to 24-year-old age group (Pfeffer 1988). One study of 27 adolescent suicide victims found that one-third had a blood alcohol level greater than 0.1% (Brent et al. 1988). A psychological autopsy study of completed suicides determined that 70% of the adolescents had drug or alcohol problems (Shafii et al. 1985). Other authors have cited the rising prevalence of substance abuse as a significant contributor to the increasing number of youth suicides (Marzuk and Mann 1988; Murphy 1988).

As disturbing as these statistics are for both adults and adolescents, they are likely underestimations; it is unclear how many injuries or deaths (e.g., the 200,000 annual alcohol-related deaths in the United States) are actually suicide attempts. Some authors have suggested that overdoses, propensity for accidents, needle sharing, risky drug buying practices leading to homicides, and general lack of self-preservation efforts by some substance abusers are actually covert or passive suicidal acts (Frances et al. 1987; Marzuk and Mann 1988). Indeed, one study of fatally injured pedestrians reported that one-third tested positive for alcohol in their blood (Combs-Orme et al. 1983).

The Link Between Substance Abuse and Suicidal Behavior

As shown in Table 6–1, the potential relationships between substance abuse and suicide are multifactorial and interrelated. For example, the depression that so frequently occurs in chemically dependent patients may increase the risk of suicide. However, depression may coexist with substance abuse as a predisposing factor or as a symptom of another disorder (e.g., borderline personality disorder or bulimia nervosa). Moreover, depression may occur as a sequela of a substance use disorder for a number of reasons, including a direct toxic drug effect, a reaction to

Table 6–1. Links between substance abuse and suicidality

Depression
Other comorbid psychiatric disorders
Poor medication compliance (medical and/or psychiatric)
Poor judgment, aggressiveness, impulsiveness, and disinhibition during acute or chronic intoxication or withdrawal
Personal and psychosocial losses, including social supports, home, job, health, and finances

interpersonal loss, or a response to comorbid medical problems (Jaffe and Ciraulo 1986).

Despite the fact that it may frequently be difficult to separate the links between substance abuse and suicidality into discrete categories, we will attempt to outline some of the ways in which substance abuse may predispose an individual to suicidal behavior.

Depression

It is well known that depression increases the risk of suicide; studies of suicide cases have revealed depression rates of 30% and above (Sainsbury 1986). Moreover, the coexistence of a substance use disorder and depression increases the risk of suicide even further (Fowler et al. 1980). The widespread prevalence of depressive symptoms in chemically dependent patients has been well documented, with up to 98% of newly admitted alcoholics reporting some depressive symptomatology (Keeler et al. 1979). As Jaffe and Ciraulo (1986) have noted, the presence of depressive symptoms in alcoholics can have numerous etiologies, including the direct toxic effects of alcohol, impaired hepatic function, poor nutrition, withdrawal symptoms, head trauma, losses, coexisting character pathology, and affective illness. Chemically dependent patients (in particular, intravenous drug users) are also at risk to exhibit depressive symptoms as a result of human immunodeficiency virus infection (Holland and Tross 1985).

The frequent coexistence of substance abuse and depression has led a number of researchers to try to understand the relationship between these two disorders. Schuckit (1985), for example, distinguished between primary and secondary depression according to the age of onset of the two disorders. In his studies of alcoholics, he found that although primary depression was relatively uncommon (3–10%), a substantial number of alcoholics experienced secondary depression during the course of their alcoholism. Other studies of alcoholics have shown higher rates of major depression, with women more likely to suffer from depression prior to the onset of their alcoholism and men more likely to experience alcoholism first (Hesselbrock et al. 1985).

Studies of cocaine abusers have estimated that approximately 10–30% of this population suffers from major depression, although the overall prevalence rate of affective illness in this group appears to have declined somewhat recently (Gawin and Kleber 1986; Weiss et al. 1988). A similar prevalence rate of current major depression has been found in studies of opioid addicts; lifetime studies of the latter group have revealed that more than half of opioid addicts in treatment have experienced major depression (Khantzian and Treece 1985; Rounsaville and Kleber 1986).

Research on community populations of substance abusers has shown a lower incidence of comorbid depression than was found in the studies of treatment populations mentioned above. Analysis of the Epidemiologic Catchment Area study data revealed that nearly half of the alcoholic population suffered from another psychiatric disorder, most commonly antisocial personality disorder, drug abuse, or mania. Major depression and dysthymia, however, were not as strongly associated with alcoholism as expected (Helzer and Pryzbeck 1988). Alcoholics with coexisting depression may be more likely to enter treatment, thus explaining the higher prevalence rates reported in clinical studies.

A study comparing untreated opioid addicts in the community with opioid addicts seeking treatment showed a significantly higher level of depressive symptoms and major depression in the latter group (Rounsaville and Kleber 1985). These results indicate that the presence of depressive symptoms in substance abusers may be an important precipitant for seeking treatment, thus highlighting their clinical importance.

Other Comorbid Psychiatric Disorders

In the past several years, there has been a great deal of research interest in the relationship between substance abuse and psychopathology. One of the major reasons for this increased interest is the accumulating evidence that diagnosis and treatment of coexisting psychiatric illness in a chemically dependent patient can also improve the prognosis of the substance use disorder (Gawin and Kleber 1984; Kofoed et al. 1986; Weiss et al. 1985). Although a great deal of attention has been focused on depressive illness in substance abusers, a number of other psychiatric disorders frequently coexist with substance abuse and may increase the likelihood of suicidal behavior. Anxiety disorders, bipolar disorder, schizophrenia, and disorders of impulse control have all been found more frequently in substance abusers than would be expected in the general population (Allen and Frances 1986).

In addition to the high prevalence rate of DSM-III-R (American Psychiatric Association 1987) Axis I disorders in this population, several studies have shown a link between substance abuse and personality disorders. Antisocial personality disorder has been shown to be the most prevalent Axis II disorder in this population, with borderline, narcissistic, and histrionic personality disorders also being relatively common (Hesselbrock et al. 1985; Khantzian and Treece 1985; Weiss et al. 1986).

Antisocial personality disorder alone carries a significant risk for suicidal behavior, since individuals with this disorder experience severe mood swings, irritability, aggressiveness, and impulsiveness, particularly in the context of loss (Cadoret et al. 1984; Khantzian 1985; Schuckit 1983). Patients with borderline, narcissistic, and histrionic personality disorders may also have an increased rate of suicide because of their propensity to exhibit labile mood, erratic behavior, and depressive symptoms.

Poor Medication Compliance

One major problem that clinicians encounter in treating patients who have substance abuse problems as well as psychiatric illness is the fact that these patients typically exhibit poor compliance with their medication regimens (Drake et al. 1989). Possible reasons for this include confusion, poor memory, denial of their psychiatric illness (perhaps in addition to denial of their chemical dependency), altered metabolism of their medication as the result of substance use, impulsiveness, or poor self-care. Failure to treat the comorbid disorder adequately may exacerbate overall psychiatric symptoms and thus increase the likelihood of suicidal behavior. Since suicide risk has been found to correlate with the overall level of psychopathology (regardless of the specific nature of the particular disorder), poor medication compliance increases that risk.

Results of Acute Intoxication

In addition to the long-term adverse sequelae that frequently occur in substance abusers, the acute effects of many of the drugs of abuse may increase the risk of suicidal behavior. For example, acute intoxication with alcohol or stimulant drugs can increase aggressiveness, impair judgment, and lead to disinhibited impulsive behavior. The frequent association between alcohol use and criminal behavior may, in part, be related to these factors (Brain 1986). Since suicide has been described by some as an aggressive act against the self (Buie and Maltsberger 1989), use of a drug that increases aggression may facilitate the transition from ideation to action. Acute withdrawal syndromes may also be associated with depression and desperation about being unable to attain abstinence, both of which may increase suicide risk. Withdrawal from stimulants in particular has been linked with potentially serious levels of depression (Gawin and Kleber 1986).

Acute intoxication is likely a major factor in a number of deaths that could alternately be considered accidents, passive suicide attempts, or semi-intentional suicidal acts. Examples of this phenomenon include motor vehicle accidents that occur while the driver is intoxicated (particularly single car accidents), and the aforementioned finding that a high percentage of pedestrians killed in traffic accidents had been drinking (Combs-Orme et al. 1983). Interestingly, a substantial percentage of homicide victims also test positive for alcohol in their blood (Evans 1986). Although there are numerous potential explanations for this, it is likely that a subpopulation of this group may engage in high-risk activities while intoxicated, thus increasing the likelihood of a lethal outcome.

A more recent risk engendered by substance abusers is the engagement in either needle-sharing behavior or risky sexual practices while intoxicated, both of which increase the likelihood of contracting human immunodeficiency virus infection. Although these behaviors probably represent active or even passive suicidal acts only in a small minority of individuals, it is likely that a sense of desperation and hopelessness could increase the potential for this high-risk behavior.

Drug overdoses may also sometimes be classified as "accidental" suicidal behavior. For example, when it becomes known in the illicit-drug-using community that a particular individual has died from a heroin overdose, a certain subpopulation of heroin addicts will make great efforts to seek out heroin from the same supply that caused the lethal overdose. As one such patient said, "You figure the stuff is either going to give you an unbelievable high or it's going to put you under. You hope for the high, but if it doesn't work out, it doesn't work out." This type of fatalistic thinking, unfortunately quite common among certain drug addicts, can obviously increase the mortality rate. Although such a death would not generally be considered an active suicide attempt, it represents a form of desperate, high-risk behavior.

Loss

It is well known that alcoholics and drug-dependent patients experience numerous losses: physical health, vocational functioning, financial status, psychological well-being, and memory are some of the more commonly affected areas in the substance abuser's life. Studies of alcoholics and drug abusers who commit suicide have shown that interpersonal loss may exert a very powerful influence on suicidal behavior (Murphy and Robins 1967; Rich et al. 1988). One study (Murphy and Robins 1967) of 134 consecutive urban suicides revealed that half of the individuals who were also alcoholic had experienced a loss of a close interpersonal relationship within a year prior to the suicide. In contrast, less than 20% of the patients with depressive illness who committed suicide had experienced an analogous loss. Even more striking is the fact that one-third of the alcoholics who committed suicide had experienced the disruption of an important interpersonal relationship within 6 weeks of their death. Similar results have been found in studies of drug-dependent individuals (Rich et al. 1988). Thus the role of interpersonal loss may be critical in precipitating suicidal behavior in this population.

Is There a High-Risk Profile for the Suicidal Substance Abuser?

As described above, a recent history of interpersonal loss places the chemically dependent individual at increased risk for suicide. Galanter and Castaneda (1985) listed several other risk factors for suicide in alcoholics. According to their research, white males between ages 45 and 65 are at higher risk, with acute intoxication and recent loss of socioeconomic status or occupational role also contributing to that risk. Suicide in drug addicts tends to occur at a younger age, with many taking place in the third and fourth decades. It is unclear to what extent this difference is merely due to the general younger age of drug abusers, or whether other factors are involved as well.

Evaluation of Suicide Risk in Substance Abusers

Evaluation of suicide risk in substance abusers can be quite difficult, since the manifestations of suicidal behavior may range from a provocative display of suicidal behavior by an intoxicated individual in an emergency room to a series of telephone calls from desperate family members of a rapidly deteriorating alcoholic or addict. As is the case with many psychiatric evaluations, asking the question "Why is this occurring now?" may provide important information. In particular, a history of recent interpersonal loss or conflict, threatened or actual loss of a job, recent physical illness, legal or financial problems, or a recent relapse to substance abuse is particularly relevant. Exploration of the patient's sense of hopelessness and suicidal ideas or plans in response to these events is particularly important, since there is some evidence (albeit controversial) that hopelessness in alcoholics may be a good predictor of later suicidal behavior (Beck et al. 1976, 1989).

A comprehensive drug and alcohol history should be obtained, preferably in collaboration with the patient's family or friends. In addition, the patient should be evaluated for comorbid psychopathology and, in particular, depression. The presence and severity of depressive symptoms should be monitored carefully. The coexistence of substance abuse and depression in the context of a recent loss should be cause for great concern. Although depressive symptoms in the majority of this population will abate within several weeks of achieving abstinence (Brown and Schuckit 1988; Mirin et al. 1984), it is important to remember that even brief periods of depression in the context of active substance abuse can precipitate suicidal behavior. Moreover, some patients continue to experience symptoms of depression and anxiety for months after stopping substance use (Pottenger et al. 1979).

In addition to taking a careful substance abuse and psychiatric history, another important indicator of suicide risk is a past history of suicide attempts (Hirschfeld and Davidson 1988). A positive family history of substance abuse, affective disorder, or suicidal behavior adds further weight to the aforementioned risk factors (Marzuk and Mann 1988). In addition, the clinician should inquire carefully about the availability of the means to attempt suicide. In particular, access to firearms should be determined and dealt with promptly.

Inquiry about the substance abuser's life-style and attitudes can help to evaluate the level of self-care. Obtaining a history of accidents, overdoses, risky drug-buying practices, needle sharing, medical complications, and dwindling efforts to preserve major relationships and personal standards may provide clues of nonverbalized or passive suicidality. Table 6–2 summarizes some of the areas that are helpful to explore in evaluating suicide risk in drug- and alcohol-dependent patients.

Management of the Substance Abuser at Risk for Suicide

In attempting to lower the risk of suicidal behavior in chemically dependent patients, the first priority should be to help the patient to achieve and maintain sobriety. Suicide in substance abusers is far more likely to occur during periods of active use than during recovery (Frances et al. 1987). Thus the best way to reduce the likelihood of suicide, as with many other complications of substance abuse, is to help patients become abstinent.

A discussion of comprehensive substance abuse treatment is beyond the scope of this chapter. However, treatment strategies should be individualized, typically consisting of some combination of individual, group, and family therapy, self-help groups, education about the nature of addiction, attention to vocational issues, and, in some cases, random urine toxicologic screening. Adjunctive pharmacotherapy may be helpful in some chemically dependent patients. One drug commonly used in the treatment of alcoholism, disulfiram, should be used with caution in potentially suicidal individuals (Pary et al. 1988), since ingestion of

Table 6–2. Evaluation of the substance abuser for suicide risk

"Why now?" with particular attention to recent losses
Current and comprehensive drug and alcohol history
Presence and severity of coexisting psychiatric illness
Positive family history of suicide, affective disorder, or substance abuse
Past history of suicide attempts
Availability of means, especially firearms
Poor self-care

alcohol while taking disulfiram can precipitate a severe (and potentially fatal) toxic reaction.

Identification and treatment of comorbid psychiatric disorders, some of which may themselves be associated with a high suicide risk, can help to improve the prognosis of both the substance use disorder and the coexisting illness (Gawin and Kleber 1984; Weiss et al. 1985). Sometimes, however, it can be quite difficult to diagnose a coexisting psychiatric illness (e.g., affective disorder). Although standardized clinical interviews and self-report rating scales have shown some promise as diagnostic screening instruments (Rounsaville et al. 1979; Weiss et al. 1989), repeated interviews are often needed to determine whether patients need more specific treatment for depression. Indeed, it is often necessary to wait for several weeks or more (depending on the specific drug use pattern and the disorder to be diagnosed) before one can convincingly make a diagnosis other than substance abuse. In such cases, thymoleptic treatment of carefully diagnosed substance abusers can be quite helpful.

A major challenge in treating substance abusers with suicidal behavior is determining when to recommend hospitalization. The following clinical situations may warrant at least a brief hospital stay: 1) the presence of several suicidal risk factors, especially recent losses; 2) feelings of hopelessness; 3) acute worsening of the addiction, particularly when accompanied by a lack of self-preservation efforts; and 4) exacerbation of comorbid psychiatric illness.

For those who are hospitalized, the immediate posthospitalization period is the time of highest likelihood of relapse (Gilbert 1988). Thus designing a comprehensive individualized aftercare plan is critical in helping to minimize the risk of relapse. In addition, careful attention should be paid to the patient's previous reactions to relapses. These reactions can precipitate feelings of failure and hopelessness and lead to suicidal thoughts. Marlatt (1982) has described the importance of assisting the patient to reframe "lapses" cognitively into positive learning experiences rather than seeing them as a justification and confirmation of hopeless feelings.

Summary

One of the many potential complications of alcohol and drug abuse is the increased likelihood of suicidal behavior. Although there are many links between chemical dependency and suicide, the most powerful treatment intervention is one that addresses the primary issue of the patient's substance abuse. In patients with dual disorders, a comprehensive approach integrating the treatment of the chemical dependency and the comorbid psychiatric illness is needed to decrease the likelihood of a potentially tragic outcome.

References

Allen MH, Frances RJ: Varieties of psychopathology found in patients with addictive disorders, in Psychopathology and Addictive Disorders. Edited by Meyer RE. New York, Guilford, 1986, pp 17–38

American Psychiatric Association: Diagnostic and Statistical Manual of Mental Disorders, 3rd Edition, Revised. Washington, DC, American Psychiatric Association, 1987

Beck AT, Weissman A, Kovacs M: Alcoholism, hopelessness, and suicidal behavior. J Stud Alcohol 37:66–77, 1976

Beck AT, Steer RA, Trexler LD: Alcohol abuse and eventual suicide: a 5- to 10-year prospective study of alcohol-abusing suicide attempts. J Stud Alcohol 50:202–209, 1989

Brain PF (ed): Alcohol and Aggression. London, Croom Helm, 1986

Brent DA, Perper JA, Goldstein CE, et al: Risk factors for adolescent suicide. Arch Gen Psychiatry 45:581–588, 1988

Brown SA, Schuckit MA: Changes in depression among abstinent alcoholics. J Stud Alcohol 49:412–417, 1988

Buie DH, Maltsberger JT: The psychological vulnerability to suicide, in Suicide: Understanding and Responding. Edited by Jacobs D, Brown HN. Madison, CT, International Universities Press, 1989, pp 59–71

Cadoret R, Troughton E, Widmer R: Clinical differences between antisocial and primary alcoholics. Compr Psychiatry 42:161–167, 1984

Combs-Orme T, Taylor JR, Scott EB, et al: Violent deaths among alcoholics: a descriptive study. J Stud Alcohol 44:938–949, 1983

Drake RE, Osher FC, Wallach MA: Alcohol use and abuse in schizophrenia: a prospective community study. J Nerv Ment Dis 177:408–414, 1989

Evans CM: Alcohol and violence: problems relating to methodology, statistics and causation, in Alcohol and Aggression. Edited by Brain PF. London, Croom Helm, 1986, pp 138–160

Fowler RC, Liskow BI, Tanna VL: Alcoholism, depression, and life events. J Affective Disord 2:127–135, 1980

Frances RJ, Franklin J, Flavin DK: Suicide and alcoholism. Am J Drug Alcohol Abuse 13:327–341, 1987

Galanter H, Castaneda R: Self-destructive behavior in the substance abuser. Psychiatr Clin North Am 8(2):251–261, 1985

Gawin FH, Kleber HD: Cocaine abuse treatment: open pilot trial with desipramine and lithium carbonate. Arch Gen Psychiatry 41:903–909, 1984

Gawin FH, Kleber HD: Abstinence symptomatology and psychiatric diagnosis in cocaine abusers: clinical observations. Arch Gen Psychiatry 43:107–113, 1986

Gilbert FS: The effect of aftercare follow-up on treatment outcome among alcoholics. J Stud Alcohol 49:149–159, 1988

Helzer JE, Pryzbeck TR: The co-occurrence of alcoholism with other psychiatric disorders in the general population and its impact on treatment. J Stud Alcohol 49:219–224, 1988

Hesselbrock MN, Meyer RE, Keener JJ: Psychopathology in hospitalized alcoholics. Arch Gen Psychiatry 42:1050–1055, 1985

Hirschfeld RMA, Davidson L: Clinical risk factors for suicide. Psychiatric Annals 18:628–635, 1988

Holland JC, Tross S: The psychosocial and neuropsychiatric sequelae of the acquired immunodeficiency syndrome and related disorders. Ann Intern Med 103:760–764, 1985

Jaffe JH, Ciraulo DA: Alcoholism and depression, in Psychopathology and Addictive Disorders. Edited by Meyer RE. New York, Guilford, 1986, pp 293–320

Keeler MH, Taylor I, Miller WC: Are all recently detoxified alcoholics depressed? Am J Psychiatry 136:586–588, 1979

Khantzian EJ: The self-medication hypothesis of addictive disorders: focus on heroin and cocaine dependence. Am J Psychiatry 142:1259–1264, 1985

Khantzian EJ, Treece C: DSM-III psychiatric diagnosis of narcotic addicts. Arch Gen Psychiatry 42:1067–1071, 1985

Kofoed L, Kania J, Walsh T, et al: Outpatient treatment of patients with substance abuse and coexisting psychiatric disorders. Am J Psychiatry 143:867–872, 1986

Marlatt GA: Relapse prevention: a self-control program for the treatment of addictive behaviors, in Adherence, Compliance, and Generalization in Behavioral Medicine. Edited by Stuart RB. New York, Brunner/Mazel, 1982, pp 329–378

Marzuk PM, Mann JJ: Suicide and substance abuse. Psychiatric Annals 18:639–645, 1988

Mirin SM, Weiss RD, Sollogub A, et al: Affective illness in substance abusers, in Substance Abuse and Psychopathology. Edited by Mirin SM. Washington, DC, American Psychiatric Press, 1984, pp 58–77

Murphy GE: Suicide in alcoholism, in Suicide. Edited by Roy A. Baltimore, MD, Williams & Wilkins, 1986

Murphy GE: Suicide and substance abuse. Arch Gen Psychiatry 45:593–594, 1988

Murphy GE, Robins E: Social factors in suicide. JAMA 199:303–308, 1967

Murphy GE, Wetzel RD: The lifetime risk of suicide in alcoholism. Arch Gen Psychiatry 47:383–392, 1990

Pary R, Lippman S, Tobias CR: Depression and alcoholism: clinical considerations in management. South Med J 81:1529–1533, 1988

Pfeffer CR: Risk factors associated with youth suicide: a clinical perspective. Psychiatric Annals 18:652–656, 1988

Pottenger M, McKernon J, Patrie LE, et al: The frequency and persistence of depressive symptoms in the alcohol abuser. J Nerv Ment Dis 166:562–569, 1979

Regier DA, Myers JK, Kramer M, et al: The NIMH epidemiologic catchment area program: historical context, major objectives, and study population characteristics. Arch Gen Psychiatry 41:934–941, 1984

Rich CL, Fowler RC, Fogarty LA, et al: San Diego suicide study, III: relationships between diagnoses and stressors. Arch Gen Psychiatry 45:589–592, 1988

Robins E, Murphy GE, Wilkinson RH, et al: Some clinical considerations in the prevention of suicide based on a study of 134 successful suicides. Am J Public Health 49:888–899, 1959

Rounsaville BJ, Kleber HD: Untreated opiate addicts. Arch Gen Psychiatry 42:1072–1077, 1985

Rounsaville BJ, Kleber HD: Psychiatric disorders in opiate addicts: preliminary findings on the course and interaction with program type, in Psychopathology and Addictive Disorders. Edited by Meyer R. New York, Guilford, 1986, pp 140–168

Rounsaville BJ, Weissman MM, Rosenberger PH, et al: Detecting depressive disorders in drug abusers: a comparison of screening instruments. J Affective Disord 1:255–267, 1979

Sainsbury P: The epidemiology of suicide, in Suicide. Edited by Roy A. Baltimore, MD, Williams & Wilkins, 1986, pp 17–40

Schuckit MA: Alcoholic patients with secondary depression. Am J Psychiatry 140:711–714, 1983

Schuckit MA: The clinical implications of primary diagnostic groups among alcoholics. Arch Gen Psychiatry 42:1043–1049, 1985

Schuckit MA: Suicidal behavior and substance abuse. Drug Abuse and Alcoholism Newsletter 18:8, 1989

Shafii M, Carrigan S, Whittinghill JR, et al: Psychological autopsy of completed suicide in children and adolescents. Am J Psychiatry 142:1061–1067, 1985

Vaillant GE (ed): The Natural History of Alcoholism. Cambridge, MA, Harvard University Press, 1983

Weiss RD, Pope HG Jr, Mirin SM: Treatment of chronic cocaine abuse and attention deficit disorder, residual type, with magnesium pemoline. Drug Alcohol Depend 15:69–72, 1985

Weiss RD, Mirin SM, Michael JL, et al: Psychopathology in chronic cocaine abusers. Am J Drug Alcohol Abuse 12:17–29, 1986

Weiss RD, Mirin SM, Griffin ML, et al: Psychopathology in cocaine abusers: changing trends. J Nerv Ment Dis 176:719–725, 1988

Weiss RD, Griffin ML, Mirin SM: Diagnosing major depression in cocaine abusers: the use of depression rating scales. Psychiatry Res 28:335–343, 1989

Chapter 7

Evaluating and Treating Suicidal Behavior in the Borderline Patient

Douglas Jacobs, M.D.

Freud (1926), who actually wrote very little about suicide, had this to say about a suicidal case: "What weighs on me in this case is my belief that unless the outcome is very good it will be very bad indeed. What I mean is that he would commit suicide without any hesitation. I will, therefore, do all in my power to avert that eventuality." This statement has particular relevance for the work with the suicidal borderline patient and is exemplified in the following case example:

> A 41-year-old female, never married, with a long history of suicidal preoccupation and several episodes of overt behavior had been in treatment for 11 years. She was sexually abused by her father and uncle and alienated from her mother, a depressed alcoholic. This patient had been contemplating suicide since the age of 8, when she made her first suicide attempt by putting her head in a plastic bag. She initially sought psychiatric help following the death of her father. The first 5 years of treatment dealt with mounting waves of self-hate and persistent suicidal ideation. She had easy access to medication and medical paraphernalia through her job. During this phase of treatment, her psychiatrist collected from the patient more than 1,000 pills, several bottles of saline, iv tubing, and ampules of diazepam. Nevertheless, the patient always stated that she had a secret method for suicide that she considered as her last hope. Over 6 years, with a combination of psychotherapy, pharmacotherapy (including the recent use of fluoxetine), and four inpatient hospitalizations, her chronic depression and self-hate had been alleviated and her sexual abuse addressed, ending her accumulation of pills. Despite this progress, she held on to her secret method until one vacation, when a dramatic event occurred. Prior to her doctor's vacation, the patient developed septic arthritis.

She refused to be hospitalized (medically), which was the recommendation of her internist. Although her psychiatrist was away, he contacted her and convinced her to go to an emergency room on a daily basis and get the necessary treatment (e.g. iv antibiotics), which she did. Her septic arthritis was treated successfully. When her psychiatrist returned from vacation, she thanked him and surprised him with a gift, her secret method, succinyl choline.

Borderline patients present clinicians with a multitude of issues, like the patient described above, such as developmental issues, depression, abuse, self-destruction, and hopelessness (Perry 1989). How do we organize our assessment of suicide in a patient population for which suicide and suicidal behavior is significant (Friedman et al. 1983; Fyer et al. 1988; Gardner and Cowdry 1985)?

I propose a tripartite model of assessment of suicide in the borderline patient (Figure 7–1). This model integrates three general areas that need to be analyzed to assess objectively the potential for suicide in the borderline patient. Blumenthal and Kupfer (1986) proposed an overlapping model with five domains that offer generalizable treatment strategies for suicidal behavior. I have adapted their model to the borderline patient in a way I believe is more specific to this population. This model focuses on three areas: 1) borderline psychopathology—the specific dynamics, characteristics, and psychopathology of the borderline patient that places the person at risk for suicide; 2) coexistence of psychiatric disorders to identify the specific relationship to, or overlap with, other major psychiatric disorders that may increase the risk of suicide (e.g., depressive disorders and substance abuse); and 3) suicide perspective, which consists of three interrelated components (i.e., objectification of suicidal intent and behavior, identification of specific psychological commonalities of suicide, and determination of psychodynamic formulation).

Borderline Psychopathology

The first segment of the tripartite model involves the psychopathology of the borderline patient. It is documented in the literature that the borderline patient represents a heterogeneous population (Gunderson 1984). However, there are specific psychopathologic risk factors of the borderline personality that place the person at high risk for suicide (Kernberg

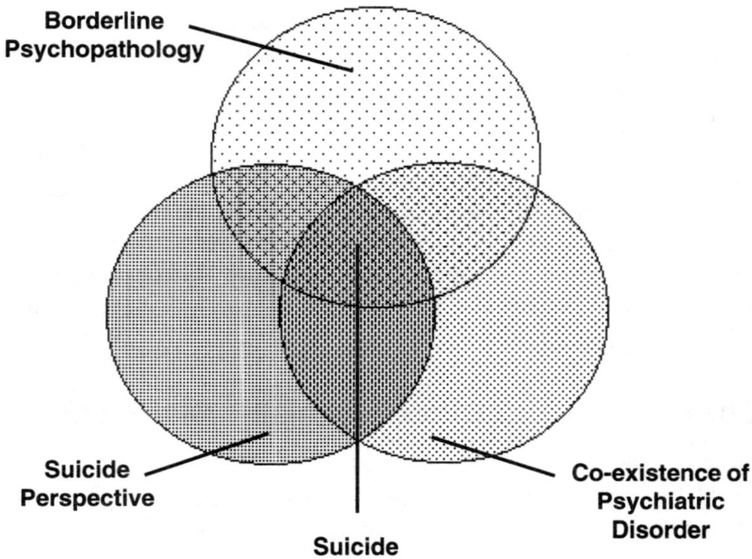

Figure 7–1. Tripartite model.-suicide assessment in the borderline patient

1984). They include impulsivity; hopelessness-despair; antisocial features (with dishonesty); interpersonal aloofness or "malignant narcissism"; self-mutilating tendencies emerging during the course of treatment, which may represent a negative therapeutic reaction; and psychosis with bizarre suicide attempts.

It is the combination of these risk factors that are particularly relevant for the clinician to note in the patient. In particular, when there is the combination of impulsivity and hopelessness, the likelihood of a patient acting on the despairing state is increased. An interesting and complicating aspect of borderline psychopathology is the propensity for wrist cutting. Himmelhoch (1988) offered an interesting thesis about the concept of threshold. He suggested that wrist cutting, when it occurs in the context of depersonalization, serves as a protective mechanism for the patient reestablishing contact. Furthermore, he stated that "a suicidal denouement seems dependent upon the ineffectiveness of wrist cutting and reestablishing contact for such patients, who often descriptively fit Gunderson and Singer's criteria for borderline syndrome" (p. 48). When treating periods of psychosis, the clinician should be aware of the vulnerability for suicide in borderline patients, which can occur as they are clinically improving and are discharged prematurely.

Clinical experience teaches us that there are aspects of the borderline personality that are associated with diminished risk, particularly those of clinging, dependency, and the use of suicidal behavior as a way to maintain connections. Patients of this type include the masochistic personality and the infantile personality with hysterical features, who displays honesty about his or her suicidal ideation. This observation has been verified by Kaplan and Klein (1989) in their work on the relationship between gender and suicide.

Coexistence With Other Psychiatric Disorders

There are four DSM-III-R (American Psychiatric Association 1987) Axis I disorders that should be considered in an evaluation of the borderline patient: affective illness, substance abuse (primarily alcoholism), eating disorders, and posttraumatic stress disorder. The clinician must carefully evaluate affective symptomatology in the borderline patient to rule out the possibility of major affective illness (Gunderson and Elliott 1985). However, a question emerges—does the coexistence of major affective illness increase the incidence of suicide? The evidence is inconclusive (Table 7–1).

In the Stone and colleagues (1987) study, in which there were 19 suicides in the 250 patients studied, there was not found to be an overrepresentation of depressive illness in the suicide group. Other studies found an overlap with depression of 40–60%, but also no overrepresentation of suicide (Akiskal et al. 1985; McGlashan and Heinssen 1988; Pope 1983). In 25% of the suicides of the Stone study, however, there was a concurrence of major affective illness, drug abuse and alcoholism, incest, chaotic family life, and impulsivity. This significant observation emphasizes the point that it is the combination and interplay of forces that lead to suicide.

It is interesting to note that Stone and colleagues (1987) cited the occurrence of incest given the recent work that has found an increased incidence of childhood trauma in patients with borderline personality disorder (Herman et al. 1989). This is why posttraumatic stress disorder has been included in this section. Herman and colleagues investigated 30 patients with borderline personality disorder and/or traits and found more

Table 7–1. Studies of completed suicide in borderline patients

Study	Length of follow-up	Number of patients	Incidence of suicide (%)
Stone et al. 1987 (Cornell)	16 years	250	8
Akiskal et al. 1985 (University of Tennessee)	6 months–3 years	100	4
Pope 1983 (McLean Hospital)	4–7 years	33	7
McGlashan and Heinssen 1988 (Chestnut Lodge)	15 years	94	3

than 75% had significant childhood trauma. However, these patients did not manifest symptoms of posttraumatic stress disorder and, in fact, were found to have accommodated to the abuse to the point where it was felt to be ego-syntonic.

The implications of these observations for their relationship to suicide and suicidal behavior are several. First, it has been hypothesized that when these patients are reexposed to trauma, there may be a release of endogenous endorphins (van der Kolk 1987). Although this is a preliminary hypothesis that needs to be validated by further data, it may explain the calm that is reported during repeated cutting episodes. This idea might well strengthen Himmelhoch's (1988) notion of a threshold concept. Second, chronic stress adversely affects the neurotransmitter system (Rubinstein 1986). One might speculate as to how this alteration impacts the documented observation that low levels of 5-hydroxyindoleacetic acid are found in suicide victims and those who make violent suicide attempts (Åsberg et al. 1976). Third, clinical experience suggests that in a subgroup of borderline patients, self-destructive behavior may progress from less lethal self-destructive acts (perhaps during early phases of reexposure to trauma), to increasingly life-threatening suicide attempts (as the stress becomes chronic). Although the biochemistry needs to be understood further, the importance of inquiring about childhood trauma and the necessity and importance of early intervention are clear.

There is equivocal evidence regarding the association of suicide with eating disorders. Stone found a diminished risk, while Shearer and colleagues (1988), in their study of 40 female borderline patients, noted an increased association. The Shearer study, however, focused on near-lethal attempts and not completed suicides. The hypothesis that there is an increased incidence of suicide in patients that have eating disorders is questionable because they did not have any completed suicides. However, what one can extract from this study is that the occurrence of a near-lethal attempt should alert the clinician to the possibility of a coexisting Axis I disorder, such as a major affective illness or an eating disorder, and the patient should be treated accordingly.

Suicide Perspective

The suicide perspective contains three subcomponents: 1) to objectify suicidal intent and behavior, 2) to identify specific psychological commonalities of suicide, and 3) to determine the psychodynamic formulation. It is this component of the tripartite model that allows the clinician specifically and objectively to assess suicidal intent.

Objectify Suicidal Intent and Behavior

The official classification of suicidal behavior contains three elements: suicidal ideation, suicide attempts, and completed suicide. It is well known that the occurrence of suicidal behavior in the borderline patient is significant. For example, more than 80% of hospitalized patients with borderline personality disorder will make a suicide attempt at some point during their treatment (Gunderson 1984). A survey from the epidemiologic catchment area study revealed that more than 50% of depressed patients have suicidal ideation, with close to 20% making attempts at some point during their treatment (Moscicki et al. 1988). Since both ideation and attempts are frequent occurrences, how do we further refine our assessment of these phenomena to help determine suicidal risk?

An objective approach is to measure the intent and lethality, which relate to how serious the patient is about ending his or her life (Beck

1979). Although it has been reported that low suicide intent may not always correlate with lethality, the presence of high suicide intent can serve as a useful dispositional guideline (Beck et al. 1975).

How do we measure suicide intent? The clinician needs to 1) determine the persistence of and ability to control suicidal thoughts and the reasons for living and dying; 2) determine the deterrents to carrying out the act, such as the impact of family (e.g., children under age 18) (Fawcett et al. 1987); 3) distinguish between active suicidal thoughts, which are volitional or deliberate, from passive suicidal thoughts, which are experienced as compulsive-automatic or intrusive (Ringel 1976); and 4) determine the degree of planning that has occurred. When assessing the existence of a suicide plan, it is important for the clinician to inquire not just about the method, but to inquire about the details, which include the method, place, time, available means, and risk-rescue issues (Weissman and Warden 1972).

The determination of suicidal intent has both clinical and legal ramifications, as well as serving as a guide to standardizing methods of communication between clinicians who must further determine the lethality of the contemplated act. The lethality is determined by an objective assessment of the danger to life from a medical-biological perspective. Clinicians should assess in an objective manner the intent and lethality of the suicidal behavior as opposed to the more subjective and sometimes misleading characterization of suicidal behavior as gestures and/or manipulations. A word of caution is needed here because despite our efforts to assess intent and lethality objectively, it should always be remembered that in a subgroup of patients there can be a rapid development of high intent and lethality.

Identify Specific Psychological Commonalities of Suicide

Psychologist Ed Shneidman (1985) summarized his three decades of work in the area of suicide by identifying 10 commonalities of suicide:

1. The common purpose is to seek a solution.
2. The common goal is cessation of consciousness.
3. The common stimulus is intolerable psychological pain.
4. The common stressor is frustrated psychological needs.
5. The common emotion is hopelessness-helplessness.

6. The common internal attitude is ambivalence.
7. The common cognitive state is constriction.
8. The common action is egression.
9. The common interpersonal act is communication of intention.
10. The common consistency is with lifelong coping patterns.

I believe that five of these factors have particular relevance for the borderline patient: intolerable psychological pain, hopelessness-helplessness, ambivalence, constriction, and egression. The intolerable psychological pain is experienced in the borderline patient as emptiness, panic, or shame. Repeated studies have demonstrated that hopelessness is correlated more with suicide than depression (Beck et al. 1985; Fawcett 1988). Ambivalence is particularly prevalent in the borderline patient and is manifested in the well-known psychological phenomenon of splitting. Thought constriction refers to dyadic thinking, black or white, either/or, and manifests itself as a lack of perceived options, which again is unfortunately quite common in borderline patients. The last notion of egression focuses on the borderline patient's propensity for action. When existing together, these factors heighten the likelihood of a lethal outcome and should be used by a clinician to guide appropriate intervention.

Determine Psychodynamic Formulation

There are three aspects of a psychodynamic formulation. These include 1) the vulnerability to painful affects; 2) the motivational aspects of suicide; and 3) the meanings of suicide and the relationship to death, which help us objectify why, when, and under what conditions a borderline patient may be more at risk for suicide.

The psychodynamic features of the borderline patient include an inner sense of badness, poor ego control, and fear of being alone (Gunderson 1984). These features contribute to one of the cardinal vulnerabilities in the suicide-prone individual: the lack of affect regulation. Maltsberger (1986) referred to three central affects that are found in suicide-vulnerable individuals: aloneness, self-contempt, and murderous rage. I add a fourth: shame-panic.

Patients who experience these affects will attempt to use external resources to ward off these feelings. This may work for a while. These resources include significant others, work, the body, and even pets. The risk of suicide will be increased when there is a loss of these resources or an inability to use them.

The seminal work of Menninger (1938) identified three motives for suicide: 1) to kill, aggress; 2) to be killed, guilt; and 3) to die, escape. The importance of distinguishing among these motives may be critical in assessing the risk of completion. In studies of suicide, 75% of completed suicides belong in the escape category, whereas 25% belong in the aggressive category (Maris 1981).

The psychodynamic meaning of suicide, which includes rebirth, reunion, and identification, are discussed in Chapter 3 (Dulit and Michels, this volume). However, the specific meaning of death is often a neglected part of the evaluation. How a patient views death may alert the clinician to the patient's lethality.

As death takes on a more positive and peaceful meaning, the prospect of suicide is near. The tortured life and suicide of Sylvia Plath is an example of this (McCullough and Hughes 1982).

Treatment Strategies

The treatment of the suicidal borderline patient requires a tripartite assessment, a flexibility and creativity regarding treatment decisions, a special attention to the patient-therapist relationship vis-à-vis suicide and borderline dynamics, rational use of pharmacotherapy, an application of the technique of empathy, a consideration of the value and limitations of contracts, and a strategy to approach chronic suicidal behavior.

Hospitalization

In the absence of a strong therapeutic relationship, patients who engage in suicidal behavior should be hospitalized. Hospitalization may allow for the development of a long-term relationship and an assessment of the therapeutic alliance. There are times when suicidal behavior develops secondary to treatment. This may signify a transference problem and the possibility of a "negative therapeutic reaction" (Kernberg 1984) and deserves outside consultation or hospitalization to flesh out the issues.

Pharmacotherapy

It is well known that borderline patients comprise a heterogeneous population. Therefore, patients suffer from affective symptomatology, anxiety, and even psychotic symptoms. Therefore, a variety of psychotropic agents have been found to be useful (Cowdry and Gardner 1988; Soloff 1981). It is particularly important for the clinician to be aware of recent evidence that shows the relationship of panic disorder and panic symptoms in suicide attempts (Fawcett 1988; Weissman et al. 1989). These observations should inform the clinician to target specific symptoms that can reduce suicidality. A specific issue related to suicide in the borderline patient has to do with the dilemma we face as psychiatrists in prescribing potentially lethal medication to a patient who without that medication will suffer increased symptomatology. Further discussions of this issue occur in Chapter 2 (Goldblatt and Schatzberg, this volume) and Chapter 9 (Gutheil, this volume). The issues to be considered when prescribing medication for the borderline patient have to do with a careful assessment process, including the therapeutic alliance, rather than merely arbitrary limits as to the size of prescriptions. As has been stated previously (Bursztajn et al. 1985), we cannot protect patients from suicide by merely limiting the size of prescriptions.

Empathy

A specific psychological tool in working with the suicidal borderline patient is empathy. Empathy informs the therapeutic approach and can be useful in attacking the problem of despair and anger. The empathic response to anger is to use limit setting as a way to signify caring, not to allow the angry outburst to lower self-esteem further.

How does empathy turn despair around (Jacobs 1989)? The mere act of being with another and listening to and sharing his or her pain can mean acceptance. Mack and Hickler (1981) emphasized the central role that self-worth plays in the development of the suicidal state. Doubting one's value or feeling that one has no value is incompatible with life. Death must follow. A role of the therapist is to convey to the patient that the patient matters. By accepting and understanding the patient, we affirm to the patient that he or she is understandable. In this way, empathy offers validation to someone who may not be feeling valid. Another mechanism is empathic sharing, in which sharing is defined as dividing into portions (i.e., you take some, I take some). This was one of the curative elements in the patient described in the beginning of this chapter. We help the despairing person by momentarily accepting a portion of their miserable state, which reduces the intensity of the affect

(Havens 1972). Empathy also permits a connection to be established and maintained. It is this aspect of empathy that is the most crucial in turning despair around. By maintaining connections with suicidal patients who are on the verge of losing their sense of self, they can find themselves through their ability to find others (Havens 1965, 1967).

Contracts

Contracts should not be structured literally as an antisuicide contract, but rather as a mechanism that encourages open communication between the patient and the doctor. In utilizing a contract with a patient, it is first and foremost important for the psychiatrist to determine that the patient is competent. It is useful when the psychiatrist determines that the patient has the potential for or exhibits a strong working alliance. In negotiating the contract, it is important not to eliminate the need to feel suicidal. It acknowledges to the patient that suicide is a serious matter and that the psychiatrist is willing to tolerate dependent behavior. It also highlights the idea of a shared responsibility for communicating suicidal feelings.

However, contraindications do exist for contracts. They should not be used with an agitated, psychotic patient or a highly impulsive patient. A contract is ill advised when there is a coexistence of substance abuse or when suicidal behavior occurs secondary to treatment (i.e., negative therapeutic reaction). The danger here is communicating to already sensitive, rejection-prone patients, the possibility of rejection (Assey 1985; Maltsberger and Buie 1989).

The Use of Consultation

With a borderline patient, a second opinion can be important to help diagnose a negative therapeutic reaction. In addition to minimizing liability, it can provide an objective assessment as to the severity of suicidality (Gutheil 1985).

Countertransference

Unrecognized countertransference reactions can have a destructive impact in the work with suicidal borderline patients. Maltsberger and Buie (1974) outlined the specific countertransference responses elicited in the therapist. The destructive impact comes not from the fact that these countertransference responses occur, but rather from the failure of the therapist to recognize, tolerate, and use the responses in a therapeutic manner. The common countertransference responses include reaction formation, projection, and the ominous denial of countertransference hatred, which includes malice and aversion. As Maltsberger and Buie (1989) pointed out, borderline patients may have a greater capacity to tolerate sadistic impulses than therapists. However, it is the aversion, the wanting to withdraw or terminate prematurely that is the most likely to precipitate suicidal action. By failing to acknowledge these countertransference responses, acting out can occur, leading to: 1) unrealistic and untherapeutic limit setting, 2) omnipotence, and 3) premature termination (the most serious), which may be the direct result of unconscious aversion.

Chronic Suicidal Behavior

We know there are patients who are prone to repetitive self-destructive acts. It is important to determine if it has become a way of life (Schwartz 1979). As stated above, in some patients repetitive suicidal acts may be protective against suicide (Himmelhoch 1988). The psychiatrist must be able to diagnose when the behavior is being used for "emotional blackmail" in an effort to get the therapist not only to care, but to assume total responsibility (Bassecu 1965). The therapist's fear of suicide may interfere with what is needed most, which is openness and availability.

In the mid-1960s, Stone and Shein wrote classic papers on the treatment of the seriously suicidal patient (Shein and Stone 1969; Stone 1960; Stone and Shein 1968). Their recommendations still have value for our work today. They emphasized the critical nature of talking openly about suicide and helping to objectify reality and clarify any reality distortions—something that happens in borderline patients and tends to cloud the issues. The issue of clarifying distorted reality has to be counterbalanced by what Les Havens (personal communication, Grand Rounds, Cambridge Hospital, 1983) described as "restoring the perceptual accuracy of our patients." This has particular relevance for patients with a history of abuse, who have the fear that no one will believe them.

Summary

Work with the suicidal borderline patient is demanding, difficult, and at times frightening. Working from a model to help us assess the patient should result in a more informed treatment and the increased likelihood of a successful outcome. By appreciating the borderline psychopathology, the clinician can distinguish those borderline patients who are at high risk for suicide. The relevance of coexisting psychiatric disorders inform the treatment, which helps us decide when a patient may be more at risk for suicide. The specific suicide perspective with its multiple components helps the clinician objectively assess suicide in an in-depth manner. Although suicide as a rare event cannot be predicted nor on a statistical basis prevented, all patients suffering from self-destructive thoughts and impulses can be offered a therapeutic intervention.

References

Akiskal HS, Chen SE, Davis CC, et al: Borderline: an adjective in search of a noun. J Clin Psychiatry 46:41–48, 1985

American Psychiatric Association: Diagnostic and Statistical Manual of Mental Disorders, 3rd Edition, Revised. Washington, DC, American Psychiatric Association, 1987

Åsberg M, Träskman L, Thorén P: 5-HIAA in the cerebrospinal fluid: a biochemical suicide predictor? Arch Gen Psychiatry 33:1193–1197, 1976

Assey JL: The suicide prevention contract. Perspect Psychiatr Care 23:99–103, 1985

Bassecu S: The threat of suicide in psychotherapy. Am J Psychother 19:99–105, 1965

Beck AT: Assessment of suicidal intention: the scale for suicidal ideation. J Consult Clin Psychol 47:343–352, 1979

Beck AT, Beck R, Covaks M: Classification of suicidal behaviors, I: quantifying intent and medical lethality. Am J Psychiatry 132:285–287, 1975

Beck AT, Steer RA, Kovacs M, et al: Hopelessness and eventual suicide: a ten year study of patients hospitalized with suicidal ideation. Am J Psychiatry 142:90–95, 1985

Blumenthal ST, Kupfer DF: Generalized treatment strategies for suicidal behavior. Annals N Y Acad Sci 487:327–340, 1986

Bursztajn H, Gutheil TG, Brodsky A, et al: "Magical thinking," suicide, and malpractice litigation. Bull Am Acad Psychiatry Law 16:369–377, 1985

Cowdry RW, Gardner DL: Pharmacotherapy of borderline personality disorder. Arch Gen Psychiatry 45:111–119, 1988

Fawcett J: Predictors of early suicide: identification and appropriate intervention. J Clin Psychiatry 49:7–8, 1988

Fawcett J, Scheftner W, Clark D, et al: Clinical predictors of suicide in patients with major affective disorders: a controlled prospective study. Am J Psychiatry 144:35–40, 1987

Friedman RC, Arnoff MS, Clarkin JF, et al: History of suicidal behavior in depressed borderline patients. Am J Psychiatry 140:1023–1026, 1983

Freud S: Psychoanalysis and Faith (1926). New York, Basic Books, 1963, pp 101–102

Fyer MR, Frances AJ, Sullivan T, et al: Suicide attempts in patients with borderline personality disorder. Am J Psychiatry 145:737–739, 1988

Gardner DL, Cowdry RW: Suicidal and parasuicidal behavior in borderline personality disorder. Psychiatr Clin North Am 8:389–404, 1985

Gunderson JG: Borderline Personality Disorder. Washington, DC, American Psychiatric Press, 1984

Gunderson JG, Elliott GR: The interface between borderline personality disorder and affective disorder. Am J Psychiatry 142:277–288, 1985

Gutheil TE: Medicolegal pitfalls in the treatment of borderline patients. Am J Psychiatry 142:9–14, 1985

Havens LL: The anatomy of a suicide. N Engl J Med 272:401–406, 1965

Havens LL: Recognition of suicidal risks through the psychological examination. N Engl J Med 276:210–215, 1967

Havens LL: The development of existential psychiatry. J Nerv Ment Dis 154:309–331, 1972

Herman JL, Perry JC, Van der Kolk BA: Childhood trauma in borderline personality disorder. Am J Psychiatry 146:490–495, 1989

Himmelhoch JM: What destroys our restrains against suicide? J Clin Psychiatry 49:46–52, 1988

Jacobs DC: Psychotherapy with suicidal patients: the empathic method, in Suicide: Understanding and Responding: Harvard Medical School Perspectives. Edited by Jacobs D, Brown HN. Madison, CT, International Universities Press, 1989, pp 329–342

Kaplan AG, Klein PS: Women and suicide, in Suicide: Understanding and Responding: Harvard Medical School Perspectives. Edited by Jacobs D, Brown HN. Madison, CT: International Universities Press, 1989, pp 257–282

Kernberg OF: Clinical management of suicidal potential in borderline patients, in Severe Personality Disorders. New Haven, CT, Yale University Press, 1984, pp 254–263

Mack JE, Hickler H: Yivienne: the Life and Suicide of an Adolescent Girl. Boston, MA, Little, Brown, 1981

Maltsberger JT: Suicide Risk: The Formulation of Clinical Judgement. New York, New York University Press, 1986

Maltsberger JT, Buie DH: Countertransference hate in the treatment of suicidal patients. Arch Gen Psychiatry 30:625–633, 1974

Maltsberger JT, Buie DH: Common errors in the management of suicidal patients, in Suicide: Understanding and Responding: Harvard Medical School Perspectives. Edited by Jacobs D, Brown HN. Madison, CT: International Universities Press, 1989, pp 285–294

Maris RW: Pathways to Suicide: A Survey of Self-Destructive Behaviors. Baltimore, MD, Johns Hopkins University Press, 1981

McCullough F, Hughes T (eds): The Journals of Sylvia Plath. New York, Dial Press, 1982

McGlashan TN, Heinssen RK: Hospital discharge status and long-term outcome for patients with schizophrenia, schizoaffective disorder, borderline personality disorder and unipolar affective disorder. Arch Gen Psychiatry 25:363–368, 1988

Menninger K: Man Against Himself. New York, Harcourt Brace, 1938

Moscicki EK, O'Carroll P, Rae DS, et al: Suicide attempts in the epidemiologic catchment area study. Yale J Biol Med 61:259–268, 1988

Perry JC: Personality disorders, suicide and self-destructive behavior, in Suicide: Understanding and Responding: Harvard Medical School Perspectives. Madison, CT, International Universities Press, 1989, pp 157–169

Pope HG Jr, Jonas JM, Hudson JI, et al: The validity of DSM-III borderline personality disorder: a phenomenologic, family history, treatment response, and long-term follow-up study. Arch Gen Psychiatry 40:23–30, 1983

Ringel E: The presuicidal syndrome. Suicide Life Threat Behav 6:131–145, 1976

Rubenstein DH: A stress-diathesis theory of suicide. Suicide Life Threat Behav 16:100–115, 1986

Schwartz DA: The suicidal character. Psychiatr Q 5:64–70, 1979

Shearer SL, Peters CP, Quaytman MS, et al: Intent and lethality of suicide attempts among female borderline inpatients. Am J Psychiatry 145:1424–1427, 1988

Shein HM, Stone AA: Psychotherapy designed to detect and treat suicidal potential. Am J Psychiatry 125:1247–1251, 1969

Shneidman E: Definition of Suicide. New York, John Wiley, 1985

Soloff PH: Pharmacotherapy of borderline disorders. Compr Psychiatry 22:535–543, 1981

Stone AA: A syndrome of serious suicidal intent. Arch Gen Psychiatry 3:331–339, 1960

Stone AA, Shein HM: Psychotherapy of the hospitalized suicidal patient. Am J Psychother 22:15–25, 1968

Stone MR, Stone DK, Hurt SW: Natural history of borderline patients treated by intensive hospitalization. Psychiatr Clin North Am 10:185–206, 1987

Van der Kolk BA: Psychological Trauma. Washington, DC, American Psychiatric Press, 1987

Weissman AD, Warden W: Risk-rescue rating in suicide assessment. Arch Gen Psychiatry 26:553–560, 1972

Weissman MM, Klerman GL, Markowitz JS, et al: Suicidal ideation and suicide attempts in panic disorder and attacks. N Engl J Med 321:1209–1214, 1989

Chapter 8

Environmental, Educational, and Psychological Interventions in Suicidal Adolescents

Pamela Cantor, Ph.D.

The rate of suicide among adolescents in the United States has increased by 72% in the last 20 years (Curran 1987), making suicide the second leading cause of death among 15- to 24-year-olds (Cantor 1982; Cohen et al. 1988). The United States now has one of the highest rates of suicide for adolescents and young adults in the world, with reports indicating that between 9% and 15% of American high school students have shown suicidal behavior in the past 12 months (Rubenstein et al. 1989). One study, which used an anonymous questionnaire, had even placed this figure as high as 20% (Rubenstein et al. 1989). What is even more disturbing, however, is that 75% of these suicidal high school students received no therapeutic intervention during this time period (Rubenstein et al. 1989).

> Bruce was one of the adolescents who did not receive any intervention and who became a suicide statistic. He came to his high school one morning in November and walked straight to the nurse's office. She asked him how he was feeling, because he had been absent a lot lately. He pushed her aside and asked to use her phone. She tried to talk to him; he ignored her. He dialed a crisis center and told the man who picked up the phone that he had everything under control. Bruce thanked him for listening, but said that he would not be needing to call anymore. He had it all figured out. He hung up the phone as the bell rang and walked to class. As he went down the hall, he tried to gather the kids who would follow him. He said, "Follow me, you do not want to miss this. You do not want to miss the most sensational act of the century. Come with me." He walked into the classroom, opened his

> desk, pulled out a gun, and shot himself. Half the kids ran from the room, the other half stayed to watch. The teacher stood helpless at the front of the classroom. After a few agonizing days in the intensive care unit, Bruce died. (Cantor 1987)

Bruce did not need to die. He needed treatment. Bruce could have benefited from the traditional forms of treatment (e.g., inpatient, outpatient, individual, family, substance abuse, and pharmacologic), and he also could have benefited from educational and environmental interventions. Experts believe that the suicide deaths for adolescents could be reduced by as much as 20% through public education (Holinger 1984) based on studies of the impact of education in the areas of child abuse, discrimination, and drunk driving (Cantor 1989). In this chapter, I will discuss educational and environmental interventions as well as a model for psychological intervention with suicidal adolescents.

Environmental Intervention: Limitation of Availability of Lethal Agents

Since adolescent suicide is often an impulsive act, it has been proposed that limiting access to methods that are commonly used in suicide attempts in the United States could reduce the suicide rate (Cantor 1989). There is some empirical support for this notion from other countries. In Great Britain, for example, the suicide rate by carbon monoxide poisoning declined from 40% to less than 10% when the British converted their home heating method from a highly lethal coke gas to a natural gas of low lethality (Cantor 1989). The overall suicide rate in Great Britain also dropped by 33% as a result of this change, and this low rate remained constant despite the bleak economic picture in Great Britain (Kreitman 1982; Seiden 1983).

In Australia, the placement of restrictions on the quantity of hypnotics also resulted in a substantial decline in the suicide rate in that country between 1960 and 1980 (Oliver and Hetzel 1973). These two studies are significant because they suggest that individuals do not necessarily switch to other highly lethal methods of killing themselves when access to one such method is restricted (Cantor 1989).

Firearms are the most obvious target for restriction in the United States. The recent increase in adolescent suicide in the United States can be accounted for almost entirely by firearms (Boyd 1983). The suicide rate by firearms is increasing more rapidly than the suicide rate by other methods (Brent 1989; Brent et al. 1987; Shaffer and Fisher 1981), and the use of firearms since the 1970s has become the primary method of suicide for younger persons of both sexes (Blumenthal 1988; Brent et al. 1987; Shaffer et al. 1988). According to one study, 65% of all teenage suicides are committed with firearms (Cantor 1985).

Brent (1989) reported that "the suicide rate by firearms is correlated directly with the production, sales, and ownership of guns and inversely with the restrictiveness of gun control laws" (p. 269). This is also supported by Lester and Murrell's (1980) study, which found that the strictness of gun control laws was significantly correlated with the suicide rates in those states (see Boyd 1983), and Brent and colleagues' (1988) study, which found that the homes of suicide victims are still more likely to contain firearms than the homes of hospitalized adolescents who have attempted suicide even after controlling for demographic and diagnostic variables.

Approximately 25 million households in the United States have handguns, and one-half of these owners keep their handguns loaded (Cantor 1985). These firearms are often readily located in the garage or in a cabinet in the den or living room. Browning (1974) found that 83% of all firearm suicides were committed with handguns (see Boyd 1983), and Cantor (1989) reported that approximately 70% of young gun victims could not have obtained their weapons if handgun regulations had been in effect. This is significant; half of these teens—and maybe Bruce—might not have chosen to proceed with another method (Holinger 1984). However, Brent and colleagues (1988) cautioned that "the restriction of accessibility to firearms by altering the method of storage may not be as effective as simply removing all firearms from the home" (p. 587).

While the elimination of handguns clearly would not solve the underlying problems that motivate adolescents to suicide, mandatory safety training and laws that make guns less accessible could result in fewer deaths (Cantor 1985). In fact, one study hypothesized that limiting accessibility to firearms would result in 20% less adolescent suicides (Holinger 1984). The reasoning in this case is similar to that of legislation in states that require drivers to wear seat belts—that is, although seat belts do not make people better drivers, they do improve the chances of surviving a collision.

Alcohol is significantly correlated with suicide by firearms in youth (Brent et al. 1987), and the increase in the suicide rate among adolescents has been hypothesized to be related to an increase in the prevalence of alcohol abuse. Brent (1987) thus advocated the legislation of more effective restrictions on the availability of alcohol and firearms to minors, and Shaffer and colleagues (1988) in fact went so far as to posit that "it would be sensible to deny ownership of firearms to individuals who share a household with a substance abusing or an alcoholic member" (pp. 679–680). Although Shaffer and colleagues' restriction may be difficult to implement, the argument does have some logical validity.

Not only are alcoholic substances readily available to today's adolescents, but so are prescription drugs. Adolescents are known to stockpile medication, gathering painkiller prescriptions from specialists for headaches of mysterious origins or chronic menstrual disorders. They also hoard medications that do not belong to them, and the medicine cabinets of their parents and their friends provide readily available sources. In the United States, 11.3% of young people commit suicide each year by poisoning, usually with prescription medication, making suicide by poisoning the second most common method of suicide among adolescents (Cantor 1989). Being cognizant of the availability of prescription medication to the adolescent is thus important.

Educational Intervention

Awareness of Risk Factors

Treatment can also mean watching for signs of high risk; a number of risk factors have been identified for adolescent suicide. For example, the group at highest risk for teenage suicide are boys who have made a previous suicide attempt or who are depressed (Shaffer et al. 1988). Bruce's death, for example, might have been averted if anyone had noticed that he had bruises on his neck; these may have been indicative of earlier repeated attempts at hanging himself. Or he may have been saved if anyone had paid attention to the fact that he had been absent a great deal and had not been handing in his homework; the inability to concentrate on one's studies is the first sign of depression in younger people (Toolan 1975). He may have lived if anyone had noticed that he had been giving away prized possessions, such as his favorite tapes, or calling a hot line (Cantor 1987).

Although predicting suicide based on the symptoms and clues a young person gives may have its limitations, most of the suicide risk factors are amenable to intervention, and thus "a significant portion of adolescent suicide may be preventable" (Brent et al. 1988, p. 581). However, treatment not only means educating the mental health professional as to the risk of suicide, but also telling the adolescent's family how to protect the young person from harm. To Brent and colleagues (1988), the prevention of adolescent suicide is not only "dependent on the ability to identify populations at high risk," but also on the ability to "offer interventions that modify these risk factors before suicide ensues" (p. 581).

The Dilemma of Diagnosis

The most important factor in treatment planning is reputed to be diagnosis. Practitioners need to know that a young person may be very depressed, yet never mention depression in the doctor's office. As Toolan (1975) wrote, depression is "often masked by acting-out tendencies" in younger people and "the psychiatrist performing such an evaluation must bear in mind that many youngsters will appear more angry than depressed, unlike older patients who usually appear more overtly depressed" (pp. 341–342).

The influence of biology in various diagnostic categories is presently in a state of flux. For example, schizophrenia and bipolar disorder have recently been attributed to biochemical dysfunctions (Roy and Linnoila 1990). Depressive reactions, obsessive-compulsive disorders, and phobias, which traditionally have been considered solely from psychodynamic perspectives, have demonstrated biochemical mediation (Arana and Hyman 1989). Furthermore, current research is investigating biochemical alterations in impulsivity in the borderline and narcissistic patient (Linnoila et al. 1990).

The finding that biochemical markers correlate with suicidal behavior rather than with syndromal diagnoses, such as major depression or borderline personality disorder, suggests that suicidal behavior is a symptom and not a disease entity (Cohen et al. 1988). Suicidal behavior can appear in many diagnostic categories. It is a symptom of alcohol or drug abuse—as 70% of adolescent suicide victims suffer from alcohol or substance abuse problems (see Blumenthal 1988)—as well as anorexia, bulimia, or truancy.

Researchers have also postulated that pharmacologic treatments may eventually be specifically targeted at suicidal behavior rather than at psychiatric diagnoses (Cohen et al. 1988). Thus classifying a young person only by the psychiatric categories of schizophrenia, depression, or borderline can obscure the problem of suicide and impede treatment. The emphasis for patients considering suicide should be dual: primarily on the level of perturbation but also on their psychiatric disorder. As is emphasized by Goodwin and Runck (Chapter 1, this volume) as well as by Shneidman (1990), the father of suicide prevention, there is not always a direct correlation between suicide and diagnostic categories; as Shneidman (personal communication) aptly stated, "I am convinced that that kind of reductionism is not the answer to suicide."

Medication Issues

In treating the suicidal adolescent, there is always the question of whether to use medications to relieve anxiety or depression. Adolescents are prone to hoard medications without the therapist's knowledge, which increases the possibility of overdose. Medications have been found to be useful for youngsters in suicidal states only if they are indicated for a specific underlying disorder. In situations of depression, the benefits must be weighed against the risks. The considerations for prescribing practices outlined by Goldblatt and Schatzberg (Chapter 2, this volume) should be followed with adolescents with the added caveat of their heightened potential for impulsivity.

Hospitalization Issues

Hospitalization is necessary if suicidal adolescents are in danger of harming themselves or others or if their family is not available, not supportive, or disruptive. A period of hospitalization has a number of advantages. It can allow for a period of adjustment to medication and can engage the adolescent in therapy. It can afford the therapist time to evaluate the young person and the family situation before making treatment plans. Furthermore, brief use of a hospital allows the parents a safety net and a respite in their constant vigilance and worry about a suicidal youngster and can assure a young person that the cries for help have been taken seriously and are not dismissed as an attention-getting maneuver.

On the other hand, however, certain hospital stays can also be experienced as depersonalizing and punitive, depending on the unit available and the staff. A difficult situation can arise when an adolescent needs to be hospitalized yet is so frightened that he or she threatens, "I'll commit suicide if you put me in a hospital"—and you are fearful the adolescent will commit suicide if you do not. If the situation seems equivocal, a consultation can help resolve the dilemma. However, if a hospital is not used, an extensive support system must be available. This includes frequent therapy appointments, very frequent phone contact, the cooperation of family and friends, as well as the removal of lethal weapons from the house.

Psychological Intervention: A Proposed Model

Outpatient therapy might take any of the following forms: supportive psychotherapy, insight-oriented therapy, psychoanalytic psychotherapy, family therapy, or group therapy. In my opinion, the most appropriate choice for treatment of suicidal adolescents is supportive psychotherapy, which reinforces defenses and helps control disturbing thoughts and feelings with reassurance, suggestion, persuasion, or empathy, followed by insight-oriented psychotherapy or family therapy. However, as I will reiterate later, the manner in which treatment is conducted is much more important than the specific choice of treatment type.

Supportive Psychotherapy

Supportive psychotherapy has been defined by the American Psychiatric Association (1984) as "a type of psychotherapy that aims to reinforce defenses and help suppress disturbing psychologic material. . . . It avoids probing the patient's emotional conflicts in depth" (p. 129). It may be the most effective initial treatment for any young person who is under stress and has a reduced capacity to cope (Cantor 1990). Thus a therapist uses supportive psychotherapy in response to a young person's dealing with a life crisis or a regressive episode, and it seems to be used most effectively when a youngster is experiencing extreme stress or turmoil or when a person with psychotic potential becomes overtly psychotic. In my view, this approach is particularly applicable as an initial approach with the suicidal adolescent suffering developmental crises or self-esteem or behavioral problems.

The Initial Visit: Establishing Communication

The adolescent's first visit with the therapist must establish enough of a communication to allow the adolescent to want to come again. This is often tough, as many of these kids have "had it" with authority and punitive adults who do not appear to understand. Each therapist develops his or her own technique to accomplish this elusive task, but the principle remains the same. Adolescents are looking for someone they can trust and who will be consistent. They mistrust bureaucracy and tend to be put off by the cold impersonal atmosphere of clinics and intimidated by doctors and the rituals of making appointments and filling out forms. Those who are in helping roles are often seen by young people as too old, too outmoded, too irrelevant, too formal, too inflexible, and too unavailable.

I also invite the adolescent to be present at the first session with the parents so that there is no question of a breach of confidentiality. I have found that most adolescents elect not to be there. The initial session with parents, if possible, should include both parents. Too often therapists either underestimate the importance of fathers or allow them to opt out of participating because of scheduling difficulties. Typically, the mother reports over the phone that the father really is not very involved with the children, or that the father protests about having to see a psychiatrist, and they all agree the mother can give any pertinent information about the child. It is important to note, however, that the mother cannot give all the information, let alone give us a feeling for the father's personality, attitude, or degree of involvement. By excusing the father, the therapist may give tacit permission for the father to absent himself further from his adolescent's life (Cantor 1983).

Difficulties arise when one parent has pressured the other parent or family members into coming into treatment. This intensifies resistance, and typically one or more members of the family refuse to come or will come and drop out, leaving the therapist with the patient and the mother. In training, I was taught if one member of the family cannot come, the session must be canceled. Although this may work in theory, in reality it is impossible. There is rarely one week in one month when one child is not sick or one parent is not out of town.

Family Intervention

Family intervention is used when an adolescent's difficulties reflect ongoing difficulties within the family and is particularly useful when there is identifiable pathology in other members. The focus on family treatment is not on the individual but on the family process, and the goal is to help the family become aware of the underlying emotional configurations that keep them stuck in destructive patterns and to open up the potential for change (Cantor 1990). Adolescents are usually brought to treatment, often unwillingly (Nicholi 1978). Since it is the parents who insist on the treatment, it is the parents who can disrupt treatment at any time. Often an adolescent's parents will disrupt therapy precisely when the adolescent is most involved because they feel threatened and can sabotage therapy when the adolescent most needs help. While this threatened loss or actual break can precipitate a suicide attempt, which gives the parents the chance to say, "I knew your therapist was not doing you any good," alternatively, it can give the therapist a chance to get a renewed commitment from the adolescent and the parents.

If a youngster is living at home, it is extremely important that the parents be involved in the evaluative process. According to Toolan (1975):

> [Many parents] will be angry with their child for such behavior, while others may deny any suicidal intention on the part of their child . . . [and] there are times when some youngsters may be impelled to make suicidal attempts to convince their parents that they are truly unhappy and depressed. (p. 341)

Although clinicians have traditionally been taught that an initial diagnostic session with parents should occur before talking with the adolescent, I believe that it is preferable to see the adolescent first, perhaps even three or four times, and only after a relationship of trust is established should the therapist see the parents. The exceptions are if the therapist decides the adolescent is at risk, in which case the parents must be seen to ensure the safety of the adolescent, or if a decision to hospitalize must be made. Otherwise, seeing the adolescent first greatly increases the chance that the adolescent will view the therapist as an ally and not as an emissary of his or her parents.

Attitude

Regardless of the form of therapy, the attitude of the therapist is critical. The cornerstone of treatment with depressed or anxious adolescents is to be involved, protective, and constant. This requires an approach and a personality that tolerates, and even encourages, the youngster's needs for dependency and attachment. Although some therapists maintain neutrality to ensure appropriate distance as well as to foster the transference, this approach is not always beneficial to a suicidal adolescent. If a non-suicidal adult patient asks where I am going for a vacation, I might turn the question around and reply, "Why do you ask?" I would not, however, do this with a suicidal adolescent, because most adolescents are sensitive to adult nuances and could misinterpret such a response as a rejection. If I need to find out if the adolescent fears abandonment or if I want to know how the adolescent feels about his or her mother or father not being around, all I need to do is ask. Usually, the adolescent will have no difficulty at all in telling me, and what I may gain in my understanding of the patient's dynamics by withholding this vacation information, I gain twice over by disclosing and developing the therapeutic alliance through a trusting relationship.

On the other hand, a therapist's desire to be active may cause the therapist to ask too many questions. In anxiety, one can bombard a suicidal youngster with "When did you do it? How did you do it? Are you going to do it again?" This is counterproductive; it conveys the message that all the therapist is interested in is the "suicidal event" rather than the adolescent, defeats the purpose of exploring the adolescent's actions, and blocks any catharsis. According to Toolan (1975), "Patience is a prime requirement on the part of the therapist" (p. 341), and the treatment of adolescents is difficult because adolescents are "frequently provocative and will often test the therapist's patience and tolerance. . . . They want a close relationship but at the same time are frightened of it, as they fear its loss as they have lost previous relationships" (p. 343). If a therapist asks too many questions in a desire to learn, the therapist will not learn anything.

While traditionally therapists are taught to listen empathically through silence and tears and to keep quiet and be insightful, one must do all of that and more with suicidal adolescents. Therapists must be responsive and give in to the desire to provide solace and let the patient know that the therapist shares and hears the adolescent's pain without blocking the flow of emotion. This can be done, for example, simply by offering tissues. The therapist must also recognize that the patient is confused, embarrassed, or humiliated, and put the patient at ease. The adolescent may be terrified; the doctor may appear to be an awesome stranger who holds the secret to the future with the seeming power to declare sanity versus insanity, to decide whether the adolescent returns to school or goes to a hospital, and to have control over life and death. A simple handshake, which conveys warmth and respect, will often help to alleviate these fears.

I often go beyond this gesture of physical contact and work at making my young patients feel "at home." My office is in my home, and while separate from the living area, I have tried to make it look like a warm oasis filled with green plants and sunshine. Frequently, my patient and I will eat or drink something together. I sit directly across from my patient. There is an attitude of our being in this together, which removes some of the aura of omnipotence and distance.

A key to success to working with suicidal adolescents is to be warm and responsive, without being familiar or effusive. This is a most difficult line to walk. The risk of blurring the boundaries between a professional and a social relationship is often a problem for the therapist of an adolescent patient. I have discovered that the more involved I become in the life of the patient, the more success I have. Therapy with teenagers requires a deep involvement, with perhaps more focus on the relationships in the adolescent's life and less focus on the relationship between therapist and patient. In this sense, therapy with a suicidal adolescent should look more like an insight-oriented therapy, which primarily focuses on the patient's life situation and only secondarily on the therapeutic relationship.

The focus of therapy with the suicidal adolescent is not only on evaluation and treatment, but should go further and involve the therapist in the patient's life. This may seem in opposition to traditional therapeutic neutrality. The therapist of a suicidal adolescent should want to be seen as a friend, an ally in a common struggle, and a source of wisdom. But as with therapeutic neutrality, the therapist should not want the patient to be involved with the therapist's needs. Depending on the personality of the therapist, I see nothing wrong in accepting select invitations to important events in the patient's life, such as graduations, weddings, or school plays.

Many youngsters do see their therapist as a powerful source of wisdom. Otherwise, why would they come? But many suicidal young people want to see their therapists as more than powerful; they want to see them as omnipotent. I tell my patients that as much as I want to help them and be there for them, I cannot read their minds or be immediately available at the precise moment they want me to intervene (Cantor 1983).

In my view, the most important clinical guideline in working with suicidal adolescents is to listen to them and to what is going on around them, without trying to pass judgment on what they say. This is a hard lesson to learn, as a therapist (and as a parent). What is going on is just the suicide event, and the therapist wants to convey an interest in the whole person. It is usually unproductive to ask why the adolescent thought about or attempted suicide. Such questions will be seen as accusations. It is better to ask about the circumstances of the adolescent's life, school, work, family, dates, and friends. The therapist needs to make the adolescent feel comfortable, reach out as an ally, go below the surface issues, and encourage the adolescent's responsibility in the treatment. The therapist wants to avoid embarrassing the adolescent about being brought to a "shrink" or blame the adolescent for having to come or give any excuse to decide that therapy or the therapist is irrelevant to the adolescent's needs or insensitive to his or her problems.

Countertransference Issues

Therapy with an adolescent involves very stormy periods, just as parenting an adolescent does. Therapists (and parents) are building a dependent relationship of trust and caring and then trying to decrease the very dependent relationship they tried so hard to build. The adolescent's intense dependence-autonomy conflicts with parents will be activated in therapy with such strength that the therapist may at times feel that the adolescent is intent on making the therapist feel miserable. Fears of dependency may make it difficult for the young person to express gratitude and may lead to criticism or demanding behavior. At the very least, the adolescent will test the limits by frequently changing and breaking appointments.

All of these behaviors can leave the therapist feeling incompetent and useless. The therapist may feel defensive or hostile toward the adolescent. As Maltsberger and Buie (1989) emphasized, it is important to recognize, tolerate, and use these countertransference responses to avoid countertherapeutic responses on the part of the therapist. Can a therapist show concern, offer support, and get involved in a young person's life if the therapist does not like the youngster in question? Most people have some trait that others do not like, such as aspects of immaturity or defects of character. The careful clinician makes distinctions between symptoms of the patient he or she does not like and the actual person and will try to understand and help the patient. The therapist should not work with the patient if the negative feelings of the therapist are so strong as to interfere with professional objectivity and empathy. Adolescents are sensitive to hypocrisy, and suicidal adolescents, in particular, are convinced that no one really likes them. Working with a therapist who questions how much he or she likes the adolescent can result in further damage to the self-esteem the therapist needs to build.

Course of Treatment

The optimal course of outpatient treatment with the suicidal adolescent is as follows. First, the therapist must establish a warm and caring relationship with the suicidal patient, which both the adolescent and family can accept. Second, the therapist should allow, and even encourage, dependency and regression. Third, the treatment should try to foster emotional growth and self-sufficiency in order to help the youngster become more self-reliant without stirring fears of abandonment. Finally, the therapist must help the adolescent to detach from the therapist and establish a better relationship with parents, siblings, and friends (Cantor 1977).

Thus the therapist is actually asking the adolescent to repeat the developmental tasks of infancy, childhood, adolescence, and young adulthood with the help of a supportive parent-like therapist. No therapist can do this if he or she does not like the patient, nor can the therapist do this if he or she does not get involved. The course the therapist has to maintain between giving in to excessive demands for attention and affection while maintaining an empathic stance to the teenager's despair and anger requires the combined talents of humor, an even disposition, and patience. The therapist's ability to maintain this balance is probably the single most important aspect of treatment and the most crucial predictor of success.

Summary

In conclusion, the intervention strategies that appear to have the greatest impact on youth suicide are the limitation of the availability of firearms, an awareness of specific risk factors and treatment issues, and effective psychological intervention. Our intervention strategies must be supplemented by educating young people to help each other and teaching adults who parent or work with adolescents how to recognize a young person in crisis. Secondary prevention efforts coupled with the limitation of the availability of firearms can help prevent a suicide like that described in the beginning of the chapter.

However, a final word of caution is in order. Working with suicidal patients is a difficult task; working with suicidal adolescents is an even more difficult task. It has been stated that no therapist should handle more than three or four suicidal patients at one time (Motto 1985). In my clinical experience, even that number may be too many.

I have chosen to work with suicidal young people and have been involved in the field of suicidology for more than 20 years. At times, it has been frightening, demanding, and draining. Yet the experience of connecting with a young person who is struggling with whether to continue on with the rest of his or her life and helping the adolescent reach a positive decision makes all the work worth the effort.

References

American Psychiatric Association: A Psychiatric Glossary. Washington, DC, American Psychiatric Association, 1984

Arana GW, Hyman S: Biologic contributions to suicide, in Suicide: Understanding and Responding: Harvard Medical School Perspectives. Edited by Jacobs D, Brown HN. Madison, CT, International Universities Press, 1989, pp 73–86

Blumenthal SJ: A guide to risk factors, assessment, and treatment of suicidal patients. Med Clin North Am 72:937–971, 1988

Boyd JH: The increasing rate of suicide by firearms. N Engl J Med 308:872–874, 1983

Brent DA: Correlates of medical lethality of suicide attempts in children and adolescents. J Am Acad Child Adolesc Psychiatry 26:87–89, 1987

Brent D: Suicide and suicidal behavior in children and adolescents. Pediatr Rev 10:269–275, 1989

Brent DA, Perper JA, Allman CJ: Alcohol, firearms, and suicide among youth: temporal trends in Allegheny County, Pennsylvania, 1960 to 1983. JAMA 257:3369–3372, 1987

Brent DA, Perper JA, Goldstein CE, et al: Risk factors for adolescent suicide: a comparison of adolescent suicide victims with suicidal inpatients. Arch Gen Psychiatry 45:581–588, 1988

Browning CH: Suicide, firearms and public health. Am J Public Health 64:313–317, 1974

Cantor P: Suicide and attempted suicide among students: problem, prediction, and prevention, in Understanding a Child's World: Readings in Infancy Through Adolescence. Edited by Cantor P. New York, McGraw-Hill, 1977, pp 433–443

Cantor P: Suicide and depression, a case study: "too sad to live." in TV and Teens: Experts Look at the Issues. Edited by Schwartz. Reading, MA, Addison-Wesley, 1982, pp 175–186

Cantor P: Depression and suicide in children, in Handbook of Clinical Child Psychology. Edited by Walker CE, Roberts MC. New York, Wiley-Interscience, 1983, pp 741–759

Cantor PC: Testimony before United States Subcommittee on Juvenile Justice. Washington, DC, April 30, 1985

Cantor PC: Young People in Crisis: A film and training program presented by the National Committee on Youth Suicide Prevention, The American Association of Suicidology in consultation with Harvard Medical School, Dept. of Psychiatry, The Cambridge Hospital, 1987

Cantor P: Intervention strategies: environmental risk reduction for youth suicide. Report of the Secretary's Task Force on Youth Suicide, Vol 3: Prevention and Interventions in Youth Suicide (DHHS Publ No ADM-89-1623). Washington, DC, U.S. Government Printing Office, 1989, pp 285–293

Cantor P: Symptoms, prevention, and treatment of attempted suicide, in Depressive Disorders: Facts, Theories, and Treatment Methods. Edited by Wolman B, Stricker G. New York, John Wiley, 1990, pp 189–202

Cohen LS, Winchel RM, Stanley M: Biological markers of suicide risk and adolescent suicide. Clin Neuropharmacol 11:423–435, 1988

Curran DK: Adolescent Suicidal Behavior. Washington, DC, Harper & Row, 1987

Holinger P: Suicide prevention and intervention, in Carter Center, Closing The Gap Project. Atlanta, GA, Centers for Disease Control, 1984

Kreitman N: How useful is the prediction of suicide following parasuicides? Bibl Psychiatr 162:77–84, 1982

Lester D, Murrell ME: The influence of gun control laws on suicidal behavior. Am J Psychiatry 137:121–122, 1980

Linnoila M, Virkkunen M, Roy A, et al: Monoamines, glucose metabolism, and impulse control, in Violence and Suicidality: Perspectives in Clinical and Psychobiographical Research: Clinical and Experimental Psychiatry (Monogr No 3). Edited by Praag HM, Plutchik R, Apter A. New York, Brunner/Mazel, 1990, pp 218–241

Maltsberger JT, Buie JT: Common errors in the management of suicidal patients, in Suicide: Understanding and Responding: Harvard Medical School Perspectives. Edited by Jacobs D, Brown HN. Madison, CT, International Universities Press, 1989, pp 285–294

Motto J: Treatment concerns in preventing youth suicide, in Youth Suicide. Edited by Peck ML, Farberow NL, Litman RE. New York, Springer, 1985, pp 91–111

Nicholi AM Jr: The adolescent, in Harvard Guide to Modern Psychiatry. Edited by Nicholi AN. Cambridge, MA, Harvard University Press, 1978, pp 519–541

Oliver RG, Hetzel BS: An analysis of recent trends in suicide rates in Australia. Int J Epidemiol 1:91–101, 1973

Roy A, Linnoila M: Monoamines and suicidal behavior, in Violence and Suicidality: Perspectives in Clinical and Psychobiographical Research: Clinical and Experimental Psychiatry (Monogr No 3). Edited by Praag HM, Plutchik R, Apter A. New York, Brunner/Mazel, 1990, pp 141–183

Rubenstein JL, Heeran T, Housman D, et al: Suicidal behavior in "normal" adolescents: risk and protective factors. Am J Orthopsychiatry 59:59–71, 1989

Seiden R: Death in the West: A spatial analysis of the youthful suicide rate. Address to the American Association of Suicidology, Dallas, TX, 1983

Shaffer D, Fisher P: The epidemiology of suicide in children and young adolescents. Journal of the American Academy of Child Psychiatry 20:545–565, 1981

Shaffer D, Garland A, Gould M, et al: Preventing teenage suicide: A critical review. J Am Acad Child Adolesc Psychiatry 27:679–680, 1988

Shneidman E: A death in life: notes of a committed suicidologist, in A History of Clinical Psychologists in Autobiography. Edited by Walker CE. Pacific Grove, CA, Brooks/Cole, 1990, pp 225–291

Toolan JM: Suicide in children and adolescents. Am J Psychother 29:339–344, 1975

Chapter 9

Suicide and Suit: Liability After Self-destruction

Thomas G. Gutheil, M.D.

As the other chapters of this book have demonstrated, suicide is a complex phenomenon on the brink of life with many factors that serve as its etiology, many factors that serve as its mitigators, and many factors that constitute appropriate clinical interventions. The treating mental health professional of the patient who committed suicide during or shortly after treatment, however, has more than his or her own sense of catastrophic bereavement with which to contend. In today's climate, the loss of the patient may be followed by the various losses (e.g., narcissistic, financial, social) that follow from being the target of a malpractice suit flowing from the suicide of that very patient.

Suicide is nationally the number one claim against mental health professionals, usually by a factor of two or more than the next most common claim. For example, some years ago, the American Psychiatric Association Insurance Trust identified its first 1,200 claims (Klein and Glover 1983). Suicide specifically led the list. Clinicians must recall, however, that a liability claim is an attorney's conceptualization of what constitutes the wrongdoing by the physician. Thus I suspect that suicide issues may have appeared under other headings in the same listing, including attempted suicide, misdiagnosis, inadequate diagnosis, and even fracture (the last relevant when a patient attempts suicide by jumping from a window and breaks bones, thus permitting only a case under the claim of "fracture," albeit the context has all the obvious trappings of a suicide attempt). The purpose of this chapter is to examine the medicolegal dimensions of suicide as they impact on the practitioner from a series of viewpoints, including a brief introduction to some legal theoretical issues that are relevant to some cases, practical discussions of how suicide litigation actually works, and broadly relevant approaches to liability prevention or risk management.

Fundamentals of Malpractice

Malpractice has specific defining elements in the context of tort law, that aspect of the law dealing with civil wrongs or harms and the compensation of victims of the same. In a traditional analysis, malpractice consists of four elements, each of which must be proven by the plaintiff (in this context, usually the estate of the decedent or suicidal person) by a preponderance of the evidence; that is, that the plaintiff is more likely than not to have a case (Gutheil and Appelbaum 1982). Some theorists describe this standard of proof as representing "51% likelihood" that the proposition in question is true. Each of these four propositions will be specifically addressed as follows.

Clinician-Patient Relationship

Professional malpractice requires, first and foremost, that a professional relationship exist between the defendant accused in the matter and the patient in question, now usually deceased. The "usually" derives from the fact that a patient who has been badly injured in a serious suicide attempt may yet, paradoxically, bring suit against the treating clinician for failure to prevent the attempt. So, in a logical enigma, a patient, while alive, may sue the doctor for failure to prevent suicide (i.e., an attempt). While it is most common for physicians to be the target of such litigation—the extent of their insurance coverage, after all, is the largest—mental health professionals of all disciplines have been either the sole defendant in such litigation or one of the named defendants. Hence I will speak in this context most broadly of the clinician-patient relationship.

The first burden on the plaintiff, then, is to prove that the clinician in question had a professional relationship with the patient and that this relationship carried with it certain duties as follows.

Negligence or the Breach of Duty

The second claim that the plaintiff advances in the case is that the physician's professional duty, flowing from the clinician-patient relationship, was somehow breached because of negligence—"a sin of omission"—whereby the clinician in question failed to exhibit that degree of care and skill of the average reasonable practitioner in that specialty. It is important to note that the reference standard, by which a clinician is judged to have been or not been negligent, is neither the shining stars of the field nor the worst examples of that particular professional discipline. Rather, it is those individuals in the "middle of the Gaussian curve," as it were, in relation to which the skill that constitutes the "standard of care" is defined.

The exact wording of the standard is subject to regional variation; terminology such as "average reasonable practitioner," "average prudent practitioner," and "practitioner at that level of training and specialization taking into account the advances in the field" is common. It is probably not essential for clinicians to know the exact wording of the standard in their jurisdiction since that is a matter for expert witness testimony; but the general thrust of the standard, more or less nationally, will convey some variation on the above terminology.

In sum, the patient is claiming that the clinician's performance on the case was below that of the average professional peer group in regard to the case in question.

Damages or Harm

Contrary to what many clinicians believe, negligence alone, in the sense of negligent practice, does not inherently trigger liability. The negligence in question must result in specific damages or harms, which, in the context of suicide, would represent death and its accompanying losses or injuries encountered in a suicide attempt. In the process of litigation, such harms are given specific monetary value, and experts (e.g., economists) may attach dollar values to the deceased person's future earning capacities, employment benefits, and the like. These calculations, which assign a monetary value to what most clinicians think of as unpredictable imponderables, may certainly seem bizarre in a clinical context, but they are bread-and-butter procedures in determining the monetary cost of someone's death.

Causation

The fact that a clinician was negligent in some area of practice in regard to the patient and the fact that then the patient committed suicide in and of itself do not inherently represent malpractice unless the specific element of causation is demonstrated; namely, that there is a direct causal connection between the negligence in relation to the case and the patient's suicide. It is important to understand that the legal concept of causation is distinctly different from the medical notion, the latter more closely matching the idea of "etiology." To illustrate this difference, I will attempt to use a metaphor.

Metaphoric example. Consider a camel with serious osteoporosis of the spine, whose back is laden with straw. A final piece of straw (the proverbial "last straw") is placed on the back, and the camel's back breaks. In undertaking a clinical analysis of the situation, the clinician would consider the preexisting condition of the camel and its back, the burden posed by the preexisting straw, and the final straw leading to a condition of clinical decompensation.

The legal viewpoint, however, focuses only on the last straw in question, which is referred to as the "proximate cause." This is best understood by a model used in legal teachings to convey the notion of proximate cause: the "but for" test. This test takes the following form: "But for this last straw, the camel's back would not have been broken."

Although this is true in a narrow sense, the clinician usually finds much to argue about in this rather simplistic formulation. This model has dominated legal thinking for decades, however, because to the last straw, in its nonmetaphoric form, can be affixed the name, and to the name can be affixed the blame, and to the blame can be affixed the claim. It is this chain of connections that pulls the engine of malpractice litigation.

In suicide, the situation becomes even more bewildering to the clinician. The plaintiff claims that it was the clinician's negligence that "caused" the suicide. The clinician is inclined to protest that the patient had many more things on his or her mind than the clinician's negligence, whatever that may have been, and that the suicide was caused by the underlying depression, the patient's despair, his or her life situation—in short, all the many features addressed elsewhere in this book. From a viewpoint of proximate causation, however, one can see the model employed by the law: but for the clinician's negligence, the patient would not have had—the plaintiff claims—the opportunity to take suicidal action.

This point will be examined in more detail below. Note the interesting fact that prior to the early 1940s, the patient's suicidal action was considered to break the causal chain between the clinician's negligence and the patient's death. That is, even had the clinician been negligent, the patient's actions—suicidal intent put into practice—interceded as the intervening cause and became the new proximate cause in the patient's damages (i.e., death from suicide). Thus prior to the early 1940s, the clinician would not be held liable. For reasons too complex to be of interest to any but legal scholars, this model changed after that point, and clinicians began to be held liable for negligence that actually led to suicide. At present, then, the plaintiff's attorney will be attempting to prove the causal connection between the clinician's negligence and the patient's death.

For mnemonic purposes, the elements of malpractice are most easily retained as the "Four D's" of Malpractice: **D**ereliction of a **D**uty **D**irectly causing **D**amages. Proof of these elements constitutes the plaintiff's side of the case.

The Psychology of Liability

The foregoing discussion represents a quick distillation of the legal elements of malpractice. It is essential to understand, however, that—like many of the phenomena envisioned in legal theory—the realities of suicide litigation bear little resemblance to these elements: the latter do not capture the "Why" of litigation. Most clinicians can test the wisdom of this proposition by reflecting on their own experience and that of colleagues. They are aware of appallingly bad clinical care that did not result in litigation and equally aware of top-level care that did so. This awareness alone should be sufficient to convince clinicians that the level of care is not the defining factor in lawsuits.

I suggest that the true origin of lawsuits may be understood from a model developed by the Program in Psychiatry and the Law at the Massachusetts Mental Health Center, co-directed by myself and Dr. Harold J. Bursztajn. The program suggests that malpractice litigation results from the malignant synergy of a bad outcome (in this case, serious injury or death through suicide) and what we refer to as "bad feelings" (Gutheil et al. 1984).

Thus we are suggesting that litigation in this worst of all possible outcomes flows from accompanying bad feelings, a model that respects the fact that suicide as a clinical event leaves among the worst feelings in its wake. This clinical reality helps account for the primacy of suicide litigation in claims against mental health professionals.

The bad feelings in question are fairly specific to suicide when a litigation issue arises. The most common one is *guilt,* particularly the phenomenon of guilt among survivors, another form of guilt that is extremely common in suicidal litigation along the following lines: husband leaves (separates from, divorces, threatens to divorce) wife; wife kills herself; husband sues wife's treating clinician. Of course, the gender roles could as readily be reversed, but the psychological mechanism is extremely transparent. If a spouse or loved one commits suicide just after your termination or your threat to leave the relationship, you feel inescapably extremely guilty as having yourself "caused" the suicide.

It is extremely natural as a human reaction to wish to transplant this guilt through a mechanism of displacement onto others. The tort system provides a ready and psychologically acceptable vehicle for such displacement of affect, where the legal system serves intrapsychic ends. Indeed, in my experience, this particular scenario is the most prevalent one for suicide litigation and is, of course, not limited to specifically marital relationships.

A second trigger of litigation from an emotional viewpoint is *rage* at the clinician. This rage may take several forms. One version is outrage at the clinician's pre- or postsuicide arrogance, unavailability, insensitivity, and unresponsiveness. A variant of this rage may occur when the clinicians have been experienced as particularly blaming of the suicide survivors in a way which triggers retaliatory blaming fantasies in those individuals.

Another important feeling in suicide litigation is the feeling of *grief.* While grief would be an understandable and natural response, for multiple reasons, survivors of suicide may resist feelings of grief, loss, and depression and may wish to avoid experiencing these most painful of affects. One of humanity's oldest "antidepressants" has been energetic activity (e.g., throwing oneself into the funeral ceremonies), and litigation occasionally appears to serve the role of such avoidance-providing activity. Plaintiffs can become so immersed in the complexities and phenomena of litigation as to achieve significant emotional distance from any direct sense of loss.

Another affect that may play a role is the emotion of *surprise.* Families of individuals who have shown long-standing depressive or suicidal preoccupations and inclinations are rarely prone to such a response, but a number of suicides do occur in contexts where the death catches everyone (not uncommonly, the clinician as well) entirely without warning. The feeling of surprise and shock may take the form "this wasn't supposed to happen" and this emotion, as well, may be blamed on the clinician by the plaintiffs in question.

Another important affect is *psychological abandonment.* As an expert witness in a number of cases, I have had the strong impression that a certain amount of litigation flows from family members simply wishing to find out what happened—what actually happened—to their loved one. Clinicians' natural guilt responses may combine with well-meant advice from old-fashioned attorneys to keep physicians and family members separated in the context of threatening litigation. An unfortunate result of this approach may be to produce an air of mystery, uncertainty, and ignorance about what actually occurred—an atmosphere that may itself foment litigation as a means of simply having the family members' questions answered.

Family members, despairing of repeated attempts to talk to clinicians or administrators, turn in desperation to attorneys to break through the wall of silence around the final fate of their loved ones. It is here that interpersonal management and outreach to the bereaved survivors become particularly important in liability prevention, as will be addressed in the final segment of this chapter. It is important to realize that none of the foregoing is intended to suggest that families who sue after suicide are all crazy or that physicians never do anything wrong. The proposition that actual litigation flows from bad outcomes and bad feelings in combination is an empirical description of the realities of the psychology of litigation, nothing more.

Suicide Liability Issues in Practice

Although I will be focusing here primarily on outpatient suicide issues, I will for completeness address the in-hospital and postrelease or postescape suicide as well. Indeed, these three settings exhaust the possible locales of suicide where personal litigation occurs. Each locale of suicide is determinative of the particular medicolegal issue that will be asked in the service of determining negligence. So powerful is this connection that, by merely describing the location and context of the suicide, the essential question and a rough outline of both sides of the case can be sketched out.

Outpatient Suicide

As might be imagined, the critical question here is, should the patient have been offered hospitalization or—if such an offer occurred and the patient refused—should the patient have been committed to the hospital? Outpatient suicide is an extremely low base rate phenomenon and therefore poses many statistical and other problems in terms of its prediction.

A variant of outpatient suicide is the most problematic context of all: the single evaluation in clinic, office, or emergency room settings, where neither an extensive knowledge of the patient over time nor a lasting therapeutic alliance exist to be drawn on as resources. Hence, such "one shot" evaluations ought to require the most careful, sensitive, and intuitive assessment of all. Regrettably, such evaluations, often by their very nature, take place in high turnover settings (e.g., emergency rooms) where all too little time tends to be available to permit such careful determinations.

In-Hospital Suicide

The clinical question that arises here usually turns on assessment of the patient's potential for suicide and whether the patient was sufficiently closely watched. Since the legal system is deeply invested in documents, procedures, and protocols, clinicians as a rule should have some familiarity with their own hospital's suicide precaution procedures, with the minimum requirements of those procedures, and with details of what nurses on the case are required or instructed to do when a patient is on such precautions.

Thus, a physician who admits a patient from the outpatient department and orders the patient placed on suicide precautions should understand the extent and limitations of this particular category and should be familiar with the question of whether this status has various levels of severity and the like. Since, as a practical rule of thumb, clinicians rarely read procedure manuals in any great detail if at all, it is important to determine from inpatient staff what kinds of monitoring or scrutiny are involved. As will later be addressed in this chapter, both the decision to utilize or not to utilize such status precautions should be reflected in documentation of the decision making.

Suicide After Release or Escape

Suicide litigation in these contexts turns on questions such as: Should the patient have been released or discharged at all? Should the plans, monitoring, or aftercare have been adjusted in some form? Should additional precautions have been taken to keep the patient from escaping and then committing suicide?

It is important to note under this heading that, despite the precision of the definition of malpractice given above, courts and juries are not necessarily bound by these formal models. It has been my impression that if there is a generally sloppy, negligent feeling about the case, the jury will feel the urge to punish the physician who has handled the case in such a manner, regardless of what may be the narrow requirements of that jurisdiction for the finding of fault. This is an argument for scrupulousness even in fairly irrelevant-seeming details and an incentive not to take too much for granted when it comes to documentation.

The Question of Outpatient Medications

In one of the psychopharmacologic ironies peculiar to psychiatric treatment, the most lethal medications in the pharmacopoeia—antidepressants—are normally prescribed for those conditions most likely to evoke their lethal misuse—depressions. This factor plays a significant role in the common use of antidepressants (especially of the tricyclic sort) for suicide through overdosing. An additional factor that probably but not provably plays a role in the use of antidepressants for suicide is the decline in use of electroconvulsive therapy as the treatment of initial choice. Many centers today would not consider beginning the course of treatment of a suicidal patient with electroconvulsive therapy and would instead tend first to see if medications work and then use electroconvulsive therapy as an alternative backup. As a result, patients may become just better enough under antidepressants to mobilize sufficient energy to destroy themselves before the full antidepressant benefit has been realized.

In addition, since the overwhelming majority of treatment of depression takes place on an outpatient basis, the outpatient use of tricyclics is by far the dominant form of such prescription. To cope with the dilemma of the associated risk in this situation, a number of clinicians use the mechanism of short-term prescribing: supplying the patient with only so many actual pills or alternatively with a prescription designed to last only for a specific length of time, commonly a week at a time. This model is designed to ensure that the patient possesses at any given moment only a sublethal amount of the medication in question as an aid to overcoming the impulse to overdose that may come on such a patient (Gutheil and Appelbaum 1982).

Although this approach certainly has a commonsense validity, there are a number of pitfalls in its use that should be kept in mind by the clinician taking this path. First, if such a measure is attempted, it should always be done in the context of the doctor's alliance with the healthy side of the patient against the "illness in the patient," particularly self-destructive impulsivity (Gutheil 1985). One attempts to convey to the patient something like the following:

> You and I can see together from your history that impulsivity has been a problem for you and one that you and I are working to help you control or resolve. We should discuss together whether limiting the amount of medication you have on hand at any one point may be of help to you in controlling these impulses toward hurting yourself with this medication.

An additional mechanism that may be useful is to conceptualize the medications themselves as representing temptations to action that need to be controlled: "one effect of these medications is that they sometimes tempt people to take too many" (Bursztajn et al. 1988, p. 375). These models make it clear that the physician is working with the healthy side of the patient against impulsivity, rather than that the physician, in a more oppositional manner, sees the patient as an adversary to be out-foxed, as a needy person to be withheld from in the name of the clinician's self-protection, or as some other kind of individual outside the alliance.

An additional pitfall in the use of such an approach as short-term prescribing is that it may lull the physician and the patient into a sense of certainty that they have a tight grip on suicidal action: that the situation is "under control." Although both clinician and patient are inclined to focus fairly explicitly on medication as something flowing, as it were, from physician to patient and carrying with it all the emotional freight of feeding, nurturance, and so on, the real world is filled with alternative methods for suicide; a patient may scrupulously adhere to the precise medication regimen suggested by the physician and still use a gun from home to commit suicide.

As a rule, the notion of an alliance-based negotiation over these issues through discussion with the patient should represent the model for *all* suicide precautions, including restrictions of space, hospitalizations, and the like. Whenever the clinician feels that he or she is operating *on* the patient rather than *with* the patient, an introspective phase should ensue whereby this posture—antithetical to the clinical work—is carefully scrutinized and remedied in the appropriate manner.

Legal Conceptualizations of the Patient

In actual litigation, the burden of proving that the doctor was negligent lies with the plaintiff; thus the plaintiff is essentially creating a new case. Certain portrayals of the patient are commonly invoked by the plaintiff's attorneys as a way of having the jury see the case from the viewpoint favorable to the plaintiff's side. These models are of more than academic interest, moreover, since, as will later be described, they have risk management implications for the clinician's practice. As educational background, then, I will outline the models of the patient in question.

The most common vision of the patient that the plaintiff's attorney attempts to convey is that of the patient as a child, regardless of the patient's actual age, cognitive clarity, or competence to function. From this model, the patient is not at all responsible for any actions, just as a child is not really considered responsible; it is the clinician—portrayed as the bumbling, incompetent parent—who has allowed this child to "slip through his or her fingers," as it were, and this has resulted in a suicide. The patient's depression and suicidality are portrayed as independent factors afflicting the patient rather than as the patient's state of feeling or intention. By this model, then, the clinician's failure to watch the patient closely enough, say, allowed the patient's illness to win the battle; the negligence thus caused the harms. Such models attempt to portray the clinician's job in a "puppeteer" fashion, where the inert patient merely responded to the clinician's tugs on various strings. It appears easier for a jury to see the clinician as negligent from this viewpoint rather than feeling that suicide, after all, is something the patient does to him- or herself. Great emphasis in such cases is laid on the physician acting in "parentalistic" ways from a very authoritarian model, despite the reality of how the therapeutic alliance actually occurred.

A second model, rarely addressed explicitly, is of a kind of "product liability" model in a metaphoric sense. This is particularly common in postrelease suicide cases. Here the patient is portrayed as something that the hospital has released on the unknowing public and that the "product" was defective insofar as the patient committed suicide. Here, scrutiny of the aftercare situation is a powerful factor in determining the success of this case.

Finally, tort law, under which malpractice issues lie, is fundamentally a mechanism explicitly recognized as a means of compensating victims. Either plaintiff's attorneys (or appellate court judges, when cases are appealed) may be consciously or unconsciously inclined to treat the physician's actuarially determined insurance policy as a sort of victim compensation superfund, whereby this money, seen as somehow separate from the physician, is used to compensate victims of a loss. This mechanism (formally described in law as "strict liability" or liability without fault) (Gutheil and Appelbaum 1982) represents the rock on which all malpractice defenses founder; that is, all medical malpractice juries, not just psychiatric ones, may be swayed to take the "just give the money" position as an alternative to doing direct mental battle with the thorny causal issues at stake in a case. Against such a position, there is no defense under the control of the physician, but, fortunately, this is not the most common outcome.

Indeed, physicians can take some comfort from the fact that, of the relatively small amount of cases that actually get to trial (some estimates place this as low as 6%), the majority—80% in some estimates—continue to be won by clinicians. These data suggest that juries persist in seeing the patient's suicide as the act of the patient inspired by the illness, neither of which are the physician's fault. Note, however, that it would be an error to determine risk management principles by these data alone, which, no matter how comforting, are only statistical in nature. In the next section of this chapter, I address the actual strategies for liability prevention in terms of guidelines for the clinician.

Approaches to Liability Prevention

While the previous chapters in this textbook contain material directly relevant to the appropriate assessment of suicidality and intervention therein, a somewhat concentrated review of some of these points will occur here under the general rubric that good practice is and has always been the best liability preventative. Specific issues in risk management will be addressed under five headings: assessment, intervention, durable documentation, consultation, and outreach to the survivors.

Assessment

At this point in history, in part because of the existence of masked depressions and suicides without depressed mood, the initial assessment of every patient, no matter what the chief complaint, should include a determination of that patient's suicidal ideation, intent, or risk. Even the patient who comes in with, say, an elevator phobia and appears annoyed—but neither distressed, depressed, nor despondent about this symptom—should be asked whether the patient has ever felt desperate about this symptom, whatever it may be, and whether, in the context of such feelings, he or she has ever felt like harming him- or herself. Thus appropriate intake or screening interviews at the beginning of a course of treatment appropriately include inquiry, in a specific sense, about suicidal ideation in a psychiatric "review of systems." Clinical observations, such as to how depressed the patient seems in the office (or, in an adjunctive way, how depressed the patient makes the evaluator feel [Gutheil et al. 1983]), are important elements of early assessment. Second, the various known risk factors, described by Weiden and Roy (Chapter 5, this volume) in great detail, should be specifically addressed as well. Recent changes in move of residence, employment, and marital status, as well as basic demographic risk factors should be explicitly noted and addressed. Two areas often omitted by excessively casual initial evaluations include the presence of concomitant substance abuse and the availability of weapons, not limited to firearms and including miscellaneous medications.

It is important to underscore the value of subjective data in the assessment of the patient (Gutheil et al. 1983), particularly in light of the fact that the evaluator has special exposure to the patient: seeing, smelling, hearing, observing facial expressions and body language in ways that are not always captured—or indeed, capturable—in ordinary documentation. The empathic responses to the patient as well as "gut" feelings are appropriate clinical data and merit recording, just like more concrete or objective material from the interpersonal dialogue. An explicit attempt should be made to record these phenomena since they play a recognized and sometimes definitive part in a clinician's actual decision making but may be absent from recorded data (to the detriment of the clinician's later claim of thoroughness). Buie (1981) made a complementary point that, while such responses are extremely important in the assessment, they should not represent the only factors taken into account. Indeed, Buie suggested what he called "cerebration" to accompany the empathic response, since individuals in states of acute suicidal danger may be cut off from their own despair and thus may leave a "smooth surface" as the only thing open to empathic contact. In short, subjective information must be joined and integrated with direct observational data, history of losses, trauma to the patient, and the like.

An important area insufficiently addressed in a systematic manner in most suicide evaluations is the question of the patient's competence or capacity to participate in the work with the clinician (Gutheil et al. 1986). This capacity has several dimensions. Can the patient participate with the clinician in the self-scrutiny required for the therapeutic process, or do depression, psychosis, paranoia, or other phenomena get in the way? Can the patient form a therapeutic alliance with the clinician to permit collaborative work on resolution of depressive or suicidal symptoms from a joint perspective? Can the patient participate in treatment planning in a reasonable manner with a clinician, particularly if treatment is to take place on an outpatient basis?

Although many clinicians make an automatic implicit assessment of the patient's credibility or authenticity in the interview, such an intuitive perception does not travel well to later retrospective assessment and, at worst, litigation. The work of the Program in Psychiatry and the Law in this area (Gutheil et al. 1986) suggested that a specific determination be made as to whether the patient had the capacity (or competence) to weigh the risks and benefits of giving or withholding information about suicidal intent on the one hand and the capacity to control suicidal impulses on the other. This information might be determined by specific questions, of which the following are examples:

- Do you realize I can't help you if you don't level with me?
- Do you understand the only way I'll know what's on your mind is if you tell me?
- Do you know what to do if things turn bad on you when you are outside the hospital?
- Do you know what to do if you feel the impulse to hurt yourself getting stronger?

- Do you have some plans as to what to do if you find your suicidal feelings coming back while you are on this pass?
- Do you know whom to call and do you have the number for the hospital (or the emergency room, the clinician, the ambulance service, etc.)?

This model of the patient as retaining certain capacities, despite the presence of either depression or suicidal ideation, has several advantages, including serving as a solid refutation of the plaintiff's attorney's model of the patient as a helpless child. That is, the patient who is participating with the clinician in a collaborative, foresighted, and competent planning approach cannot be the child envisioned by the other side's attorney. Thus it is extremely important to record the nature and extent of the patient's participation in this discussion. If the patient, indeed, cannot appropriately answer these questions or demonstrate these capacities, then clearly much more restrictive and protective interventions must be invoked.

Careful attention to this area is extremely helpful in coping with the largest dilemmas in clinical work: chronic suicide, manipulative suicide, and suicide in patients with character disorders, where neither simple depression nor unequivocal psychosis appears to provide the driving force. The important issue here is for the clinician to take steps to distinguish the patient who "can't" ask for help (because of severe depression, psychosis, or other clinical factors) from the patient who "won't" or "chooses not" to ask for help, which is an entirely different matter. For perspective and orientation, recall that the *competent* patient is able to refuse life-saving treatment. In a similar manner, a competent patient can refuse to turn for help to the available sources of this aid, despite knowing where and what these sources are.

The strength of this competence-based model lies not in its representing a kind of legal dodge, but in its firm clinical foundation: the patient who is, indeed, unable to recall or figure out how to ask for help inherently requires a much more protective or parental approach than the patient who knows full well where the sources of help may lie. As always, effective risk management rests solidly on the clinical foundation of good practice.

Clinical experience demonstrates that an important element in this overall approach to the patient is obtaining a kind of "informed consent" to the patient's own condition; for example, this may mean obtaining a borderline patient's informed consent to facing the intrinsic risks of that disorder. In practice, this means the clinician and patient place squarely on the table the patient's suicidal impulsivity, for example, or chronic suicidal ideation. Very often the candor that this achieves may itself decrease the antialliance tensions in the relationship (Gutheil et al. 1984). Some examples follow:

- I wish I had a guarantee that this psychotherapy would be sure to keep you alive.
- I wish we knew in advance whether you'd ever be tempted impulsively to take all these medications, as happened in the past.
- I hope you don't use these medications (or other means) to hurt yourself, but I'm well aware of the fact that there are real limits to whether I can stop you or not.
- Let's agree that I'm going to work for the side of you that wants to stay alive and do the best we can with that.

Such communications can be liberating for both clinician and patient, where the former frankly faces the limits of the capacity for intervention, and the latter comes to accept that staying alive is not simply a question of doing a favor for the doctor.

Intervention

Interventions are appropriately detailed throughout this volume. Clinicians should recall as a kind of conceptual foundation that one can always do the conservative thing: one could always hospitalize the patient, one could always place the patient on suicide precautions or various forms of close observation if the condition required it. All too many clinicians, however, are inhibited from this basic realization by fear that their conservative practice will be later second-guessed through litigation for false imprisonment or civil rights violations. In actual practice, the slightest demonstration of reasonable assessment and good faith easily refutes these charges. Admittedly, if a clinician hospitalizes the husband and runs off with the wife, this would raise some question about the good faith dimensions of the intervention; but short of such egregious circumstances, conservative practice can always be defended. One implication of the foregoing is that when the clinician is making a judgment call in the direction of a *less* conservative step (e.g., the decision *not* to hospitalize the patient), slightly more care and attention are required, as the following sections will indicate.

Durable Documentation

For the expert witness in a liability context, the issue of documentation is almost always the "make or break" issue in a case. Not only is the documentation the only pathway to contemporaneous clinical assessments, but the nature and quality of the documentation may profoundly influence the jury's sense of the general "decor" of the case. Here, my earlier comments about sloppiness and a broad feeling of negligence may be particularly relevant.

Durable and effective documentation, however, is not identical with the notion of "writing more" or simply writing reams of material about every aspect of the case. Not only is this functionally impractical, but it is often ineffective in a genuine risk management sense. Documentation, to be effective, should focus on three main areas, which, if carefully addressed, may suffice to maintain good clinical care as well as to serve as a powerful shield against the imputation of negligence.

The first area to be addressed is the risk-benefit analysis of the intervention or approach chosen by the clinician. Empirical experience suggests that an area that clinicians insufficiently address here is the question of the risks and benefits of "the road not taken." That is, if the physician is planning to give the patient medications, attention clearly focuses on the risks and benefits of the medications themselves; but it should be considered—and as well documented—that the *failure* to use medication has significant risks of its own. Similarly, the decision not to hospitalize invokes certain risks, but hospitalization has risks of its own, and outpatient treatment has detectable benefits.

The point here it that a risk-benefit analysis of both forks of the branch of the decision tree—the risks and benefits of the chosen course and risks and benefits of alternative courses—captures an assessment of the situation that is relatively clearly not negligent, despite the fact that the clinician's decision may be proven in hindsight to be wrong. Clearly, if a patient has committed suicide, something bad has happened and possibly something wrong has also happened. But the issue in the courtroom turns on the question of negligence, and this in turn will relate to the clinician's analysis of the decision making.

The second essential area for documentation is in the exercise of a clinician's judgment at critical decision points. This means not only identifying the assessments in all their detail, but making explicit the clinician's *use* of these data in the decision making, which should also be outlined in the record. It is one thing if the progress note states, "See next week" and quite another if the note relates, "Moderate level of patient suicidal ideation; solid impulse control; and positive future plans; suggest elective hospitalization; may be deferred for one more week while we continue to assess; patient able to weigh risks and benefits of calling me if condition worsens." Relevant decision points might include the prescription of medication in whatever form it takes, hospitalization, release from the hospital, or the decision not to hospitalize in a tricky situation.

Finally, the patient's capacity or competence to participate in decision making—and particularly to weigh risks and benefits of giving information to the clinician about his or her own suicidal condition—should also be explicitly recorded. The rationale for this was given earlier and is further developed by Jacobs (Chapter 7, this volume). This last point bears specific relevance to the widely used concept of the so-called nonsuicide contract. Like other phenomena in the generally obsessional world of mental health practice, such notions are in danger of taking on a life of their own. A nonsuicide contract, as generally envisioned, represents a kind of moral commitment not to harm oneself during a specified time interval. Such approaches represent a counterattack on the suicidal patient's depressive vision of burdensome life stretching into the indefinite future without end in the same state of pain with which he or she now presents.

Asking the patient to hold off on self-destruction for a limited period of time may provide some relief because the patient, unable to promise a lifetime without suicide, may be able to envision holding together for a day (or even, in extreme cases, for an hour). Inexperienced clinicians, however, are in danger of viewing this moral commitment as some kind of guarantee or warranty such as that which comes with an appliance. No such thing, of course, is intended. In addition, the issue of a patient's competence or capacity to participate in such a contract is all too rarely specifically assessed and recorded. No matter how nonformal such contracts are, the patient's capacity to participate in them is a natural prerequisite for their use.

Consultation

If recorded in the chart, consultation with a colleague, no matter how informal, represents a powerful antidote to the accusation that the intervention in question deviated from the standard of care. Although a consultant who does not see the patient (e.g., in a telephone review of the case with a colleague) does lose the subjective data available to the direct assessor, the consultant may have available the perspective and detachment to offer valuable objective insights. A plan of action that seems reasonable to several practitioners within a particular field offers a strong challenge to the claim that the average reasonable practitioner would not have pursued the approach in question. Dulit and Michels (Chapter 3, this volume) addressed further the value of consultation in resolution of an impasse.

Consultation should be recorded in the chart despite the possibility that the consultant may be named in the litigation. If a case is presented anonymously to a consultant ("I have a 35-year-old married male here who . . ."), the consultant may be able to validate the consultee's plan without specifically acquiring a duty to anyone beyond the consultee; absent duty, liability cannot follow. Colleagues working in the same environment can and perhaps should frequently perform this service for each other. Frequent peer review, in addition to providing liability prevention, is a significant factor in maintaining high standards of care.

Outreach to Survivors

Clinicians whose patients have committed suicide often describe themselves as emotionally devastated and often as unambiguously bereaved as individuals who have suffered any other loss. Clinicians should, however, recall that the family of the suicidal patient has had a catastrophic event occur to them as well; struck by such lightning, they are in need of the clinician's efforts, which should continue to be therapeutic in nature. These include offering of condolences; meetings with family; and support for, and occasionally actual treatment or referral of, survivors and others. Maltsberger (Chapter 10, this volume) succinctly outlined the dynamics of the resistances that clinicians may have to overcome to accomplish this outreach.

At the Massachusetts Mental Health Center, we recommend that the clinician on the case and others who may have worked with the family (e.g., the social worker) should attend the funeral or, at the very least, meet with the family and send condolences. This support not only helps the family cope and deal with the catastrophe they have just experienced but also de-adversarializes the relationship between treatment staff and the family—a liability-preventing as well as humanitarian dimension of such outreach. The appropriateness of outreach to family members should not prevent the clinician from immediately notifying an insurer in the case of this or any other bad outcome, but the adversarialization that occasionally supervenes after a catastrophe should be scrupulously avoided. As earlier indicated, families uninformed about the context of a suicide may develop idiosyncratic and even paranoid fantasies of what actually happened and who did what to whom; the best antidote toward this potentially litigious posture is a supportive review of the matter with family members.

As a final note, careful attention should be paid to review of the matter from a quality-assurance perspective, as in a morbidity or mortality conference, where attention should be paid both to whether such material is protected from later scrutiny and whether additional forums should be employed for discussion of the case. Over and above such medicolegal or administrative requirements, treatment staff are often denied an essential opportunity to terminate with the lost patient, and efforts should be made to provide such an experience. Attending the funeral or clinical, hospital-based memorial services may also serve this extremely valuable function.

Summary

The primacy of suicide in mental health litigation should not lead to clinicians' responding through fear, defensive practice, or other adversarializing reactions. Rather, good clinical care augmented by the principles reviewed above should represent the core of a preventive approach to the unfortunate possibility of liability after suicide.

References

Buie D: Empathy: its nature and limitations. J Am Psychoanal Assoc 299:281–307, 1981

Bursztajn H, Gutheil TG, Brodsky AS, et al: "Magical thinking," suicide and malpractice litigation. Bull Am Acad Psychiatry Law 16:369–377, 1988

Gutheil TG: Medicolegal pitfalls in the treatment of borderline patients. Am J Psychiatry 142:9–14, 1985

Gutheil TG, Appelbaum PS: Clinical Handbook of Psychiatry and the Law. New York, McGraw-Hill, 1982

Gutheil TG, Bursztajn H, Brodsky A: Subjective data and suicide assessment in the light of recent legal developments, part 1: malpractice prevention and the use of subjective data. Int J Law Psychiatry 6:317–329, 1983

Gutheil TG, Bursztajn H, Brodsky A: Malpractice prevention through the sharing of uncertainty: informed consent and the therapeutic alliance. N Engl J Med 311:49–51, 1984

Gutheil TG, Bursztajn H, Brodsky A: The multidimensional assessment of dangerousness: competence assessment in patient care and liability prevention. Bull Am Acad Psychiatry Law 14:123–129, 1986

Klein JI, Glover SI: Psychiatric malpractice. Int J Law Psychiatry 6:131–157, 1983

Chapter 10

The Implications of Patient Suicide for the Surviving Psychotherapist

John T. Maltsberger, M.D.

The impact of patient suicide on the surviving psychotherapist has been scantily addressed and, when reported, reported scantily. Possibly this is the consequence of denial and other defenses that such a loss may call into play. Some therapists bereaved by suicide may respond with melancholia-like symptoms. Others develop atonement reactions marked by reaction formation and undoing. Others yet exhibit avoidance reactions colored with denial, projection, and distortion. These reactions and their prophylaxis will be reviewed here.

The psychotherapist who loses a patient to suicide is faced with a formidable adaptational challenge like that which confronts other near survivors. We know that the future welfare of family members assaulted by suicide is endangered by such an event (Roy 1983). Less appreciated is the extent to which psychotherapists may be emotionally compromised, personally, to be sure, but also in the way they perform professionally, when patients kill themselves (Rotov 1970; Woods 1973). Goldstein and Buongiorno (1984) interviewed 20 psychotherapists who had at some point in their careers lost at least one patient to suicide. All of the psychotherapists demonstrated "considerable affect" in the course of these research interviews, although in some instances the suicides were probably not recent. The psychotherapists reported expectable emotional distress at the time immediately following their patient's suicide, yet all 20 considered that they had "recovered" from the suicide at the time of the interview. Nevertheless, 7 of the subjects recontacted the authors to report a change in sleep pattern after the interview. It is noteworthy that one of the group no longer worked with actively suicidal patients, and one (possibly the same person) no longer worked with depressed patients. It seems likely that the self-assessment of "recovered from the suicide," which all 20 reported, is excessively sanguine and that it reflects a considerable degree of denial. Litman (1965) noticed the prevalence of denial among psychotherapists bereaved by suicide; to acknowledge that a patient's suicide had resulted in persisting injury, that it had impaired professional functioning, would increase the distress the suicide itself was already causing. One might expect some degree of denial in such circumstances.

Other authors have remarked on the tendency to deny other details concerning patient suicide. For example, Brown (1987) commented on the tendency to minimize both the incidence and the impact of suicide on trainees in psychiatric facilities. Between one-third and one-half of psychiatric residents are likely to lose a patient to suicide in the course of their training. Although Brown's psychiatrists-in-training resembled the psychotherapists in the previous study—both tended to disavow lasting ill-effects—it is plain that the emotional consequences were not trivial. One reported his sense of professional competence required 2 years to rebuild after a suicide and that personal treatment and further training had been important in his recovery. Another had decided no longer to accept patients where suicide was a "chronic" concern. Psychiatrists, veterans of medical and surgical departments by the time they begin residency training, are probably better prepared to withstand patient death through suicide (or other causes) than trainees from other disciplines, such as psychology or social work. I am unaware of any studies that detail the impact of suicide on nonmedical psychotherapists specifically.

Litman (1965) interviewed 200 psychotherapists shortly after their patients committed suicide and reported on their emotional reactions. While neither he nor other authors have systematically studied the more lasting effects of suicide on psychotherapists (I am unaware of any long-term follow-up studies in the literature), he nevertheless offered a useful perspective on therapist response to what is always a professional catastrophe.

In reviewing acute bereavement responses, Litman (1965) found that "therapists react to the death of a patient personally, as human beings, in much the same way as do other people. They react secondly, in accordance with their special role in society" (p. 572). According to the degree of personal commitment to the patient who abandons the psychotherapist through suicide, the psychotherapist, like others, may be expected to respond with sadness, denial, depression, self-blame, anger, blaming others, lowered self-esteem, partial identification with the patient, repression, grief, and mourning. These phenomena are well discussed elsewhere and require no special elaboration here (Alexander 1977; Holden 1978; Kolodny et al. 1979; Levinson 1972). Such responses are usual, and, while painful, not pathologic if they do not persist for long periods of time and if they give way as the work of normal grieving proceeds. Clinical judgment may be impaired during the immediate bereavement period, however, just as it may in other circumstances of severe personal upset.

Litman's (1965) second class of responses, those that belong to psychotherapists because of their special role in society, are of particular professional interest because they are likely to shape future patterns of practice and to color relationships with other patients. He commented that many of his interviewees were afraid others would blame them. Many were afraid they were professionally inadequate. Some were afraid of being sued, vilified in the newspapers, or investigated. Some were afraid that others among their patients would react badly to news reports. A number decided to do everything possible in the future to avoid working with potentially suicidal patients. Litman found that denial was the most commonly used defense mechanism used by therapists in the immediate postsuicide period.

Psychotherapists do not differ from others in their fundamental responses to loss, and losses evoke varying degrees of painful affect in everyone. Sadness, anger, and the anxiety of abandonment are the three fundamental affect states into which any bereaved person will be cast by the circumstances of loss, and, according to the defensive organization of the person's character, the psychotherapist may have greater or lesser degrees of difficulty in coping with each of these.

The anxiety of abandonment merits an explanatory comment. Even though it is commonplace in situations of loss, its descriptions in the professional literature are usually partial. Subjectively, some bereaved persons experience nothing worse than lonesomeness, a condition that suggests mild dejection and longing. Others may have to deal with greater or lesser degrees of a more distressing form of abandonment anxiety, aloneness, different from lonesomeness not only in degree of distress it produces, but in quality.

Those who have experienced difficulty in the mastery of separation anxiety in the course of development may respond with intense anxiety of this kind when a patient commits suicide (Buie and Adler 1982). At its most intense, aloneness is a state of panic in which self-annihilation seems imminent. In less extreme degrees, aloneness is the experience of a deep void, a feeling of inner emptiness, deadness, or numbness. To feel alone in this sense is to feel that one is dying. Some feel utterly and forever cut off from others. It is aloneness that animates patients in states of severe agitated depression to pluck at the clothing of passersby and beg for relief. Obviously, the aloneness experience is closely related to the affect of despair; no person can long endure aloneness of much intensity without abandoning hope. Intense aloneness experiences of the full-blown variety are probably fairly unusual in psychotherapists except for brief periods of time just after suicide takes place, but attenuated aloneness experiences are not.

A therapist's successful recovery from a traumatic loss such as suicide will involve the gradual working through of the memories and attachments to the lost patient. This is a process that will require some period of time and that will require in the process the bearing of sadness, anger, and the affects of abandonment in connection to the memories of the patient, the patient's treatment, and the circumstances of the loss. The process of mourning in the suicidal situation is particularly painful and difficult because the death of the patient is inevitably experienced as an assault and must therefore generate a very substantial angry response in the bereaved psychotherapist. The anger is likely to be defended against in ways that make it difficult to acknowledge it fully and place it into perspective; sadness may be intense, and in turn, it may be warded off through a variety of defenses. To the extent that the therapist is vulnerable to reactions of aloneness, severe discomfort occasionally tending to crescendo into short spells of psychomotor agitation may be expected.

The adaptational challenge to any bereaved person is gradually to give up the defenses that are automatically called into play in the immediate experience of loss. In the acute situation, they are needed to ameliorate the flood of feelings that threaten to overwhelm. Over time, painful affects must be experienced in tolerable doses in connection to the memories and fantasies of the person who has been lost, and for this to take place, the defenses against them must gradually be relinquished. This, of course, is the process of mourning.

Litman (1965) noticed that while some of his bereaved practitioners had little commitment to their patients, others were deeply involved. He described one practitioner who "virtually adopted an intelligent and beautiful young woman, one of his psychology students, and when she committed suicide while in psychotherapy with him, he went through weeks of deep mourning and grief" (pp. 572–573). Normal mourning may take place in cases of bereavement through suicide, but frequently it does not, because those who die by suicide reject and repudiate every other person in the world, especially those who care deeply about them. It is the experience of active rejection coupled with loss by death that is particularly difficult for survivors to bear. Rejection of this sort inflicts a serious narcissistic injury and mobilizes not only ordinary sadness, but extraordinary anger and abandonment anxiety. A psychotherapist who cares deeply about a patient who commits suicide will, like others close to the patient, be at risk to develop a pathologic grief reaction.

The loss of a patient to suicide is a qualitatively different experience for the psychotherapist from the loss of a patient to pneumonia for an internist. The principal reason for this is that the therapist brings much more of the total person to the therapeutic encounter than the usual internist does. Indeed, for the psychotherapist, the person is the principal therapeutic tool. The person of the internist is important in the treatment of pneumonia (or other illnesses), but not more important than the drugs or procedures that internist employs. While psychiatry may offer helpful medications, hospitalizations, or electroconvulsive treatment in the treatment and management of suicidal crises, these measures do not strictly belong to psychotherapy. There the therapist is actually the principal modality of treatment. Brown (1987) observed that this is especially true for trainees who in the beginning of their work know so little about psychological practice that it often seems to them they bring *only* themselves to the encounter with the patient. Thus it is that the loss of a patient to suicide raises questions of professional adequacy that cannot be separated from questions of personal adequacy.

A second qualitative difference arises from the different quality of relationship that the psychotherapist experiences with a suicidal patient in comparison to the internist and the pneumonia patient. The psychotherapeutic relationship is likely to be much more emotionally intense and to require many more hours of time and effort than the usual medical one. Suicidal patients evoke intense feelings of anxiety and ambivalence. The understanding and mastery of countertransference hate places special demands on psychotherapists that are usually less significant in the work of other physicians.

There is a third qualitative difference: suicide is a chosen death, death from pneumonia is not. When the suicidal patient chooses to die, the patient actively repudiates the therapist. In doing so, the patient hurts the therapist, and the injury the patient inflicts by choosing to die further burdens the therapist with intense countertransference anger. The internist who loses a patient to pneumonia may experience some degree of angry frustration, but the intensity is less, the death having been involuntary, and not personally directed as an unconscious attack on the physician.

Suicidal deaths are likely to be experienced differently from more ordinary deaths in medical and surgical practice in terms of quantitative distress as well. Death by suicide is comparatively rare, but with the one exception of homicide, it is the only form of death the psychotherapeutic practitioner has primary professional responsibility to prevent. Few of us see many patients die and so we are not inured to it.

There are at least three types of pathologic grief reaction to patient suicide that may interfere with the therapist's personal and professional functioning. These are the melancholiac type, the atonement type, and the avoiding type. Each is characterized by a certain constellation of persisting defenses that interfere with normal mourning and subsequent reintegration.

Melancholiac Reactions

Reactions of the melancholiac variety are rarely profound enough to contribute to fully developed melancholia in the surviving psychotherapist, although from time to time severe reactions of this sort take place. A young psychiatrist attended two patients who died by suicide; after their deaths, he made a dangerous suicide attempt himself and barely survived. Another psychiatrist who had been responsible for the care of four patients who committed suicide subsequently gave up psychiatric practice in a discouraged mood. A psychologist did away with herself after she had been involved with two patients who committed suicide (Rotov 1970).

Even though a full melancholiac reaction is unusual, a defensive constellation similar to that observed in clinical melancholia, and described by Freud (1915) in *Mourning and Melancholia,* can sometimes be observed in surviving psychotherapists. The loss of the ambivalently loved patient is followed by the introjection of the patient, the mobilization of intense aggression (anger), and the direction of the anger against the self through the agency of the superego.

Introjection of (identification with) the lost patient is sometimes signaled by the appearance of suicidal daydreaming in the surviving therapist; the postsuicide development of accident-proneness also indicates it. A therapist may get cut shaving or bruised, banged up, or scratched in small ways (Carter 1971). Evidence for identification with the lost patient is commonly found in dreams (Buie 1982; Litman 1965; Kolodny et al. 1979). To the extent that such introjections persist, the structural framework for a lasting depressive attitude is laid down.

The sudden loss of a patient sometimes reactivates in the therapist an old depressive complex never before adequately resolved. When the therapist has formed a transference to the patient that arises from an ambivalent relationship to one of the therapist's own parents, the loss of the patient may revive a persisting depressive reaction to the loss of the parent.

Introjection of the patient either by itself or because the introjection of the patient has an additive, reactivating effect on a previous introject prepares the way for anger at the abandoning patient to be turned against the self (Alexander 1977). Self-attack can be expressed not only in lowered self-esteem and the subjective experience of guilt, but in self-destructive behavior of one kind or another.

Levinson (1972) reported the case of a young psychotherapist who abruptly lost a patient to a sudden coronary occlusion. This therapist had experienced his own father's death in similar circumstances some time before but had not worked through the loss. The patient's death triggered a severe self-critical reaction in the therapist who blamed himself quite unrealistically for failing to anticipate and take steps to prevent the patient's demise. After several days of increasing agitation, the therapist resigned his residency and took up a research fellowship. (I can find no such detailed reports in the literature of melancholiac reactions following death by suicide. It is difficult to imagine that they do not occur; their scarcity or absence must reflect the pain they cause and reluctance to write about them.) Other bereaved workers, driven by unrealistic guilt, may unconsciously attempt to provoke punishment from supervisors, staff, or other survivors of the suicide. Persisting attitudes of self-discouragement may impede the development of realistic self-confidence in future years and inhibit appropriate clinical self-assertion when it is needed.

Levinson's (1972) self-recriminating psychiatric resident exhibited increasing agitation over a period of 1 or 2 days before resigning from his residency. Agitation is, of course, commonplace in full-blown melancholia and is the psychomotor correlate of moderate to severe subjective aloneness. Buie (1982) noticed that psychotherapists frequently have only incompletely mastered separation (abandonment) anxiety in the course of their own development and that they become therapists in the search for a soothing, holding environment that will assist them to allay persisting distress of this sort.

When the holding environment the therapist offers a patient is accepted, the patient is relieved of anxiety, and over time the therapist may also come to rely unconsciously on the holding derived from this relationship with the patient. When the patient rejects the therapist, however, as is manifestly the case in suicide, the therapist is deprived of the holding needed and is likely to experience a crisis of separation anxiety, as well as rage and depression. Buie (1982) discussed the countertransference implications of this state of affairs in dealing with rejecting patients in general; to the extent that a therapist cannot tolerate patient rejection, that therapist is likely to repress countertransference rage at the patient and displace it toward the patient's parents, thereby interfering with therapeutic understanding and progress.

In abandonment-sensitive therapists, the loss of a patient to suicide may give rise to clinically evident agitation. Milder anxiety reactions are probably much more common and must often go unnoticed. One of the repercussions of patient suicide might expectably be a heightened incapacity to acknowledge, understand, and use countertransference hate in treating future suicidal individuals (Maltsberger and Buie 1974). The holding environment, badly needed by the traumatized therapist, may seem too precarious and will unconsciously be protected at the expense of therapeutic progress.

Superego malformations in psychotherapists render them particularly vulnerable to pathologic grief reactions of the melancholic variety. One of the functions of good clinical training is to bring about certain changes in the ego-ideal of the apprentice therapist. The beginner is likely to feel that the test of clinical skill is the achievement of cure, and of course, some patients are beyond cure. A third-year medical student, responsible (under supervision) for the management of a debilitated woman with an overwhelming pneumococcal pneumonia, exerted himself to an extraordinary degree to make sure she received optimal care. Everything possible was done for the patient's recovery, and the treatment was carefully reviewed by the ward attending physician shortly before her demise. After the patient's death, the student developed a depression that persisted for some weeks. He reproached himself bitterly for failing to save her life. Were it not for the impossible self-demand to cure that the student's superego so omnipotently exacted, he might better have seen that although his patient had died, he had every reason to congratulate himself for putting forward the best possible effort on her behalf. Shortly after graduating from medical school, this gifted student put an end to his life in the middle of a distinguished neurology residency.

The developing clinician must relinquish the self-demand to cure, or even to save, the life of every patient. Suicidal illnesses are malignant diseases, and to them some patients will inevitably succumb. The self-demand to cure and rescue must be replaced with the determination to place at the patient's disposal the best that one can of currently available clinical science and art. It is reasonable to expect oneself to be clinically educated and knowledgeable; reasonable to expect oneself to be sufficiently aware of one's own unconscious processes so that one does not get in the patient's way of recovery; reasonable to expect oneself to be disciplined, tenacious, and devoted to the patient's treatment. But to expect oneself to cure every patient is manifestly unreasonable, and this is a difficult lesson for some trainees to learn. Learning it begins early in training with the emulation of experienced, respected teachers who have themselves already developed mature, clinically appropriate self-expectations. But it may be only in the crucible of surviving an actual patient suicide that trainees finally rid themselves of omnipotent self-demands.

Unless the professional ego-ideal of the therapist has undergone the necessary development, the loss of a patient to suicide will find the therapist vulnerable to unrealistic self-criticism and will open the way to depressive responses. Clinicians who demand the impossible of themselves cannot work comfortably with deeply disturbed patients, because in many such cases the risk of suicide may be continuous and substantial over the course of years. Good clinical work requires that therapists have the capacity to withstand the loss of a patient to suicide without turning against and blaming themselves for it in unrealistic ways.

Atonement Reactions

Atonement reactions to the loss of a patient by suicide are generated by anger at the patient for suicidal abandonment, and its reciprocal, guilt (self-punishment is demanded by the therapist's superego). The therapist will inevitably react with anger. To the extent that this becomes unbearable, therapists are likely to displace their reactions away from the patient who has deserted them and toward surviving members of the family or onto other worrisome patients where suicide is possible. The displaced anger is likely to be warded off further by reaction formation; that is, angry impulses will be transformed into their opposite and expressed by excessively solicitous behavior. Because hating the patient who has deserted remains unacceptable to the bereaved therapist's superego, the therapist is likely to engage in guilt-driven behavior designed to undo the injuries, while unconsciously wanting to inflict them on others. The anger that underlies most reaction-formation and undoing behavior is not fully warded off, however, and is likely to be acted out in one way or another, sometimes by passive-aggressive behavior. The therapist will not quite be aware of behaving inappropriately and in the grips of an atonement reaction, but those toward whom such solicitude is directed will in general recognize that there is something false in this therapist's excessive niceness.

Levinson (1972) described the case of a therapist, thrown off balance by a young man's suicide, who called on the family, expressed his condolences, and invited the surviving mother to become his patient. She accepted, but in doing so was prevented from expressing her anger at the therapist and at the institution with which he was affiliated; her son had been a patient there. Her recovery was poor and she became a chronic invalid.

A psychiatrist with responsibility for an inpatient ward lost a patient to suicide some months before the admission of a prominent young lawyer who had made a grisly, nearly successful attempt on his own life. Although the lawyer received a course of electroconvulsive therapy and signally improved, the psychiatrist, immobilized with fear of another suicide, continued to enforce rigid precautions long after they were necessary. The patient was refused permission to be alone in a small safe room with his clergyman, his consulting psychiatrist, or his own attorney, even though an attendant could stand outside and watch through a window in the door. This excessive, well-intended cautiousness alienated the patient, insulted the family, and destroyed trust between patient, family, and staff. The ward treatment team divided against itself, and the patient had to be moved to another hospital.

Less obvious yet frequently persisting atonement reactions operate in those therapists who display excessive caution and oversolicitude with other patients who are depressed but not clinically suicidal. There may be a tendency to resort too quickly and too often to hospital care. There may be too much medication prescribed. There may be difficulty in allowing necessary regression in the psychotherapy.

Reaction formation may seriously interfere in clinical judgment. Electroconvulsive therapy, surely the treatment of choice in deeply suicidal patients with psychotic depressions, is often withheld because to some therapists its prescription is unconsciously equated with sadistic attack. Such patients may then go forward to destroy themselves after inadequate treatment with antidepressant drugs and premature hospital discharge.

Avoidance Reactions

The threat of suicide provokes anticipatory sadness, anger, and abandonment anxiety. The fear of such distress causes some psychotherapists to react with the narcissistic avoidance defenses of denial, distortion, and projection in anticipation of attempted suicide. In the face of completed suicide, the same defenses may be employed to protect personal composure and to ward off pain. Therapists such as these experience great difficulty in relating empathically to suicidal patients because they need to make themselves unaware of clinical facts and their implications to protect personal equilibrium. When such psychotherapists are unfortunate enough to experience patient suicide, the tendency to react with avoidance defenses is likely to increase.

The eminent Swiss psychiatrist Ludwig Binswanger discharged a dangerously suicidal woman from the locked ward of a sanatorium and permitted her to go home under the care of her husband to kill herself. After she did so, Binswanger published a dense, philosophical, highly abstract "existential analysis" of the case (he called the patient "Ellen West") wherein his lethal decision is rationalized (Binswanger 1944). He asserted that the patient's death was not only inevitable, but appropriate. He almost ignored the highly ambivalent relationship between Ellen West and her husband and the hostility of her relatives and described no effort to make available to her a dependable and lasting sustaining personal resource. After reviewing this dismaying and barren report, Lester (1971) concluded that Binswanger's arguing the inevitability of his patient's suicide reflected his need to acquit himself of responsibility for it. The case of Ellen West thus documents a classic avoidance reaction.

Aversive acting out in the countertransference is a notorious type of avoidance reaction. One wonders how Binswanger felt about Ellen West, and how capable he was of knowing it if he hated her. When a therapist cannot endure his own hostile countertransference excitement nor the anticipatory affects aroused by possible suicide, repudiation of the patient may occur. A therapist who had grown increasingly frightened by a patient who repeatedly threatened suicide and cut her wrists finally "set limits" on the behavior by telling the patient that if such "manipulation" did not cease the treatment would stop. When the patient responded by further wrist cutting, the therapist broke off his relationship with her, and the patient committed suicide. Parallel examples of discharge from inpatient settings of patients who are too threatening for the staff to tolerate are commonplace. Harmful clinical decisions motivated by the wish to be rid of a disturbing patient can be rationalized when important facts in the patient's history and mental state examination are denied (Maltsberger 1986).

When the pain of losing a patient to suicide is too great for a therapist to bear, a scapegoat to be held responsible for the patient's death may be selected and lastingly blamed. Critical superego attitudes are deflected from the self and projected outward onto others. In this way, self-recrimination can be avoided by the device of projective devaluation.

A psychiatric resident lost a chronically suicidal schizophrenic woman to suicide. Every effort had been made to prepare the resident for this possibility as the patient was gradually allowed out of the hospital for a trial return to life as an outpatient. The only other possibility for the patient was continuous inpatient incarceration, where suicide would also have been a continuing risk. Yet when suicide took place, the resident could not tolerate the guilt (however unrealistic) and blamed his supervisor for the patient's death. This blaming attitude continued for some years afterward as the trainee, now graduated from the training program, continued to slander the former teacher in the professional community, repeating many distortions of the actual clinical events.

Another form of avoidance reaction is the denial of clinical facts after suicide has taken place to avoid the pain of acknowledging that a mistake has been made in clinical judgment. A psychiatrist who had allowed an actively deluded patient in a psychotic melancholia out of the hospital on pass took the view that nothing could have been done to prevent his patient's suicide after she killed herself. He was supported in this attitude by others on the staff of the ward where the patient had been cared for. Many suicides that take place while patients are under professional care are in fact preventable, at least for some while. Refusal to look for and acknowledge mistakes makes learning from clinical experience impossible.

Prophylaxis Against and Management of Pathologic Reactions to Patient Suicide

Supportive measures for the therapist bereaved by suicide are essential and have been described in detail elsewhere (Brown 1987; Carter 1971; Cotton et al. 1983; Kolodny et al. 1979). Ward meetings, support groups, "psychological autopsies," and conferences with experienced supervisors are all useful and necessary (Shneidman 1969). In many instances, however, the surviving psychotherapist tends to deny persisting personal and professional difficulties that are sequelae to such an injury. Because of denial, it is commonly difficult for surviving therapists to grasp the fact that they might benefit from psychoanalytic consultation. For this reason, supervisors and training directors should routinely encourage personal consultation for trainees who are suicidally bereaved, and psychotherapists who have finished their training should be prepared in the same way to consult a colleague when patient suicide occurs. Pathologic grief reactions can be prevented in this way by the promotion of normal mourning; the interests of the therapist's other patients can be protected; and narcissistic barriers against learning from mistakes can be removed. Otherwise, personal constriction and professional limitation can ensue.

References

Alexander P: A psychotherapist's reaction to his patient's death. Suicide Life Threat Behav 7:203–210, 1977

Binswanger L: The case of Ellen West (1944), in Existence: A New Dimension in Psychiatry and Psychology. Edited by May R, Angel E, Ellenberger HF. New York, Basic Books, 1958, pp 237–364

Brown HN: The impact of suicide on therapists in training. Compr Psychiatry 28:101–112, 1987

Buie DH: The abandoned therapist. International Journal of Psychoanalytic Psychotherapy 9:227–231, 1982

Buie DH, Adler G: Definitive treatment of the borderline personality. International Journal of Psychoanalytic Psychotherapy 9:51–87, 1982

Carter RE: Some effects of client suicide on the therapist. Psychotherapy: Theory, Research and Practice 8:287–289, 1971

Cotton PG, Drake RE, Whittaker AW: Dealing with suicide on an inpatient psychiatric unit. Hosp Community Psychiatry 34:55–58, 1983

Freud S: Mourning and melancholia (1915), in The Standard Edition of the Complete Psychological Works of Sigmund Freud, Vol 14. Translated and edited by Strachey J. London, Hogarth Press, 1957, pp 239–258

Goldstein L, Buongiorno P: Psychotherapists as suicide survivors. Am J Psychother 38:392–398, 1984

Holden LD: Therapist response to patient suicide. Medical Digest, January 1978, pp 23–32

Kolodny S, Binder RL, Bronstein AA, et al: The working through of patients' suicides by four therapists. Suicide Life Threat Behav 9:33–46, 1979

Lester D: Ellen West's suicide as a case of psychic homicide. Psychoanal Rev 58:251–263, 1971

Levinson P: On sudden death. Psychiatry 35:160–173, 1972

Litman RE: When patients commit suicide. Am J Psychother 19:570–576, 1965

Maltsberger JT: Suicide Risk: The Formulation of Clinical Judgment. New York, New York University Press, 1986

Maltsberger JT, Buie DH: Countertransference hate in the treatment of suicidal patients. Arch Gen Psychiatry 30:625–633, 1974

Rotov M: Death by suicide in the hospital. Am J Psychother 24:216–227, 1970

Roy A: Family history of suicide. Arch Gen Psychiatry 40:971–974, 1983

Shneidman E: Suicide, lethality and the psychological autopsy. International Psychiatric Clinics 6:225–250, 1969

Woods LW: Disaster during psychiatric treatment. Canadian Psychiatric Association Journal 18:67–70, 1973

Index